SEVENTH EDITION
GRAMMAR
IN CONTEXT BASIC

SANDRA N. ELBAUM
JUDI P. PEMÁN

NATIONAL GEOGRAPHIC
LEARNING

Australia · Brazil · Mexico · Singapore · United Kingdom · United States

National Geographic Learning,
a Cengage Company

Grammar in Context Basic, **Seventh Edition**
Sandra N. Elbaum
Judi P. Pemán

Publisher: Sherrise Roehr

Executive Editor: Laura Le Dréan

Managing Editor: Jennifer Monaghan

Director of Global Marketing: Ian Martin

Heads of Regional Marketing:

  Joy MacFarland (United States and Canada)

  Charlotte Ellis (Europe, Middle East and Africa)

  Kiel Hamm (Asia)

  Irina Pereyra (Latin America)

Product Marketing Manager: Tracy Bailie

Content Project Manager: Beth F. Houston

Media Researcher: Leila Hishmeh

Art Director: Brenda Carmichael

Senior Designer: Lisa Trager

Operations Support: Rebecca G. Barbush, Hayley Chwazik-Gee

Manufacturing Planner: Mary Beth Hennebury

Composition: MPS North America LLC

For permission to use material from this text or product, submit all requests online at **cengage.com/permissions** Further permissions questions can be emailed to **permissionrequest@cengage.com**

Grammar in Context Basic ISBN: 978-0-357-14022-2
Grammar in Context Basic + OLP ISBN: 978-0-357-14048-2

National Geographic Learning
200 Pier 4 Boulevard
Boston, MA 02210
USA

Locate your local office at **international.cengage.com/region**

Visit National Geographic Learning online at **ELTNGL.com**
Visit our corporate website at www.cengage.com

Printed in the United States of America.
Print Number: 02   Print Year: 2023

CONTENTS

WELCOME TO THE UNITED STATES

TIME AND MONEY

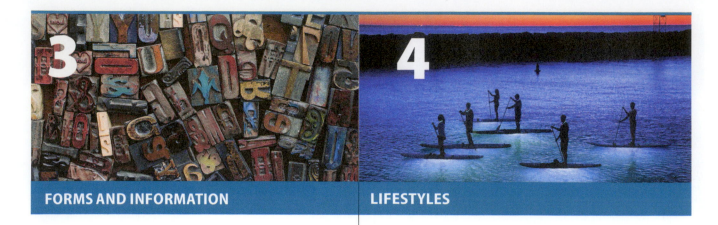

3

FORMS AND INFORMATION

4

LIFESTYLES

DRIVING

SCHOOL

7

SHOPPING

8

ERRANDS

9

CHANGES

10

CHOICES

11

CAREERS

12

VOLUNTEERING

ACKNOWLEDGMENTS

The Author and Publisher would like to acknowledge and thank the teachers who participated in the development of the seventh edition of *Grammar in Context*.

A special thanks to our Advisory Board for their valuable input during the development of this series.

ADVISORY BOARD

Andrea Gonzalez, BYU English Language Center, Provo, UT, USA

Ellen Rosen, Fullerton College, Fullerton, CA, USA

Erin Pak, Schoolcraft College, Livonia, MI, USA

Holly Gray, Prince George's Community College, Largo, MD, USA

John Halliwell, Moraine Valley Community College, Palos Hills, IL, USA

Katherine Sieradzki, FLS Boston, Boston, MA, USA

Maria Schirta, Hudson County Community College, Jersey City, NJ, USA

Oranit Limmaneeprasert, American River College, Sacramento, CA, USA

Susan Niemeyer, Los Angeles City College, Los Angeles, CA, USA

REVIEWERS

Adriana García, Institut Nord-America, Barcelona, Spain

Alena Widows, Institut Nord-America, Barcelona, Spain

Augustine Triantafyllides, So Easy, Athens, Greece

Bilal Aslam, GTCC, High Point, NC, USA

Carmen Díez, CFA Les Corts, Barcelona, Spain

David Finfrock, QU, Doha, Qatar

Deanna Henderson, LCI, Denver, CO, USA

Ellen Barrett, Wayne State University, Detroit, MI, USA

Francis Bandin, UAB, Barcelona, Spain

Jonathan Lathers, Macomb Community College, Warren, MI, USA

Karen Vallejo, University of California, Irvine, CA, USA

Kathy Najafi, Houston Community College, Houston, TX, USA

Katie Windahl, Cuyahoga Community College, Cleveland, OH, USA

Laura Jacob, Mt. San Antonio College, Walnut, CA, USA

Leah Carmona, Bergen Community College, Paramus, NJ, USA

Luba Nesterova, Bilingual Education Institute, Houston, TX, USA

Marcos Valle, Edmonds Community College, Lynnwood, WA, USA

Marla Goldfine, San Diego Community College, San Diego, CA, USA

Milena Eneva, Chattahoochee Technical College, Marietta, GA, USA

Monica Farling, University of Delaware, Newark, DE, USA

Naima Sarfraz, Qatar University, Doha, Qatar

Natalia Schroeder, Long Beach City College, Long Beach, CA, USA

Paul Schmitt, Institut d'Estudis Nord-Americans, Barcelona, Spain

Paula Sanchez, Miami Dade College, Miami, FL, USA

Paulette Koubek-Yao, Pasadena City College, Pasadena, CA, USA

Robert Yáñez, Hillsborough Community College, Tampa, FL, USA

Samuel Lumbsden, Essex County College, Newark, NJ, USA

Sarah Mikulski, Harper College, Palatine, IL, USA

Steven Lund, Arizona Western College, Yuma, AZ, USA

Teresa Cheung, North Shore Community College, Lynn, MA, USA

Tim McDaniel, Green River College, Auburn, WA, USA

Tristinn Williams, Cascadia College, Seattle, WA, USA

Victoria Mullens, LCI, Denver, CO, USA

A WORD FROM THE AUTHOR

My parents immigrated to the United States from Poland and learned English as a second language as adults. My sisters and I were born in the United States. My parents spoke Yiddish to us; we answered in English. In that process, my parents' English improved immeasurably. Such is the case with many immigrant parents whose children are fluent in English. They usually learn English much faster than others; they hear the language in natural ways, in the context of daily life.

Learning a language in context, whether it be from the home, from work, or from a textbook, cannot be overestimated. The challenge for me has been to find a variety of high-interest topics to engage the adult language learner. I was thrilled to work on this new edition of *Grammar in Context* for National Geographic Learning. In so doing, I have been able to combine exciting new readings with captivating photos to exemplify the grammar.

I have given more than 100 workshops at ESL programs and professional conferences around the United States, where I have gotten feedback from users of previous editions of *Grammar in Context*. Some teachers have expressed concern about trying to cover long grammar units within a limited time. While ESL is not taught in a uniform number of hours per week, I have heeded my audiences and streamlined the series so that the grammar and practice covered is more manageable. And in response to the needs of most ESL programs, I have expanded and enriched the writing component.

Whether you are a new user of *Grammar in Context* or have used this series before, I welcome you to this new edition.

Sandra N. Elbaum

For my loves
Gentille, Chimene, Joseph, and Joy

Grammar in Context, the original contextualized grammar series, brings grammar to life through engaging topics that provide a framework for meaningful practice. Students learn more, remember more, and use language more effectively when they study grammar in context.

ENHANCED IN THE SEVENTH EDITION

National Geographic photographs introduce unit themes and pull students into the context.

UNIT
7
Prepositions
There Is and *There Are*
Quantity Words

SHOPPING

About eighty percent of the food on shelves of supermarkets today didn't exist 100 years ago.
DR. LARRY MCCLEARY

A man who sells fish entertains customers at a fish market in Seattle, Washington, U.S.

FRESH COPPER-RIVER KING SALMON FILLETS $69.99

Unit openers include an inspirational quote to help students connect to the theme.

Updated readings introduce the target grammar in context and provide the springboard for explanations and practice.

Words to Know sections include vocabulary to help students understand what they are reading, listening to, and practicing. In this new edition these targeted words are on the audio program.

BEFORE YOU READ

1. Is it easy to make choices in a store? Why or why not?
2. Do you compare prices when you shop? Why or why not?

READ

Read the following conversation. Pay special attention to the *yes/no* questions and *wh-* questions using *there is* and *there are* in bold.

Halina and her husband, Peter, are in the supermarket.

Peter: There are many brands of shampoo. **Why are there** so many brands? Do people need so many choices?

Halina: I don't think so. **Is there** a difference between this shampoo for $3.99 and that shampoo for $10.99?

Peter: I don't know. Let's buy the cheap one.

Halina: OK. There's probably no difference.

Peter: **Are there** any other items on the shopping list?

Halina: Just two. We need sugar. The sugar is in aisle 6.

(one minute later)

Halina: This sign says 25 ounces for $1.75. That one says five pounds for $2.25. Which one is a better buy?

Peter: I don't know. What's an ounce?

Halina: It's part of a pound. There are sixteen ounces in a pound.

Peter: **Is there** a calculator on your phone?

Halina: Yes, but we don't need it. Look. There's a small sign under the sugar. The five-pound bag is about 2.8¢ an ounce. The 25-ounce bag is about 7¢ an ounce. The big bag is a better buy.

Peter: You're a smart shopper. Are we finished? **Is there** anything else on the list?

Halina: Yes. There's one more thing—dog food.

Peter: Wow! Look. There are over twenty kinds of dog food.

Halina: Dogs have choices, too.

DID YOU KNOW?
One pound = .45 kilograms
One ounce = 28.35 grams

COMPREHENSION Based on the reading, write T for *true* or F for *false*.

1. _____ There are two brands of shampoo in the store.
2. _____ An ounce is smaller than a pound.
3. _____ Halina and Peter have a dog.

WORDS TO KNOW

brand	Many companies make soap. There are a lot of different **brands**.
shampoo	I need to buy **shampoo** so I can wash my hair.
choice	There are twenty kinds of dog food, so there are many **choices**. We have to pick one.
difference between	What's the **difference between** the cheap shampoo and the expensive one?
ounce	An **ounce** is a unit of measure. Sixteen **ounces** is equal to one pound.
calculator	I have a **calculator** on my phone. It helps me do math.
better buy	The large bag of sugar is a **better buy**. We can save money.

LISTEN

Listen to the sentences about the conversation. Circle *True* or *False*.

1. (True)   False
2. True   False
3. True   False
4. True   False
5. True   False
6. True   False
7. True   False
8. True   False

7.8 *There Is* and *There Are*—*Yes/No* Questions

Compare statements and questions with *there is* and *there are*.

STATEMENT	QUESTION	SHORT ANSWER
There's a shampoo aisle.	Is there a hardware aisle in this store?	No, there isn't.
There are large bags of sugar.	Are there any small bags of sugar?	Yes, there are.
There's dog food in this aisle.	Is there any cat food in this aisle?	Yes, there is.

Notes:

1. We often use *any* in questions with noncount and plural count nouns.
2. We don't make a contraction in an affirmative short answer.
   Yes, there is.   NOT: *Yes, there's.*

New reading comprehension activities provide students a quick comprehension check to make sure they understood the reading.

COMPREHENSION Based on the reading, write T for *true* or F for *false*.

1. _____ There are two brands of shampoo in the store.
2. _____ An ounce is smaller than a pound.
3. _____ Halina and Peter have a dog.

New Fun with Grammar allows the class to practice grammar in a lively game-like way.

New Summary and Review sections help students revisit key points and assess their progress.

From Grammar to Writing gives editing advice and practice to set students up to successfully apply the grammar to writing.

FUN WITH GRAMMAR

Play Bingo. Your teacher will give you a blank Bingo card. Write the prepositions *in, on, at, to, after, before, near, next to, for,* or *out of* in each square. Some squares will have the same words. Put the prepositions in any order. Your teacher will call out a preposition. Find a square with that preposition and write a sentence in the square, using that preposition. To win the game, you have to have sentences in four squares in a row, either horizontally (→), vertically (↓), or diagonally (↗). The first person to get four correct sentences in a row says, "Bingo!" and wins the game.

SUMMARY OF UNIT 7

Time Expressions

In the morning	
in twenty minutes	three times a month
at night	
at 10 p.m.	once a week
on Saturdays	every day
after 9:30	24 hours a day
before 10:30	24/7

Prepositions of Place and Prepositions in Common Expressions

in	Rick is in the car.
near	The pharmacy is near the supermarket.
next to	The pharmacy is next to the gas station.
on	The store is on the corner. The program is on TV.
	Rick is on the phone. Toothpaste is on sale.
at	Rick is at the store.
to	Go to the pharmacy.
for	Aspirin is on sale—two bottles for $8.00.
out of	We're out of coffee.

There Is and *There Are*—Affirmative Statements

THERE	BE	A/AN OR QUANTITY WORD	NOUN	PREPOSITIONAL PHRASE
There	is	an	elevator	in the store.
	is	some	milk	in the fridge.
	are	two	clerks	in aisle 6.

There Is and *There Are*—Negative Statements

THERE	BE	NO OR ANY	NOUN	PREPOSITIONAL PHRASE
There	is	no	elevator	in the store.
	are		lightbulbs	in this aisle.
	isn't	any	coffee	in the big store.
	aren't		lightbulbs	in this aisle.

There Is and *There Are*—Questions

YES/NO QUESTION	WH- QUESTION
Are there ten items on the list?	How many items are there on the list?
Are there different kinds of shampoo?	Why are there different kinds of shampoo?
Is there any sugar?	How much sugar is there?
Is there a difference between this shampoo and that shampoo?	Why is there a difference in price?

REVIEW

Choose the correct words to complete the conversation.

A: Hello?

B: Hi, Tim. Are you still (on/at/near) work?

A: Yes, I am. I'm coming home (ou/after/in) a few minutes, though.

B: Can you please go (at/in/to) the supermarket (on/in/to) your way home? We're (after/out of/for) milk. And (there's/are there/there are) (some/one/any) other things we need, too.

A: Sure. Is the supermarket open (on/in/at) the evening?

B: Yes. It's open late (on/in/at) Thursdays.

A: OK. The supermarket (near/next to/on) the corner of 5th Street and Oak Street, right?

B: No. That one isn't open (in/at/on) night. (There's/There are/There's no) a supermarket (on/before/next to) the hardware store. Go (ta/near/for) that one.

A: OK, got it.

(30 minutes later)

A: Hi, Kate. I'm (on/at/to) the store. How many items (there are/is there/are there) on your list?

B: Not too many. (There's/There are/There is) ten items, but you don't have to get everything.

A: Oranges are (on/in/for) sale. Five (on/for/out of) a dollar. That's a good price.

B: Yes, it is. Please get oranges. (There are/There aren't/There no) any oranges in the fridge. (There are/There aren't/There is) no apples, either. Please get apples, too.

A: OK. Where's the dairy section? I don't see it.

B: (There's/There are/Is there) two dairy aisles in that store, actually. (There's/There are/Is there) one (next to/out of/for) the fruit . . .

A: Oh, yes. I see it.

B: (Is there/Are there/How much is there) any milk in that aisle?

A: Hmm. No, (there is/there isn't/there aren't).

B: OK. (There's/Is there/There are) another dairy aisle. It's (on/in/near) the meat section.

A: OK . . . Oh, there's (any/many/a lot of) milk here!

B: Great. And can you please buy coffee? There isn't (some/no/enough) here.

A: Sure. I'll be home soon!

FROM GRAMMAR TO WRITING

PART 1 Editing Advice

1. Use the correct preposition.

   Sue likes to shop ~~in~~ at night.

   Your favorite program begins ~~after~~ in twenty minutes.

2. Don't use prepositions with certain time expressions.

   Simon works five days ~~in~~ a week.

3. Don't use *to* after *near*.

   There's a convenience store near ~~to~~ my house.

4. Don't write a contraction for *there are*.

   ~~There's~~ There are fifteen students in the class.

5. Don't use *a* after *there are*.

   There are ~~a~~ good sales this week.

6. Don't use two negatives together.

   There aren't ~~no~~ any lightbulbs in this aisle.

7. Use correct word order.

   How many batteries ~~there are~~ are there in the flashlight?

PART 2 Editing Practice

Some of the shaded words and phrases have mistakes. Find the mistakes and correct them. If the shaded words are correct, write C.

Ali: I need a lightbulb for this lamp. Are there any extra lightbulbs? **[C]**

Shafia: No, there isn't. (aren't) We need to buy more.

Ali: Let's go in the hardware store. Is it open now?

Shafia: No. It's late. The hardware store isn't open in the night. It closes in 6:00 p.m. But the big store near to the bank is open very late.

Ali: There are a lot of things in sale at that store this week. Let's make a list.

Shafia: We don't need a lot of things. We only need lightbulbs.

Ali: What about batteries? Are there batteries in the house?

Shafia: There're some AA batteries.

Ali: But we need C batteries for the radio.

Shafia: There aren't no C batteries in the house.

Ali: Do you want to go to the store with me?

Shafia: My favorite show starts after five minutes. Can you go alone?

Ali: OK.

Shafia: There's no rice in the house. Can you get some rice, too?

Ali: There isn't any rice at the hardware store.

Shafia: Of course not. But the hardware store is next the supermarket. In fact, you don't need to go to the hardware store at all. There are lightbulbs and batteries at the supermarket, too.

Ali: OK. Good. There's no need to go to two stores. Is this supermarket open at night?

Shafia: Yes. It's open seven days in a week. And it's open all night.

PART 3 Write

Write five or six sentences to describe each photo. You can write affirmative statements, negative statements, or questions.

In photo A, a woman is with a sales person at a hardware store.

PART 4 Learner's Log

1. Write one sentence about each of these topics:
   - shopping in the United States
   - different types of stores
   - getting a good price

2. Write any questions you still have about shopping in the United States.

ADDITIONAL RESOURCES

FOR STUDENTS The **Online Practice** provides a variety of interactive grammar activities for homework or flexible independent study.

GO TO ELTNGL.COM/MYELT

FOR TEACHERS The **Classroom Presentation Tool** allows the teacher to project the student book pages, open interactive activities with answers, and play the audio program.

The Teacher's Website hosts the teacher's guide, audio, and ExamView® Test Center, so teachers have all the materials they need in one place.

ELTNGL.COM/GRAMMARINCONTEXTSERIES

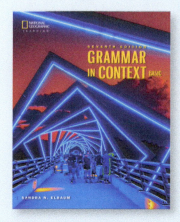
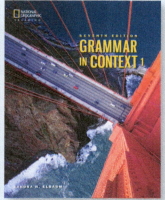
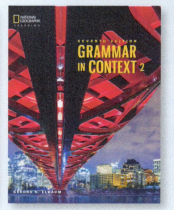
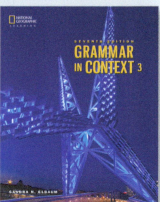

Simon and Marta, with Tina, Amy, and Ed

Halina and Peter, with Anna

Dorota

Shafia and Ali

Victor and Lisa, with Maya

Sue and Rick

Be
Singular and Plural Nouns
Adjectives

My fellow Americans, we are and
always will be a nation of immigrants.

BARACK OBAMA

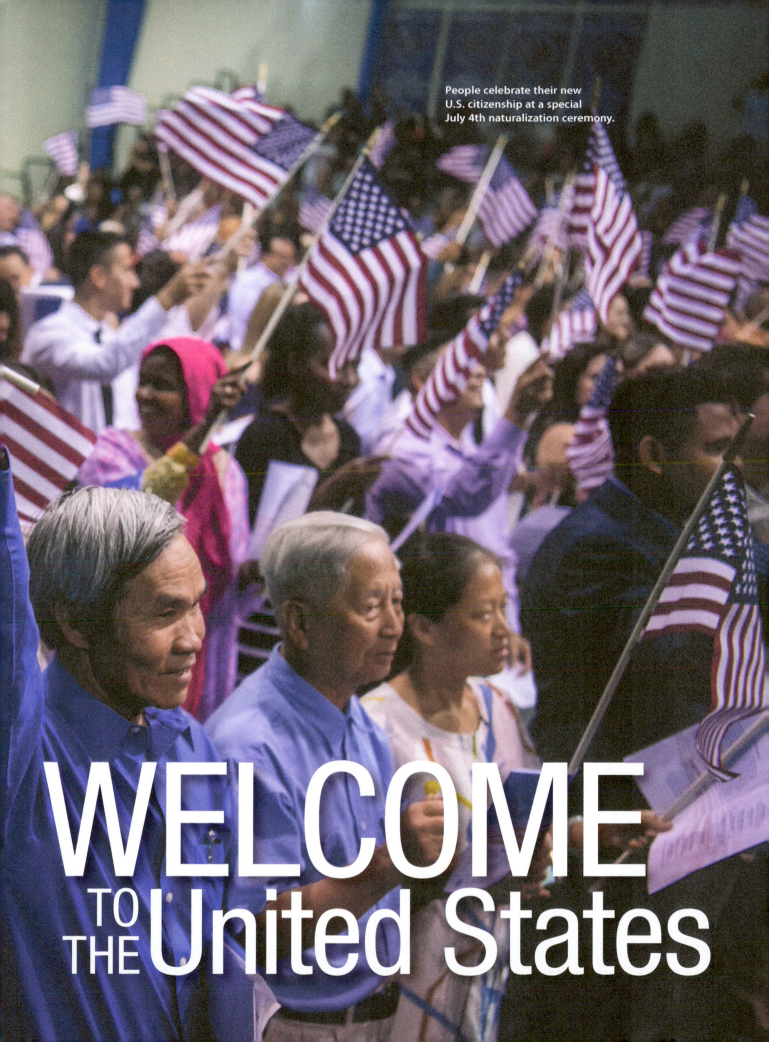

People celebrate their new U.S. citizenship at a special July 4th naturalization ceremony.

WELCOME
TO THE United States

BEFORE YOU READ

Circle *Yes* or *No*.

1. Many things are new for me in this country.   Yes   No

2. People help me with new things.   Yes   No

READ

Read the following conversation. Pay special attention to the subject pronouns, and *is, am,* and *are* in bold. 🎧 **1.1**

Dorota and Simon are at the airport.

Dorota: Welcome! My name **is** Dorota. **I am** from Poland, but **I am** a citizen of the U.S.[1] now. My first language **is** Polish. English **is** my second language. This **is** my friend, Simon. **He is** from Mexico.

Simon: Hi. My name **is** Simon. **I am** from Mexico, but **I am** a citizen of the United States now, too. Spanish **is** my first language. My second language **is** English. **We are** both here to help you. **We are** helpful.

Dorota: **You are** new in this country. **You are** immigrants from other countries. Life **is** different here. Many things **are** different for you—the supermarket **is** different, the laundromat **is** different, and the bank and school **are** different, too. Everything **is** new for you. Maybe **you are** confused.

Simon: Dorota and **I are** here to help you in new places. The laundromat and supermarket **are** the first places to go.

---

[1] *U.S.* is an abbreviation for "United States."

DID YOU KNOW?
Some supermarkets and laundromats are open 24 hours a day.

COMPREHENSION Based on the reading, write T for *true* or F for *false.*

1. _____ Dorota is from Poland.

2. _____ Simon is from Poland.

3. _____ English is Simon's first language.

WORDS TO KNOW ⏳ 1.2

citizen	Dorota is a **citizen** of the United States.
first/second	The **first** place to go is the laundromat. The next place is the supermarket. The supermarket is **second**.
both	Dorota is a citizen. Simon is a citizen, too. They are **both** citizens.
help (v.) helpful (adj.)	Dorota and Simon **help** new immigrants. They are **helpful**.
immigrant	I am from Colombia. I am new to the United States. I am an **immigrant**.
life	**Life** in the United States is new for me.
different	Simon is from Mexico. Dorota is from Poland. They are from **different** countries.
supermarket	We buy food in a **supermarket**.
laundromat	The **laundromat** is a place to wash clothes.
bank	He needs money. He is at the **bank**.
everything	**Everything** is new—the bank, the supermarket, and the laundromat.
confused	I am new here. Everything is different. I am **confused**.

LISTEN

Listen to the sentences about the conversation. Circle *True* or *False*. ⏳ 1.3

1. True   (False)   5. True   False

2. True   False   6. True   False

3. True   False   7. True   False

4. True   False   8. True   False

1.1 Subject Pronouns

EXERCISE 1 Fill in the blanks with the correct subject pronoun.

1. _____We_____ are immigrants.

2. Dorota is from Poland. _____ is a U.S. citizen now.

3. _____ am new to this country.

4. Simon is from Mexico. _____ is from Mexico City.

5. You and I are new here. _____ are from Brazil.

6. The bank is near my house. _____ is big.

7. Simon and Dorota are friends. _____ are helpful.

8. **Halina:** Thank you for your help.

   Simon: _____ are welcome.

1.2 *Be*—Affirmative Statements

SUBJECT	BE	
I	am	a citizen.
Dorota She Simon He	is	from Poland. helpful. from Mexico. in the United States.
The supermarket It	is	different. big.
We You Dorota and Simon They	are	from Japan. new here. American citizens. helpful.

Notes:

We use a form of *be* to:

1. describe the subject (*helpful, big*)
2. tell where the subject is from (*from Mexico, from Poland*)
3. classify the subject (*a citizen*)
4. show location (*here, in the United States*)

EXERCISE 2 Fill in the blanks with the correct form of *be*: *am, is,* or *are.*

1. The laundromat _____is_____ different.

2. I _____ new here.

3. You _____ a citizen.

4. We _____ here to help you.

5. Some things _____ different in the United States.

6. He _____ confused.

7. Simon and Dorota _____ helpful.

8. Dorota _____ from Poland.

EXERCISE 3 Dorota is with Halina, a new immigrant. Fill in the blanks with the correct form of *be*. Then listen and check your answers. 🎧 1.4

Halina: Hi, Dorota. I _____*am*_____ Halina.
            _{1.}

Dorota: You _____ from Poland, right?
             _{2.}

Halina: Yes. I _____ new here.
             _{3.}

Dorota: I _____ from Poland, too. I _____ here to help you. Simon _____ here to help
             _{4.}   _{5.}   _{6.}

             you, too. He _____ from Mexico. Many people here _____ from different countries.
                           _{7.}   _{8.}

Halina: I _____ a little confused. Many things _____ new for me.
             _{9.}   _{10.}

Dorota: Yes. Life _____ different here. But Simon and I _____ both here to help you.
                       _{11.}   _{12.}

ABOUT YOU Check (✓) the items that are true for you.

1. _____ I am new to the United States.

2. _____ I am new at this school.

3. _____ Life is different in a new country.

4. _____ I am confused about life in the United States.

5. _____ I am a citizen of the United States.

6. _____ I am an immigrant.

7. _____ Americans are helpful.

8. _____ I am from Mexico.

9. _____ Spanish is my first language.

10. _____ My family is in the United States.

ABOUT YOU Fill in the blanks.

1. My name is _____.

2. I am from _____.

3. _____ is my first language.

4. I am confused about _____.

5. _____ is my friend.

6. _____ is different in the United States.

7. _____ are different in the United States.

8. _____ is helpful.

A shopping center in Miami, Florida, USA

Circle *Yes* or *No*.

1. I use the laundromat.   Yes   No
2. I wash my clothes by hand.   Yes   No

READ

Read the following conversation. Pay special attention to the contractions with *be* and *this*, *that*, *these*, and *those* in bold. 🎧 1.5

Dorota and a new immigrant, Shafia, are at the laundromat.

Dorota: **This** is the laundromat.

Shafia: The **laundromat's** new for me. **I'm** a little confused.

Dorota: Don't worry. **We're** together. **I'm** here to help you.

Shafia: Thanks. My clothes are dirty. I need clean clothes. **I'm** glad **we're** here.

Dorota: **These** are the washing machines, or washers. The small machines are for small items—clothes, towels, and sheets. **Those** big machines are for big items, like blankets. Coins are necessary for the machines. Over there is the change machine.

Shafia: **Those** machines over there are different.

Dorota: Yes. **They're** dryers. They are for the wet clothes.

Shafia: Okay. Wow! **It's** hot inside the laundromat.

Dorota: **You're** right. The dryers are very hot.

Shafia: **It's** easy to wash clothes in a laundromat.

Dorota: Yes, it is.

Shafia: **These** two washers are empty. **I'm** ready to wash my clothes.

dryer
washing machine
sheets
blanket
towels
clothes
coins

DID YOU **KNOW?**

The average American family washes almost 400 loads of laundry each year.

COMPREHENSION Based on the reading, write T for *true* or F for *false*.

1. _____ The laundromat is new for Dorota.
2. _____ Shafia's clothes are dirty.
3. _____ The dryers are for the wet clothes.

WORDS TO KNOW 🎧 1.6

don't worry	**Don't worry.** I'm here to help you.
together	Dorota is with Shafia. They're **together**.
clothes	This is my shirt. Those are my pants. These are my **clothes**.
dirty	Your clothes are **dirty**. You need to wash them.
clean	My clothes are **clean**. I don't need to wash mine.
glad	I'm **glad** we're here. I'm happy.
item	These machines are for small **items**. Those machines are for bigger things.
necessary	It's **necessary** to wash clothes. You need to do it.
change machine	When you put a dollar bill in the **change machine**, it gives you coins. Four quarters is **change** for one dollar.
right	**A:** It's hot here. **B:** Yes, you're **right**. It is hot.
empty	The dryer is **empty**. It is available.
ready	**A:** It's time to go. **B:** Yes, I'm **ready**! We can go.

LISTEN

Listen to the sentences about the conversation. Circle *True* or *False*. 🎧 1.7

1. (True)   False   4. True   False

2. True   False   5. True   False

3. True   False   6. True   False

1.3 Contractions (Short Forms)

LONG FORM	CONTRACTION	EXAMPLES
I am	I'm	**I'm** here to help.
She is	She's	**She's** from Poland.
He is	He's	**He's** from Mexico.
It is	It's	**It's** hot in here.
Life is	Life's	**Life's** different.
Everything is	Everything's	**Everything's** new.
Dorota is	Dorota's	**Dorota's** from Poland.
The laundromat is	The laundromat's	The **laundromat's** hot.
You are	You're	**You're** very helpful.
We are	We're	**We're** together.
They are	They're	**They're** at the laundromat.

Notes:

1. To make a contraction (short form), we put an apostrophe (') in place of the missing letter.
2. We can make a contraction with a subject pronoun + *am*, *is*, and *are*.
3. We can make a contraction with a singular subject + *is*.
4. We cannot make a contraction with a plural noun + *are*.

   The **dryers are** empty.   NOT: The **dryers're** empty.

GRAMMAR IN USE

It is common to contract a noun or name + *be* in spoken English.

   Simon's from Mexico.

We don't usually contract a noun or name + *be* in written English.

EXERCISE 4 Write the contraction for the words given.

1. _____ I'm _____ new here.
   <u>I am</u>

2. _____ from Mexico. _____ a citizen of the United States now.
   a. <u>Simon is</u>   **b.** <u>He is</u>

3. _____ from Poland. _____ a citizen, too.
   a. <u>Dorota is</u>   **b.** <u>She is</u>

4. _____ both very helpful.
   <u>They are</u>

5. _____ big.
   <u>The laundromat is</u>

6. _____ hot in the laundromat.
   <u>It is</u>

7. _____ new here. _____ new, too.
   a. <u>You are</u>   **b.** <u>I am</u>

   _____ both new.
   c. <u>We are</u>

Warsaw Castle Square, Poland

EXERCISE 5 Ali and Peter are new immigrants. Fill in the blanks with the correct form of *be*. Use contractions when possible. Then listen and check your answers. 🎧 1.8

Ali: I 'm_____ from India. You 're_____ from Russia, right?
            1.   2.

Peter: No. I _____ from Warsaw. It _____ in Poland.
                 3.   4.

Ali: I _____ new here. I _____ confused about things.
                 5.   6.

Peter: We _____ both confused. Life _____ different here.
                 7.   8.

Ali: Yes. Many things _____ new here. The bank _____ new for me.
                             9.   10.

            The supermarket _____ new for me, too.
                            11.

Peter: I _____ glad to know Simon and Dorota. Simon and Dorota _____ from other
                 12.   13.

            countries, but they _____ both citizens now. Simon _____ from Mexico.
                                14.   15.

            He _____ helpful. Dorota _____ from Poland. She _____ helpful, too.
                 16.   17.   18.

Ali: You _____ right. They _____ both very helpful to new immigrants.
                 19.   20.

1.4 Singular and Plural

Singular means "one." *Plural* means "more than one." A plural noun usually ends in -*s*.

SINGULAR	PLURAL	SINGULAR	PLURAL
one machine	five machines	one laundromat	four laundromats
one coin	six coins	one supermarket	seven supermarkets
one towel	three towels	one friend	nine friends
one blanket	two blankets	one citizen	eight citizens

EXERCISE 6 Write the plural form of the words.

quarter 🪙

dime 🪙

nickel 🪙

dollar 💵

1. sheet	_____sheets_____	7. towel	_____
2. quarter	_____	8. item	_____
3. dime	_____	9. blanket	_____
4. dryer	_____	10. coin	_____
5. nickel	_____	11. dollar	_____
6. machine	_____	12. citizen	_____

1.5 This, That, These, Those

SINGULAR		PLURAL		EXPLANATION
This is a laundromat.		**These** are quarters.		Near →
That is a big machine.		**Those** are the dryers.		Not near Far →

Note:

Only *that is* has a contraction—*that's.*

> **That's** a big machine.

Pronunciation Note:

It's hard for many nonnative speakers to hear the difference between *this* and *these*. Listen to your teacher pronounce the sentences in the chart.

EXERCISE 7 Fill in the blanks with *this, that, these,* or *those* and the correct form of *be.* Use contractions when possible.

1.    _____This is_____ a dollar.

2.    _____ the change machine.

3.    _____ coins.

4.    _____ quarters.

5.    _____ an empty machine.

6.    _____ dryers.

EXERCISE 8 Circle the correct word.

1. The (*sheet*/*sheets*) are white.

2. The blankets (*is*/*are*) big.

3. (*These*/*This*) are the dryers.

4. (*They're*/*They*) hot.

5. (*A quarter*/*Quarters*) are necessary for the machine.

6. (*That*/*Those*) machines are empty.

7. The towels (*'re*/*are*) dry.

8. (*A dollar*/*Dollars*) is necessary for those machines.

9. There (*is*/*are*) three dryers in this laundromat.

10. (*This*/*These*) is a big washing machine.

FUN WITH GRAMMAR

Play a game in groups of five. Take turns identifying something near or far that you can see in your classroom.

    A: *That's a table.*

    B: *These are keys.*

If you can't think of a sentence or if you use the wrong word, you are out of the game.

A mother and daughter wait for their laundry at a laundromat.

Circle *Yes* or *No*.

1. I'm confused in an American supermarket.   Yes   No

2. Prices are the same in every supermarket.   Yes   No

READ

Read the following conversation. Pay special attention to the negative forms of *be*, **adjectives, and expressions with** *It* **in bold.** 🎧 1.9

Dorota and Halina are at the supermarket.

Dorota: This is the supermarket. **It's early**. The supermarket **isn't crowded**. The parking lot**'s not crowded**.

Halina: This is my first time in an American supermarket. I**'m not** sure what to do.

Dorota: **It's not hard** to use the supermarket. I'm here to help you.

Halina: Thanks. Hmmm. The prices **aren't** on the products.

Dorota: The prices are on the shelves, under the products. A bar code is on each package. Prices **aren't** the same every week. Some things are on sale each week. Look— crackers are on sale this week. They're usually $4.99 a box. This week they**'re not** $4.99 a box. They're $3.50. And look there. Apples are on sale, too. One pound for $2.15.

Halina: Look! These cookies are **free**.

Dorota: The samples are **free**, but the bags of cookies **aren't**.

(ten minutes later)

Halina: We're finished, right?

Dorota: Yes, we're finished. This checkout is **empty**.

Halina: The cashier**'s not** here.

Dorota: It's a self checkout.

DID YOU KNOW?

Many people bring their own reusable bags to the supermarket. They use the bag many times. In some supermarkets, plastic bags aren't free.

A self-service checkout at a supermarket

8 412978 000098

a bar code

COMPREHENSION Based on the reading, write T for *true* or F for *false*.

1. _____ The supermarket is crowded.

2. _____ The supermarket is new for Halina.

3. _____ Cookies are on sale.

WORDS TO KNOW 1.10

early	It's 8 a.m. It's **early**.
crowded	The store is empty. It isn't **crowded**.
parking lot	I am in the supermarket. My car is in the **parking lot**.
sure	I'm confused. I'm not **sure** what to do.
hard	It's not **hard** to use the supermarket. It's easy.
price	The **price** is 89¢ a pound.
product	The supermarket has many **products**: milk, fruit, meat.
shelf/shelves	The items are on the **shelves**.
bar code	A **bar code** is on each product. The cashier scans the bar code.
package	The cookies are in plastic **packages**.
the same	Prices aren't **the same** every week. They change.
on sale	Crackers are **on sale** this week. They're only $3.50 a box instead of $4.99.
pound	Americans use **pounds**, not kilograms. The abbreviation for pound is *lb*.
free	The cookies aren't **free**. They're $3.79.
sample	The store has **samples** sometimes. You can try the product.
bag	I bring a reusable **bag** to the supermarket. I don't use paper or plastic **bags**.
cashier	The **cashiers** are at the checkouts. They use registers and give the customers their change.
self checkout	The **self checkout** is fast. The customer scans the items.

LISTEN

Listen to the sentences about the conversation. Circle *True* or *False*. 1.11

1. True   (False)   5. True   False

2. True   False   6. True   False

3. True   False   7. True   False

4. True   False   8. True   False

1.6 *Be*—Negative Statements

Compare negative long forms and contractions.

NEGATIVE LONG FORM	NEGATIVE CONTRACTION	
I am not sure.	**I'm not** sure.	
You are not early.	**You're not** early.	**You aren't** early.
She is not a cashier. **He is not** at home. **The store is not** small. **It is not** crowded. **That is not** the price.	**She's not** a cashier. **He's not** at home. **The store's not** small. **It's not** crowded. **That's not** the price.	**She isn't** a cashier. **He isn't** at home. **The store isn't** small. **It isn't** crowded. **That isn't** the price.
We are not in the laundromat. **They are not** on sale. **The cookies are not** free.	**We're not** in the laundromat. **They're not** on sale.	**We aren't** in the laundromat. **They aren't** on sale. **The cookies aren't** free.

Notes:

1. We cannot make a contraction for *am not.*

    NOT: *I **amn't** sure.*

2. We cannot make a contraction for a plural noun + *are.*

    NOT: *The **cookies're** free.*

Compare affirmative and negative statements with *be.*

AFFIRMATIVE	NEGATIVE
We **are** at the supermarket.	We **aren't** at home.
The milk **is** fresh.	It **isn't** old.
I **am** new here.	I**'m not** sure about many things.
The samples **are** free.	The cookies in packages **aren't** free.
You **are** from the United States.	You**'re not** from Mexico.
Peter **is** a new immigrant.	Dorota **isn't** a new immigrant.

EXERCISE 9 Fill in the blanks with a negative form of the underlined form of *be.* Use contractions when possible.

1. The supermarket <u>is</u> big. It <u> isn't OR 's not </u> small.

2. The date <u>is</u> on packages. The date _____ on fruit.

3. We<u>'re</u> at the supermarket. We _____ at the laundromat.

4. Crackers <u>are</u> $3.50 this week. They _____ $3.50 every week.

5. I<u>'m</u> in the supermarket. I _____ in the laundromat.

continued

6. The store is empty. It _____ crowded.

7. You're helpful. You _____ confused.

8. Prices are on the shelves. They _____ on the products.

9. The sample cookies are free. The packages of cookies _____ free.

10. That's a bar code. That _____ the price.

EXERCISE 10 Check (✓) the true statements. Change the false statements to the negative form and add a true statement. Answers may vary.

1. _____ Supermarkets are dirty. *Supermarkets aren't dirty. They're clean.*

2. __✓__ Cashiers are helpful.

3. _____ I'm confused about supermarkets.

4. _____ Life in the United States is easy.

5. _____ Supermarkets are small.

6. _____ Americans are helpful.

7. _____ Supermarkets are crowded in the morning.

8. _____ Prices are the same every week.

9. _____ Supermarkets are hot.

10. _____ Bags are free.

1.7 Adjectives

EXAMPLES			EXPLANATION
SUBJECT	*BE*	**ADJECTIVE**	
The parking lot	**is**	**empty.**	An adjective can follow the verb *be*.
The store	**isn't**	**crowded.**	
The samples	**are**	**free.**	
Those are **free** samples.			An adjective can come before a noun.
These are **big** packages.			

Note:
Descriptive adjectives are always singular. Only the noun is plural.
    one **free** <u>sample</u>
    two **free** <u>samples</u>

EXERCISE 11 Fill in the blanks with an adjective from the box. Then listen and check your answers. 🎧 1.12

CONVERSATION A: Lisa, a new immigrant, and Dorota are at the supermarket.

new ✓	early	helpful	good
crowded	easy	big	different

Lisa: I'm _____ *new* _____ to this country. Everything is _____ for me.
1.   2.

Dorota: Don't worry. I'm here with you.

Lisa: You're very _____.
3.

Dorota: This is the supermarket. It's _____ to shop in a supermarket.
4.

Lisa: The supermarket and the parking lot aren't _____. Why not?
5.

Dorota: It's only 10 a.m. It's _____.
6.

Lisa: This supermarket is _____. In my country, stores are small.
7.

Dorota: Look! Bananas are on sale this week. They're only 59¢ a pound. That's a _____ price.
8.

CONVERSATION B: Simon is showing Lisa's husband, Victor, the laundromat.

open	different	hot	big

Simon: This is the laundromat.

Victor: It's _____ in here.
9.

Simon: Yes, it is. But the door is _____.
10.

Victor: Some machines are small, and some are _____.
11.

Simon: The big machines are for big items, like blankets.

Victor: All of these machines are the same, but those are _____.
12.

Simon: These are washing machines. Those machines are dryers.

Victor: In my country, I am the washer, and the air is the dryer!

1.8 Expressions with *It*

EXAMPLES	EXPLANATION
It's hot in the laundromat. **It**'s cold outside. **It**'s sunny today. **It** isn't rainy.	We use *it* with weather or temperature.
It's 10 a.m. **It**'s early. **It** isn't late. **It**'s Tuesday. **It**'s morning/afternoon/night.	We use *it* with time.

EXERCISE 12 Fill in the blanks with one of the words from the box.

early ✓	sunny	late	cold	7 a.m.	hot

1. It's _____ *early* _____. It's only _____.
           a.   **b.**

2. It's _____ in the laundromat. Open the door.

3. It's _____ outside. Close the door.

4. It's _____. I'm tired.

5. It's _____ today. We're at the beach.

EXERCISE 13 Fill in the blanks to make true statements. Use the words from the box in Exercise 12 or your own ideas.

1. It's _____ today. It isn't _____ today.
         a. day of week   **b. day of week**

2. It's _____ outside.

3. It's _____ inside.

4. It's _____.

ABOUT YOU Fill in the blanks to make true affirmative or negative statements. Use *am*, *is*, or *are*.

1. I _____ *am* _____ new to this country.

2. My school _____ big. My school _____ small.
                  a.   **b.**

3. In my town, the parking lots _____ crowded.

4. It _____ hot in my country right now.

5. It _____ cold in my country right now.

6. In my supermarket, the prices _____ the same every week.

7. I _____ from Poland.

1.9 Singular and Plural—Spelling Rules

SINGULAR	PLURAL	RULE
coin dime dollar	coin**s** dime**s** dollar**s**	We add -s to form the plural of most nouns.
dish watch box dress	dish**es** watch**es** box**es** dress**es**	We add -es to form the plural of nouns that end in *sh*, *ch*, *x*, and *ss*.
family baby	famil**ies** bab**ies**	We change the final *y* to *i* and add -es when a word ends in a consonant + *y*.
day toy	day**s** toy**s**	We add only -s when a word ends in a vowel + *y*.
shelf life	shel**ves** li**ves**	We take away the final *f* or *fe* and add -ves when a word ends in an *f* or *fe*.

Pronunciation Note:

Sometimes we need to pronounce an extra syllable. Listen to your teacher pronounce these words:

price—prices   *noise—noises*   *page—pages*

EXERCISE 14 Fill in the blanks with the plural form of the noun given.

1. The _____ *cars* _____ are in the parking lot.

          car

2. The _____ are under the _____.

     a. price   **b.** shelf

3. The _____ are in a blue box.

     match

4. It's Saturday, and many _____ are at the supermarket.

                family

5. The soap for washing _____ costs $2.89.

             dish

6. The _____ are on sale this week. Those _____ are on sale.

     a. cracker   **b.** box

7. Some _____ are in the supermarket today.

     baby

8. Dorota speaks two _____: Polish and English.

     language

FUN WITH GRAMMAR

Play a game of *Telephone*. With your whole class, sit in a circle. Student A, think of a sentence with *be*. It can be affirmative or negative. Whisper your sentence to Student B. Student B, whisper the sentence to Student C. Keep going around the circle. The last student says the sentence aloud. Is it the same sentence that Student A made?

SUMMARY OF UNIT 1

Be—Affirmative and Negative Statements

AFFIRMATIVE	NEGATIVE
I **am** from Poland.	I **am not** from Mexico.
You **are** early.	You **are not** late.
She **is** from Mexico.	She **is not** from Japan.
It **is** a supermarket.	It **is not** a laundromat.
We **are** cashiers.	We **are not** teachers.
They **are** late.	They **are not** early.

Contractions

LONG FORM	AFFIRMATIVE CONTRACTION	NEGATIVE CONTRACTION	
I am	I'm	I'm not	
She is	She's	She's not	She isn't
He is	He's	He's not	He isn't
It is	It's	It's not	It isn't
Everything is	Everything's	Everything's not	Everything isn't
You are	You're	You're not	You aren't
We are	We're	We're not	We aren't
They are	They're	They're not	They aren't

This, That, These, Those

SINGULAR	PLURAL
This is a laundromat.	**These** are quarters.
That is a big machine.	**Those** are dryers.

Adjectives

The parking lot is **empty**.	Those are **free** samples.

Expressions with *It*

It's hot in here.	**It**'s 10 a.m.
It's sunny today.	**It**'s Tuesday.

Singular and Plural

SINGULAR	PLURAL
one coin	two coin**s**
one dish	three dish**es**
one family	two famil**ies**
one day	four day**s**
one shelf	two shel**ves**

REVIEW

A. Choose the correct words to complete the conversation.

A: Hi. (*I'm/You're*) Anna.

1.

B: Hi, Anna. I'm Monika. (*This/These*) is my sister, Timea.

2.

A: It's nice to meet you. (*You/You're*) from Poland, right?

3.

B: No. (*We're/We aren't*) from Poland. (*We're/We*) from Slovakia.

4.   5.

A: (*I/I'm*) from Mexico. But my husband and I (*am/are*) citizens of the United States.

6.   7.

B: Everything is new for us here.

A: Don't worry. (*I'm/I'm not*) here to help. Let's start at the supermarket.

8.

Later, at the supermarket:

A: (*This is/These are*) our supermarket.

9.

B: Wow, it's (*big/free*)!

10.

A: I know. But it's (*early/late*), so it's not crowded.

11.

B: (*Those/That*) apples look good.

12.

A: Yes. But (*they not/they're not*) on sale. (*These/This*) apples are on sale. And they look

13.   14.

good, too.

B: (*We're/They're*) 99 cents a pound. Is that a (*good/helpful*) price?

15.   16.

A: Yes, it is. Oh, see (*that/these*) sign? Bananas (*is/are*) on sale this week, too.

17.   18.

B: Great. Brr, it's (*cold/nice*) in here.

19.

A: I know. Let's go to another part of the store. (*It's/They're*) warmer there.

20.

B. Fill in the blanks. Use the correct form of the words given. Use contractions where possible.

Monika _____ from Slovakia. She and Timea _____ from Poland.

              1. be   2. not be

_____ at the supermarket with Anna. _____ very helpful. The supermarket

     3. They/be   4. She/be

_____ big, but _____ crowded. Apples _____ on sale this week.

      5. be   6. it/not be   7. be

Bananas _____ on sale, too. Crackers _____ on sale. _____ cold

             8. be   9. not be   10. It/be

in the supermarket, but _____ warm and sunny outside. Anna, Monika, and Timea

                             11. it/be

_____ ready to go outside.

    12. be

FROM GRAMMAR TO WRITING

PART 1 Editing Advice

1. Use the correct form of *be*.

   You ~~is~~ *are* at the laundromat.

2. Every sentence has a subject.

   ~~Is~~ *It's* 10:15 a.m.

   ~~Is~~ *It's* hot today.

   This is Simon. ~~Is~~ *He is* from Mexico.

3. Don't confuse *this* and *these*.

   ~~This~~ *These* are big machines.

   ~~These~~ *This* is my bank.

4. In a contraction, put the apostrophe in place of the missing letter.

   ~~Your'e~~ *You're* late.

   The supermarket ~~is'nt~~ *isn't* crowded.

5. Use an apostrophe, not a comma, in a contraction.

   ~~I,m~~ *I'm* at the supermarket.

6. Don't make adjectives plural.

   These are ~~bigs~~ *big* machines.

7. Don't use *a* before a plural noun.

   This is a small machine. Those are ~~a~~ big machines.

8. Don't confuse *your* and *you're*.

   ~~Your~~ *You're* at the supermarket.

9. Don't confuse *he* and *she*.

   Dorota is from Poland. ~~He~~ *She* is from Warsaw.

   Simon is from Mexico. ~~She~~ *He* speaks Spanish.

PART 2 Editing Practice

Some of the shaded words and phrases have mistakes. Find the mistakes and correct them. If the shaded words are correct, write *C*.

Dorota and Lisa are in the laundromat.

Dorota: We,re *We're* here to wash clothes.
1.

Lisa: It's easy to wash clothes in a laundromat. *C*
2.

Dorota: Yes, it is. But is hot in here.
3.

Lisa: Your right.
4.

Dorota: The door is'nt open.
5.

Lisa: This are my blankets.
6.

Dorota: Theyr'e big. Those machines is for bigs items. This machines are for small items.
7.   8.   9.   10.

These are a quarters for the machines.
11.   12.

Lisa: Thanks. Your'e helpful.
13.

Dorota: I,m here to help. Simon's helpful, too. But is at the bank today. She's with Victor.
14.   15.   16.

PART 3 Write

Rewrite the following paragraph. Change the singular nouns and pronouns to plurals. Change other necessary words, too.

This is a green apple. It's on sale. It's very big. It's only $1.75 a pound. That's a red apple. It isn't on sale. It's not very big. It's $2.39 a pound. This is a free sample of the green apple. It's not very fresh. That's a free sample of the red apple. It's fresh. This red apple is good. That green apple isn't good today.

These are green apples. They're . . .

PART 4 Learner's Log

1. Write one sentence about each of these topics. Write affirmative and negative sentences with *be*.
   - an American laundromat
   - an American supermarket
   - items in an American supermarket

2. Write any questions you still have about the topics above.

BEFORE YOU READ

Circle *Yes* or *No*.

1. I wear a watch every day.	Yes	No
2. I have a clock in my bedroom.	Yes	No

READ

Read the following conversation. Pay special attention to the possessive forms in bold. 🎧 2.1

Victor and Dorota are in **Dorota's** car.

Victor: Hi, Dorota. I'm surprised to see you. It's **Simon's** turn to help me.

Dorota: Yes, it is. But he's with **his** kids[1] today. **His** wife, Marta, is at the hospital. **Her** father is sick. So I'm here to help you with the bank.

Victor: It's late. Look at **your** clock. It's 4:30. The bank is closed.

Dorota: No, it isn't. **My** clock is fast. It's only 4:15.

Victor: So **your** clock is broken.

Dorota: No, it isn't. **My** clock is always fast. And **my** watch is always fast, too. That way, I'm always on time.

Victor: I'm confused. **Your** clock is fast, and that's OK with you?

Dorota: Yes. I'm never late. Time is important for Americans. **Their** ideas about time are different from **our** ideas about time.

(five minutes later)

Dorota: We're here now. Oh, no. The bank is closed. Today is a holiday. It's the Fourth of July.

---

[1] *Kid(s)* is informal. *Child(ren)* is formal.

> ### DID YOU **KNOW?**
> Some American holidays are: Martin Luther King, Jr. Day (January), Memorial Day (May), Independence Day/ Fourth of July (July), Labor Day (September), Columbus Day (October), Veterans Day (November) and Thanksgiving (November).

COMPREHENSION Based on the reading, write T for *true* or F for *false*.

1. _____ Simon is with Victor today.

2. _____ Dorota's watch is broken.

3. _____ The bank is closed.

WORDS TO KNOW 🎧 2.2

surprised	Simon isn't here today. Victor is **surprised** to see Dorota.
turn	It's Simon's **turn** to help.
kid, son, daughter	Simon and Marta have three **kids**. They have a **son** and two **daughters**.
wife	Simon has a **wife**. Her name is Marta.
clock	Look at the **clock**. It's 4:30.
fast	Your clock is **fast**. It's only 4:15, but your clock says "4:30."
broken	My clock is **broken**. It doesn't work.
watch	I wear my **watch** on my wrist.
on time	You're **on time**. You're not late.
holiday	It's a **holiday** today. The schools and banks are closed.

LISTEN

Listen to the sentences about the conversation. Circle *True* or *False*. 🎧 2.3

1. (True)   False   5. True   False

2. True   False   6. True   False

3. True   False   7. True   False

4. True   False   8. True   False

2.1 Possessive Nouns

EXAMPLES	EXPLANATION
Simon's wife is at the hospital. **Marta's** father is sick.	We use noun + 's to show relationship.
Dorota's clock is fast.	We use noun + 's to show ownership.

> **GRAMMAR IN USE**
>
> Don't confuse possessive nouns and contractions with *be*.
>
> POSSESSIVE NOUN: ***Marta's** father is sick.* (Her father is sick.)
>
> CONTRACTION WITH *BE*: ***Marta's** at the hospital.* (Marta is at the hospital.)

EXERCISE 1 Fill in the blanks with *Marta's*, *Simon's*, or *Dorota's*.

1. _____Dorota's_____ clock is fast.

2. Marta is _____ wife.

3. _____ father is sick. He's in the hospital.

4. Today it's _____ turn to help, but he's with the kids.

5. _____ first language is Polish.

6. _____ first language is Spanish. He's from Mexico.

EXERCISE 2 Fill in the blanks. Put the words in the correct order. Add an apostrophe (') + *s* to make a possessive noun.

1. _____Simon's kids_____ aren't in school today.

kids/Simon

2. _____ isn't with him.

daughter/Victor

3. _____ are at home.

Simon/children

4. _____ is sick.

father/Marta

5. This is _____.

Dorota/car

6. _____ isn't fast.

Victor/watch

2.2 Possessive Adjectives

Compare subject pronouns and possessive adjectives.

SUBJECT PRONOUN	POSSESSIVE ADJECTIVE	EXAMPLES
I	my	**I** am late. **My** watch is slow.
You	your	**You** are late. **Your** watch is slow.
He	his	**He** is late. **His** watch is slow.
She	her	**She** is late. **Her** watch is slow.
We	our	**We** are late. **Our** clock is slow.
They	their	**They** are late. **Their** clock is slow.

EXERCISE 3 Fill in the blanks with *my*, *your*, *his*, *her*, *our*, or *their*.

1. You are with _____your_____ kids.

2. She is with _____ kids.

3. They are with _____ kids.

4. I am with _____ kids.

5. He is with _____ kids.

6. We are with _____ kids.

ABOUT YOU Circle *True* or *False*.

1. My watch is fast.	True	False
2. Time is important to me.	True	False
3. Money is important to me.	True	False
4. My classmate's language is different from my language.	True	False
5. My teacher's name is hard for me to say.	True	False
6. My bank is open right now.	True	False

EXERCISE 4 Simon and Dorota are on the telephone. Fill in the blanks with *my*, *your*, *his*, *her*, *our*, or *their*. Then listen and check your answers. 🎧 2.4

Simon: Hi, Dorota. This is Simon. I'm busy today. Marta's busy, too. _____Her_____ father is sick.
                                                                                    1.

   _____ kids are at home today. _____ school is closed. It's _____ turn to
   2.   **3.**   **4.**

   help Victor today, but I'm busy.

Dorota: That's OK. _____ kids need you. I'm not busy today. I can help Victor.
                           5.

FUN WITH GRAMMAR

Start a chain activity with a sentence about something that is yours.

   A: My watch is slow.

The next person (Student B) repeats the sentence, using a possessive adjective or a possessive noun, and adds his or her own sentence. Continue around the circle. Help classmates if they can't remember.

   A: My watch is slow.
   B: Your watch is slow. My shirt is blue.
   C: Dana's watch is slow. Allen's shirt is blue. My car is outside.
   D: . . .

BEFORE YOU READ

Circle *Yes* or *No*.

1.	I'm usually on time.	Yes	No
2.	My doctor is usually on time.	Yes	No

READ

Read the following conversation. Pay special attention to the *yes/no* questions in bold. 🎧 2.5

Simon comes to the bank to help Victor.

Simon: **Am I late?** Traffic is bad today.

Victor: You're not late. It's only 10:15.

Simon: Oh, I'm fifteen minutes late, then. I'm sorry.

Victor: Fifteen minutes is nothing.

Simon: In the United States, people are usually on time.

Victor: Really? **Are you serious?**

Simon: Yes, I am.

Victor: I'm surprised. **Are people on time for everything?**

Simon: For most things. They're on time for appointments.

Victor: **Is this an appointment?**

Simon: Yes, it is. I'm here to help you with the bank.

Victor: I'm confused. My doctor is never on time. She's always late.

Simon: That's different. Doctors are always late. They are very busy.

Victor: **Is it necessary to be on time with friends?**

Simon: It's not necessary, but it *is* polite.

Victor: Look. The time *and* temperature are on the clock outside the bank. **Is time always on your mind?**

Simon: Yes, it is. "Time is money." Time is always on our minds.

DID YOU **KNOW?**

Americans use Fahrenheit (F) for temperature. Other countries use Celsius (C).

COMPREHENSION Based on the reading, write T for *true* or F for *false*.

1. _____ Simon is late.

2. _____ People in the United States are usually on time.

3. _____ Doctors in the United States are usually on time.

WORDS TO KNOW 🎧 2.6

traffic	There are a lot of cars. **Traffic** is bad today.
usually	Students are **usually** on time for class. They don't arrive late.
serious	Are you **serious**? Is it true?
appointment	Victor has a 10 a.m. **appointment** with Simon.
never	Some people are **never** on time. They are always late.
polite	It's **polite** to say "please" and "thank you."
temperature	The **temperature** is 69 degrees today.
outside/inside	Victor is in the parking lot. He is **outside** the bank. He isn't **inside** the bank.
on (my, your, etc.) mind	Time is always **on my mind**. I think about it a lot.
always	Lisa **always** goes to the supermarket on Mondays. She never goes on Tuesdays.

FAHRENHEIT	CELSIUS
0	−18
10	−12
20	−7
30	−1
40	4
50	10
60	16
70	21
80	27
90	32
100	38
212	100

LISTEN

Listen to the questions about the conversation. Circle the correct answer. 🎧 2.7

1. (Yes, it is.)   No, it isn't.

2. Yes, he is.   No, he isn't.

3. Yes, they are.   No, they aren't.

4. Yes, they are.   No, they aren't.

5. Yes, it is.   No, it isn't.

6. Yes, they are.   No, they aren't.

2.3 Be—Yes/No Questions

We put a form of *be* before the subject to ask a question.

BE	SUBJECT		SHORT ANSWER
Am	I	late?	No, you aren't. OR No, you're not.
Is	traffic	bad?	Yes, it is.
Is	Simon	on time?	No, he isn't. OR No, he's not.
Are	you	serious?	Yes, I am.
Are	they	at the bank?	Yes, they are.

Note:

You can use a contraction for a negative answer. We don't use a contraction for an affirmative answer.

No, you aren't. OR *No, you're not.*   *Yes, you are.*   NOT: *Yes, you're.*

Pronunciation Note:

A *yes/no* question has rising intonation. Listen to your teacher pronounce the statements and questions above.

Am I late?

Punctuation Note:

We put a question mark (?) at the end of a question.

Compare statements and *yes/no* questions with *be*.

STATEMENT	YES/NO QUESTION
I am late.	**Am I** very late?
Time is important.	**Is time** always on your mind?
Some people are on time.	**Are some people** always on time?
It is necessary to be on time.	**Is it** necessary to be on time with friends?

EXERCISE 5 Fill in the correct form of *be* and the noun or pronoun given to make a question.

1. <u>Are Simon and Victor</u> at the supermarket? No, they aren't.
    Simon and Victor

2. _____ students? Yes, they are.
    they

3. _____ open? Yes, it is.
    the supermarket

4. _____ late? No, you're not.
    I

5. _____ good to be on time? Yes, it is.
    it

6. _____ inside the school? No, I'm not.
    you

7. _____ on time? Yes, we are.
    we

8. _____ polite? Yes, she is.
    Dorota

EXERCISE 6 Answer with a short answer, based on the conversation on page 32.

1. Is the bank open? _____ Yes, it is. _____

2. Is Simon on time? _____

3. Are Simon and Victor at the bank? _____

4. Is Simon with Dorota? _____

5. Are doctors usually on time? _____

6. Is it necessary to be on time with friends? _____

7. Is it polite to be on time with friends? _____

8. Are Americans usually late for appointments? _____

ABOUT YOU Answer with a short answer. Share your answers with a partner.

1. Are you usually on time? _____ Yes, I am. _____

2. Are you surprised about some things in this country? _____

3. Is your apartment big? _____

4. Are you a serious student? _____

5. Are you an immigrant? _____

6. Are you a parent? _____

7. Are you on time for everything? _____

8. Is this class easy for you? _____

9. Is English hard for you? _____

10. Are your classmates always serious? _____

11. Is your teacher always on time? _____

12. Are people in this city usually polite? _____

GRAMMAR IN USE

In informal conversation, we often answer a *yes/no* question with just *Yes* or *No*.

> A: *Am I late?*
> B: *No.*

EXERCISE 7 Listen to the conversations. Fill in the blanks with the words you hear. 🎧 2.8

CONVERSATION A: Victor and Dorota are at the library.

Victor: _____Am I_____ on time?
1.

Dorota: Yes, you _____.
2.

Victor: _____ at the library?
3.

Dorota: Yes, we _____. We're here to learn about the library.
4.

Victor: _____ open?
5.

Dorota: No, it _____. It's only 8:48. We're a few minutes early.
6.

CONVERSATION B: Simon and Marta are on the telephone.

Simon: Hello?

Marta: Hi, Simon.

Simon: _____ on your way home?
7.

Marta: No, I _____. I'm at the
8.
supermarket now.

Simon: _____ open now? It's 9 p.m.
9.

Marta: Yes, it _____. This store is
10.
open twenty-four hours a day.

Simon: _____ with Halina still?
11.

Marta: No, I _____. I'm alone now.
12.

Simon: We need bananas. _____ on
13.
sale?

Marta: Yes, they _____. They're only
14.
59¢ a pound this week.

Simon: We need bread, too. _____
15.
also on sale?

Marta: No, it _____.
16.

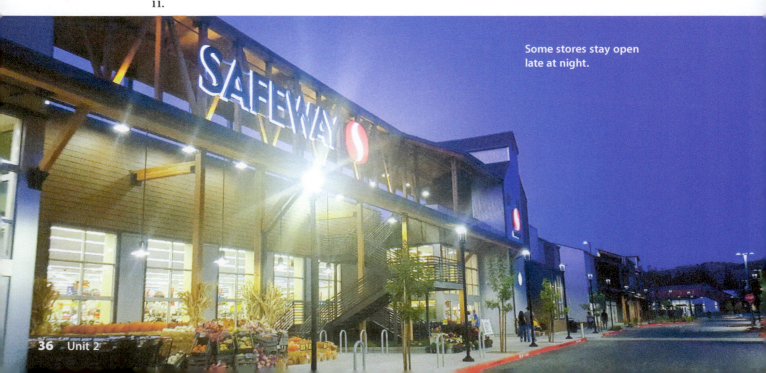

Some stores stay open late at night.

2.4 Irregular Plural Forms

SINGULAR	PLURAL	EXPLANATION
child person	children people	Sometimes the plural form is a different word.
man woman	men women	Sometimes the plural form has a vowel change.

Pronunciation Note:

We can hear the difference between *woman* and *women* in the first syllable. Listen to your teacher pronounce the singular and plural forms above.

EXERCISE 8 Fill in the blanks with the singular or plural form of the noun given.

1. The _____*men*_____ are at the bank.

man

2. One _____ is behind me. Two _____ are in front of me.

a. person   b. person

3. The _____ is with three _____.

a. woman   b. child

4. One _____ is small. The other _____ are not small.

a. child   b. child

5. A _____ is behind me.

man

6. Five _____ are in line.

woman

7. Three _____ are near the door.

man

8. There are a lot of _____ at the bank today.

person

EXERCISE 9 Fill in the blanks with the correct form of *be*.

1. The people at the bank _____*are*_____ helpful.

2. This child _____ with her mother.

3. Those children _____ with their father.

4. The woman _____ busy.

5. One person _____ alone.

6. The people in the bank _____ busy.

7. That man _____ polite.

8. Those women _____ in line at the bank.

Circle *Yes* or *No.*

1. I have a bank account.   Yes   No

2. I have an ATM card.   Yes   No

READ

Read the following conversation. Pay special attention to the *wh*-questions and the articles *a* and *an* in bold. 🎧 2.9

Dorota and Victor are at the bank.

Dorota: Hi, Victor. **How are you?**

Victor: Hi, Dorota. I'm fine, thanks. **Where is Simon?**

Dorota: He's at the supermarket already.

Victor: Is this your bank?

Dorota: Yes, it is.

Victor: **What time is it?**

Dorota: It's 7:30 p.m. The bank is closed now. We can't go inside.

Victor: **Who's that woman over there?**

Dorota: She's **a** security guard.

Victor: **When is the bank open?**

Dorota: This bank is open from 9 a.m. to 4 p.m., Monday through Thursday. It's open from 9 to 7 on Friday and 9 to 1 on Saturday.

Victor: **Why are we here,** then?

Dorota: I'm out of cash. The ATM is always open.

Victor: **What's an ATM? A** cash machine?

Dorota: **An** ATM is **an** Automated Teller Machine. And yes, it's **a** machine for cash.

Victor: **What's that?** Your bank card?

Dorota: Yes, it opens the door. And I use it to get cash. I need **a** PIN for my account, too.

Victor: **What's a PIN?**

Dorota: It's **a** Personal Identification Number.

Victor: **What's your PIN?**

Dorota: That's **a** secret!

DID YOU KNOW?

You can use mobile or online banking services to save time. You can see your monthly statement and pay bills.

COMPREHENSION Based on the reading, write T for *true* or F for *false*.

1. _____ The bank is open right now.

2. _____ The supermarket is open right now.

3. _____ On Monday, the bank is open at 5:00.

WORDS TO KNOW 2.10

security guard	The **security guard** works at the bank.
through	The bank is open Monday **through** Saturday.
out of	I'm **out of** money. I don't have any money.
ATM	The **ATM** is an easy way to get money.
cash	We are at the bank. It's easy to get **cash** at an ATM.
automated	The machine is **automated**. A computer makes it work.
teller	A **teller** works at a bank.
PIN	A **PIN** is a Personal Identification Number.
account	I have a bank **account** for my savings.
secret	No one knows my PIN. It's a **secret**.

LISTEN

Listen to the questions about the conversation. Circle the correct answer. 2.11

1. at the bank   at the supermarket

2. at the bank   at the supermarket

3. Dorota's   Simon's

4. Yes, it's late.   It's 7:30.

5. She's a bank teller.   She's a security guard.

6. twenty-four hours a day   Monday through Saturday

7. from 9 a.m. to 4 p.m.   twenty-four hours a day

8. It's a machine for cash.   It's at the bank.

9. at 10:15   to get cash

10. 924   It's a secret.

2.5 *Be*—*Wh*- Questions

Wh- questions begin with *where, when, why, who, what, whose,* and *how.* Observe the word order in a *wh-* question. *Wh-* questions are also called *information questions.*

QUESTION WORD(S)	BE	SUBJECT		ANSWER
Where	are	we?		We're at the bank.
What	is	that?		It's an ATM.
What time	is	it?		It's 10:15.
Why	are	we	here?	We're here to get cash.
When	is	the bank	open?	It's open Monday through Saturday.
Who	is	that woman?		She's a security guard.
Whose money	is	this?		It's Dorota's money.
How	are	you?		I'm fine, thanks.
How old	is	Simon's son?		He's 15 (years old).

Note:

We can make a contraction with most *wh-* words and *is.*

>   ***What's** an ATM?*   ***When's** the bank open?*   ***Why's** he here?*

Compare statements and *wh-* questions.

STATEMENT	WH- QUESTION
The bank is open.	When **is the bank** open?
We are at the ATM.	Why **are we** at the ATM?
You are a student.	How old **are you**?
I am at a bank.	Where **am I**?
She is inside the bank.	Why **is she** inside the bank?
Dorota is an immigrant.	Who **is Dorota**?
That is Dorota's money.	Whose money **is that**?
It is late.	What time **is it**?

Pronunciation Note:

Wh- questions have a falling intonation.

>   *Where is the bank?*

Listen to your teacher pronounce the statements and questions above.

EXERCISE 10 Fill in the blanks with a question word to complete this conversation between Dorota and Lisa. Then listen and check your answers. 🎧 2.12

Dorota: _____How_____ are you?
1.

Lisa: I'm fine. _____ are we?
2.

Dorota: We're at the bank.

Lisa: _____'s that?
3.

Dorota: It's an ATM.

Lisa: _____ are we here?
4.

Dorota: To learn about the bank.

Lisa: _____'s that woman?
5.

Dorota: She's the security guard.

Lisa: _____ is the bank open?
6.

Dorota: Monday through Thursday, from 9 a.m. to 4 p.m., Friday from 9 a.m. to 7 p.m.,

and Saturday from 9 a.m. to 1 p.m.

Lisa: _____ is it?
7.

Dorota: It's 8:45. We're early.

Lisa: _____'s that?
8.

Dorota: It's my ATM card.

EXERCISE 11 Complete the questions.

1. It's late. What time _____is it_____?

2. We're late. Why _____ ?

3. The ATM is near here. Where _____ ?

4. That woman is in the bank. Who _____ ?

5. That money is Dorota's. Whose _____ this?

6. Simon's 42 years old. How _____ Marta?

ABOUT YOU Answer the questions.

1. What time is it now? _____

2. Where are you from? _____

continued

3. Who's your English teacher? _____

4. How old are you? _____

5. Where's your school? _____

6. When's the school open? _____

7. Who's your friend? _____

8. Where's your English book? _____

2.6 Articles *A* and *An*

We use *a* or *an* before a singular noun.

EXAMPLES	EXPLANATION
What's this? It's **a** bank. Who's that woman? She's **a** security guard.	We use *a* before a consonant sound.
What's that? It's **an** ATM. What's this? It's **an** envelope.	We use *an* before a vowel sound. The vowels are *a, e, i, o,* and *u*.
Quarters and dimes are coins. What are those? They're pennies.	We don't use *a* or *an* before a plural noun. NOT: Quarters and dimes are *a* coins. NOT: Those are *a* pennies.
adjective adjective + noun The bank is big. It's **a** big bank.	We use *a* or *an* only if a noun follows the adjective. NOT: The bank is *a* big.

EXERCISE 12 Fill in the blanks with *a* or *an*.

1. This is ___*a*___ bank.

2. That's ___*an*___ envelope.

3. I'm _____ immigrant.

4. I'm _____ new immigrant.

5. You are _____ helpful person.

6. This is _____ new book.

7. A quarter is _____ coin.

8. Dorota isn't _____ old woman.

9. Simon's from Mexico. Mexico is _____ North American country.

10. He's _____ busy person.

EXERCISE 13 Rewrite the sentence with the adjective given. Change *a* to *an* or *an* to *a* if needed.

1. First Community is a bank. _First Community is an old bank._
                                                     old

2. That's an ATM. _____
                                                     new

3. Thanksgiving is a holiday. _____
                                                     American

4. This is a number. _____
                                                     identification

5. This is a test. _____
                                                     easy

6. That's an envelope. _____
                                                     big

EXERCISE 14 Fill in the blanks with the correct form of *be* and *a* or *an* where necessary. Use contractions when possible. Then listen and check your answers. 🎧 2.13

Halina: What's that?

Simon: It _'s an_____ ATM.
                   1.

Halina: What's an ATM?

Simon: It _____ machine for cash.
                   2.

Halina: What are these?

Simon: These _____ envelopes for checks.
                      3.

Halina: What _____ check?
                    4.

Simon: Look. This _____ check. It _____ paycheck from my work.
                         5.   6.

Halina: What _____ those?
                    7.

Simon: Those _____ drive-up ATMs.
                      8.

Halina: Americans _____ very busy. They _____ always in their cars.
                         9.   10.

Simon: It _____ easy way to use the bank. It _____ fast, too!
                   11.   12.

A man gets cash at a drive-up ATM.

SUMMARY OF UNIT 2

Possessive Nouns

USE	EXAMPLES
To show relationship	**Simon's** wife is at the hospital.
To show ownership	**Dorota's** clock is fast.

Possessive Adjectives

SUBJECT PRONOUN	POSSESSIVE ADJECTIVE	EXAMPLES
I	my	I am late. **My** watch is slow.
You	your	You are late. **Your** watch is slow.
He/She	his/her	He/She is late. **His/Her** watch is slow.
We	our	We are late. **Our** clock is slow.
They	their	They are late. **Their** clock is slow.

Be—Yes/No Questions

BE	SUBJECT		SHORT ANSWER
Am	I	late?	No, you aren't./No, you're not.
Is	traffic	bad?	Yes, it is.
Is	Simon	on time?	No, he isn't./No, he's not.
Are	you	serious?	Yes, I am.
Are	they	at the bank?	Yes, they are.

Irregular Plural Forms

SINGULAR	PLURAL
child	children
person	people
man	men
woman	women

Be—Wh- Questions

QUESTION WORD(S)	BE	SUBJECT		ANSWER
Where	are	we?		We're at the bank.
What	is	that?		It's an ATM.
What time	is	it?		It's 10:15.
Why	are	we	here?	We're here to get cash.
When	is	the bank	open?	It's open Monday through Saturday.
Who	is	that woman?		She's a security guard.
Whose money	is	this?		It's Dorota's money.
How	are	you?		I'm fine, thanks.
How old	is	Simon's son?		He's 15 (years old).

REVIEW

A. Choose the correct words to complete the conversation.

A: Hi, Marco. (*How*/*Where*) are you?
1.

B: I'm fine, thanks. How (*are*/*is*) you?
2.

A: I'm fine. I'm sorry, I'm a little late.

B: That's OK. (*Are you*/*You are*) ready to learn about the bank?
3.

A: Yes! What (*is*/*are*) that?
4.

B: It's (*a*/*an*) ATM.
5.

A: And (*who*/*what*) is that?
6.

B: This is (*her*/*my*) ATM card.
7.

A: (*Are*/*Is*) the bank open now?
8.

B: Yes, (*it's*/*it is*). It's open from 9 a.m. to 5 p.m.
9.

A: (*Are*/*Is*) all banks open from 9 a.m. to 5 p.m.?
10.

B: No, (*they are*/*they aren't*). My friend Tom has (*a*/*an*) different bank. (*His*/*He's*) bank is open from 8 a.m.
11.   12.   13.

to 4 p.m.

A: There are a lot of (*people*/*person*) in line.
14.

B: Yes, there are.

A: (*Where*/*Who*) is that woman?
15.

B: She's (*a*/*an*) teller. She works at the bank.
16.

B. Fill in the blanks to complete the conversation.

A: _____ on time?
1.

B: Yes, you are.

A: _____ are we?
2.

B: We're at the library.

A: _____ are we here?
3.

B: We're here to get a library card for you.

A: _____ library card is that?
4.

B: It's my library card.

A: _____ the library open?
5.

B: Yes, it is.

A: _____ is it open?
6.

B: It's open from 10 to 7 today.

A: _____ is it now?
7.

B: It's 10:30.

A: _____ is that woman?
8.

B: She's the librarian.

FROM GRAMMAR TO WRITING

PART 1 Editing Advice

1. *People* is a plural word. Use a plural verb.

   The new people ~~is~~ <u>are</u> late.

2. Use the correct possessive adjective.

   She is with ~~his~~ <u>her</u> father.

   They are with ~~they~~ <u>their</u> mother.

3. Don't confuse *you're* and *your*.

   What's ~~you're~~ <u>your</u> name?

   ~~Your~~ <u>You're</u> never late.

4. Use the correct word order in a question.

   Why ~~you are~~ <u>are you</u> late?

   Is ~~big the supermarket~~ <u>the supermarket big</u>?

5. Use *a* or *an* before a singular noun.

   This is <u>a</u> bank. It's <u>an</u> old bank.

6. Don't use *a* or *an* with plural nouns.

   Victor and Dorota are ~~an~~ immigrants.

7. Use *an*, not *a*, before a vowel sound.

   She is ~~a~~ <u>an</u> immigrant.

8. Use the correct plural form.

   The ~~childs~~ <u>children</u> are happy.

9. Use the correct possessive form with nouns.

   Dorota <u>'s</u> clock is fast.

PART 2 Editing Practice

Some of the shaded words and phrases have mistakes. Find the mistakes and correct them. If the shaded words are correct, write *C*.

Ali and Simon are at the bank.

Ali: <u>Are</u> we at your bank?
            1. <u>C</u>

Simon: Yes, we're at my bank. What time ~~it is~~ <u>is it</u>?
            2.

Ali: It's 9:15. Why we are here?
            3.

Simon: To learn about the ATM.

Ali: What's a ATM?
                4.

Simon: It's machine for cash.
                5.

Ali: Where's Dorota today? Why she isn't here?
                6.   7.

Simon: His son is home. She's with him.
                8.   9.

Ali: Is small her son?
                10.

Simon: No, he's not. He's an young man.
                11.   12.

Ali: How old is Dorota son?
                         13.

Simon: He's 18 years old. He's a college student.
                                   14.

Ali: Oh, look. The bank's closed today.
                         15.

Simon: Don't worry. I have a card to use the ATM.
                                 16.

Ali: Why is those people in the bank? The bank is closed, but those person are inside.
                17.   18.

Simon: They're a security guards.
                   19.

Ali: Your right.
                20.

PART 3 Write

Look at the picture. Write five *yes/no* and *wh-* questions about Marta and her daughter, Amy. Answer the questions.

Where are Marta and Amy?
They're at the doctor's office.

PART 4 Learner's Log

1. Complete the following sentences with your own ideas.

   a. People are on time for _____ .

   b. _____ are at banks.

   c. An ATM is _____ .

2. Write any questions you still have about the topics above.

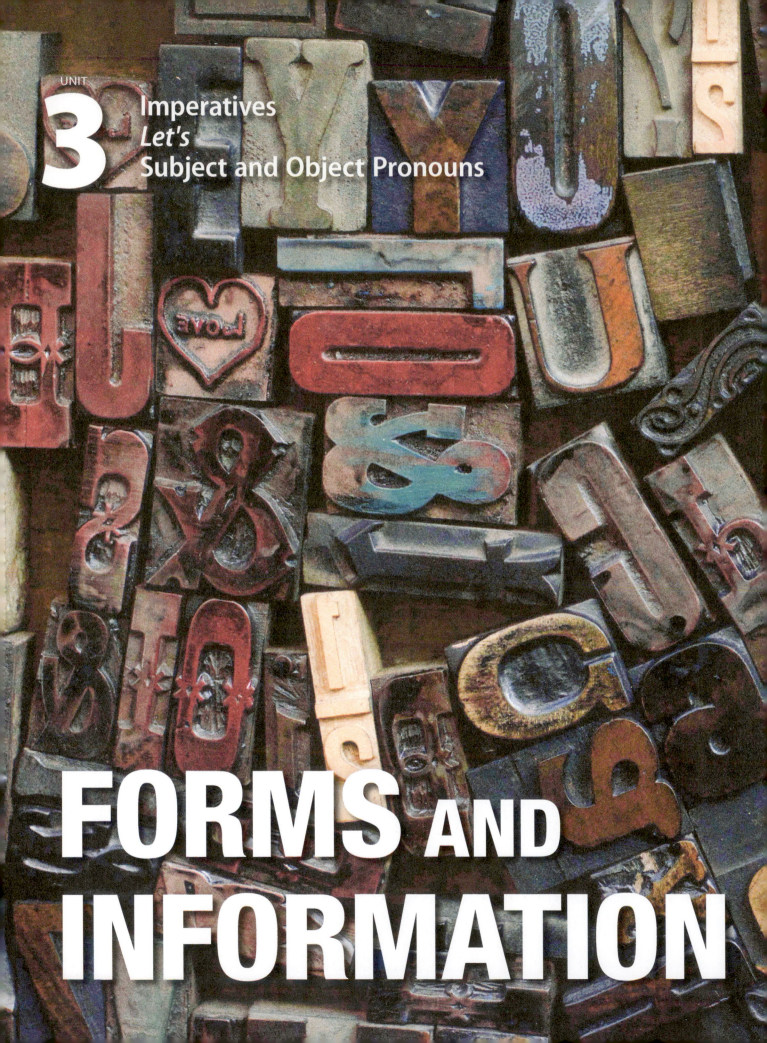

FORMS AND INFORMATION

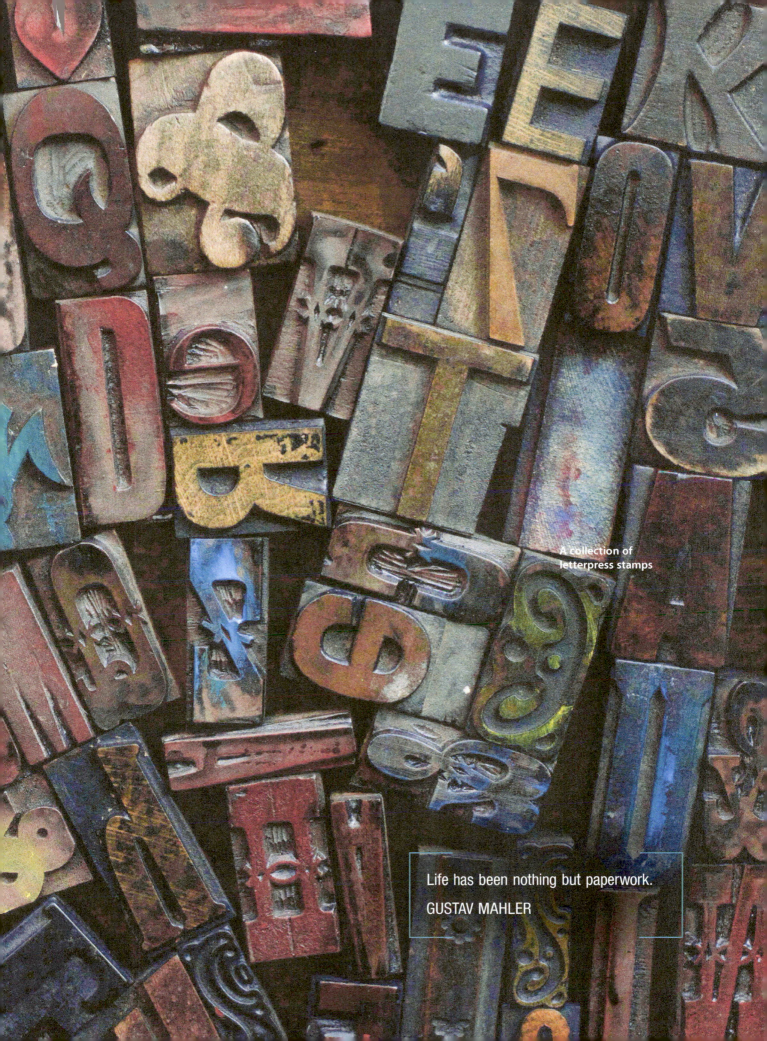

A collection of
letterpress stamps

Life has been nothing but paperwork.

GUSTAV MAHLER

BEFORE YOU READ

Circle *Yes* or *No*.

1. I have a Social Security card.   Yes   No

2. I write the month before the day.   Yes   No
   (For example: October 27 or 10/27)

READ

Read the following conversation. Pay special attention to the imperative forms in bold. 🎧 3.1

Dorota: I have something for you. **Look.**

Halina: What is it?

Dorota: It's an application. It's for a Social Security card.

Halina: I'm not sure what to do.

Dorota: **Don't worry.** It's easy. **Let** me help.

Halina: OK. I have a pencil.

Dorota: No, no. **Don't use** a pencil. **Use** a blue or black pen.

Halina: OK.

Dorota: Here's a pen. **Fill out** all the information. **Print** the information, but **sign** your name in item 17.

Halina: I'm finished.

Dorota: What's your date of birth?

Halina: 11/6/80.

Dorota: Is your birthday in November?

Halina: No. It's in June.

Dorota: **Don't write** *11/6*. **Write** the month, then the day. That's the way we write the date in the United States.

Halina: OK. 6/11/80.

Dorota: **Don't write** *80*. **Write** *1980*.

Halina: OK. I'm finished. What's next?

Dorota: **Don't forget** to sign your name. **Find** your original birth certificate. Then **go** to the Social Security office. **Take** your birth certificate and another identity document with you.

DID YOU KNOW?

Identity documents include:

- driver's licenses
- marriage certificates
- passports
- school IDs (identification cards)
- birth certificates
- state-issued IDs

COMPREHENSION Based on the reading, write T for *true* or F for *false*.

1. _____ Halina knows how to fill out the application.

2. _____ Halina's birthday is June 11.

3. _____ Halina needs to take three identity documents to the Social Security office.

application	This is an **application** for a Social Security card. Please write your information.
let	**Let** me help you. I can answer your questions.
fill out	**Fill out** the application with a pen. Please complete it.
information	The application has a lot of questions. Write the **information** on the line.
print	**Print** your name. *Halina Laski*
sign	**Sign** your name. *Halina Laski*
birthday/date of birth	Ali's **birthday/date of birth** is April 3, 1985.
forget	**Don't forget** your Social Security number. It's an important identification number to remember.
copy	This is my original birth certificate. That is a **copy**.
birth certificate	A new baby gets a **birth certificate**.
identity document	My driver's license is an **identity document**. It says who I am.

LISTEN

Listen to these instructions about how to fill out a Social Security card application. Circle *True* or *False*. 🎧 3.3

1. (True)   False
2. True   False
3. True   False
4. True   False

5. True   False
6. True   False
7. True   False
8. True   False

3.1 Imperatives—Affirmative

We use the base form of the verb for the imperative.

EXAMPLES	EXPLANATION
Use a pen. **Write** your date of birth.	We use the imperative to give instructions or suggestions.
Look at this.	We use the imperative to get someone's attention.
Help me, *please*. *Please* **help** me.	We add *please* to be more polite.

FUN WITH GRAMMAR

Play *Simon Says*. Pick one student to be Simon. Simon stands in front of the class. Everyone else stands up and looks at Simon. Simon tells the class what to do, using imperatives. Make sentences like this:

   Simon says, "Touch your nose." OR. *Touch your nose.*

Class, follow the directions ONLY if you hear "Simon says." before the imperative. If Simon doesn't say "Simon says," don't do anything. If you make a mistake, sit down. The last student standing wins.

EXERCISE 1 Match the parts of the sentences to make an affirmative imperative.

1. Make _____b_____   a. your birth certificate with you.

2. Fill _____   b. a copy of your birth certificate. ✓

3. Go _____   c. a pen.

4. Use _____   d. to the Social Security office today.

5. Write _____   e. the month before the day.

6. Take _____   f. me, please.

7. Sign _____   g. out the application today.

8. I'm confused. Help _____   h. your name in item 17.

3.2 Imperatives—Negative

EXAMPLES	EXPLANATION
Don't worry. **Don't write** 11/6 for *June 11.* **Don't be** late.	We use *don't* + the base form for the negative imperative. *Don't* is the contraction for *do not.*

GRAMMAR IN USE

Look at how we often use *don't forget.*

   The party is tomorrow. **Don't forget.**

   Don't forget <u>your papers</u> at home. (*Don't forget* + noun)

   Don't forget <u>to sign</u> your name. (*Don't forget* + infinitive)

EXERCISE 2 Rewrite the sentences. Use the negative imperative.

1. Forget your papers at home. <u>Don't forget your papers at home.</u>

2. Be late for your meeting. _____

3. Use a red pen. _____

4. Print your name. _____

5. Leave item 17 empty. _____

6. Write the day first. _____

7. Write with a pencil. _____

8. Go to the Social Security office on Sunday. _____

EXERCISE 3 Fill in the blanks with an affirmative or negative imperative. Use the verbs from the box. Answers may vary.

use	put	get	forget	write	take

1. _____Don't get_____ the application dirty.

2. _____ a pencil to fill out your application.

3. _____ to sign your application at the end.

4. _____ two forms of ID with you to the Social Security office.

5. _____ all four numbers for the year (*1980,* not *80*).

6. _____ the day first in your date of birth.

EXERCISE 4 Marta and Amy are in the kitchen. Fill in the blanks with one of the verbs from the box. Then listen and check your answers. 🎧 3.4

don't ask	don't forget	don't touch	wash	say	come
tell	make	let	be	get	

Amy: _____Get_____ me a sandwich, Mommy.
1.

Marta: I'm busy now. Later.

Amy: What's that?

Marta: It's my application. Your hands are dirty. _____ the application.
2.

Amy: What's an application? And what's that?

Marta: An application is an important form. And this is my birth certificate.

Please _____ so many questions. I'm busy now.
3.

Amy: I'm thirsty. Please _____ me a glass of milk.
4.

Marta: Later. _____ quiet now, please, and _____ me finish.
5.   6.

This is very important. . . . OK. I'm finished now. How can I help you?

Please _____ me.
7.

Amy: _____ me a sandwich.
8.

Marta: _____, "Please."
9.

Amy: Please.

Marta: And _____ your hands. _____ to use soap!
10.   11.

Amy: Ok. Please _____ with me to wash my hands.
12.

Circle *Yes* or *No*.

1. It's easy to get financial aid.   Yes   No

2. Online forms are easy.   Yes   No

READ

Read the following conversation. Pay special attention to the subject and object pronouns and *let's* + the base form in bold. 🔊 3.5

Halina and Shafia are students at the same school.

Halina: College is expensive in the United States.

Shafia: **You**'re right.

Halina: **Let's go** to the financial aid office on campus tomorrow. **Let's get** an application for financial aid.

Shafia: That's not necessary. **Let's go** online and get an application.

Halina: Is the application online?

Shafia: Yes. Let **me** show **you**. Look!

Halina: **You**'re right. Here's the financial aid website. The application is here.

Shafia: **Let's fill out** the application online. **It**'s easy. First, enter your Social Security number. Don't use dashes.

Halina: OK. What's next?

Shafia: Now enter your first and last name. Then create a password.

Halina: OK. Don't look at my password. What about this question? What's a middle initial?

Shafia: **I** don't know. **Let's call** Dorota.

Halina: **It**'s late. **Let's not bother her. I** know what *middle* means. **Let's look up** *initial* in the dictionary.

Shafia: OK. **Let's see. It** says, "the first letter of a name." So your middle initial is the first letter of your middle name.

DID YOU **KNOW?**

FAFSA (Free Application for Federal Student Aid) forms become available on October 1. It's important to fill out your form as soon as possible.

COMPREHENSION Based on the reading, write T for *true* or F for *false*.

1. _____ Halina and Shafia are at the financial aid office.

2. _____ Halina enters her middle name.

3. _____ They don't call Dorota.

WORDS TO KNOW 🎧 3.6

expensive	College is **expensive** in the United States. It costs a lot of money for many students.
financial aid	**Financial aid** is money to help pay for college.
online	The application is available **online**. It's on the Internet.
enter	**Enter** your name on Line 3 of the application.
dash	A **dash** is a short line. Social Security numbers have **dashes** between numbers: 000-00-0000.
create a password	**Create a password**. It's a secret number or word. My **password** has letters and numbers.
what about	**What about** this question? What is it?
initial	My name is Dorota Romana Nowak. My middle **initial** is *R*.
bother	He's busy. Let's not **bother** him.
look up	**Look up** *financial* in the dictionary. I want to know the meaning.

LISTEN

Listen to the sentences about the conversation. Circle *True* or *False*. 🎧 3.7

1. (True)   False
2. True   False
3. True   False
4. True   False

5. True   False
6. True   False
7. True   False
8. True   False

3.3 *Let's*—Affirmative and Negative

EXAMPLES	EXPLANATION
Let's go to the office. **Let's get** an application.	We use *let's* + the base form to make a suggestion. *Let's* is the contraction for *let us*.
Let's not call now.	We use *let's not* + the base form to make the negative.

EXERCISE 5 Fill in the blanks with *let's* or *let's not* and one of the verbs from the box.

walk	fill it out	go ✓	look up
get	call	drive	bother

1. _____Let's go_____ to the financial aid office today. I have a question about the form.

2. _____ to the financial aid office. It's far.

3. It's very cold today. _____ there.

4. It's not necessary to go to the office. _____ the application online.

5. This application is easy. _____ now.

continued

6. What's the application deadline? Where's the phone? _____ Dorota.

7. It's late. _____ her now.

8. I don't know what *password* means. _____ the word in the dictionary.

3.4 Subject and Object Pronouns

Compare subject pronouns and object pronouns.

EXAMPLES	EXPLANATION	
	Subject Pronoun	Object Pronoun
I am confused. Please help **me**.	I	me
You are not alone. I am here to help **you**.	you	you
He is at home. Call **him**.	he	him
She is at home. Call **her**.	she	her
It is your date of birth. Write **it**.	it	it
We are busy. Don't bother **us**.	we	us
They are confused. Help **them**.	they	them
I am confused. Please help **me**.	We put the subject pronoun before the verb. We put the object pronoun after the verb.	
I am finished **with** it. This application is **for you**. This question is **about** me.	We use the object pronoun after a preposition. Some prepositions are: *with, for, about, to, on, in, of, at,* and *from*.	

> **GRAMMAR IN USE**
>
> When you use *I* or *me* with a name, remember to use the correct pronoun.
>
> *Mia and **I** are at the office.*   *Please help Mia and **me**.*

EXERCISE 6 Fill in the blanks with an object pronoun.

1. I'm confused. Please help _____*me*_____.

2. Dorota is helpful. Let's call _____.

3. I'm busy. Don't bother _____.

4. We are confused. Please help _____.

5. Simon is busy. Don't bother _____.

6. I'm busy. Your father is here. Ask _____ for help.

7. Dorota and Simon are helpful. Let's ask _____.

8. The application is necessary. Let's fill _____ out.

9. This is my password. Don't look at _____ .

10. Are you confused? Don't worry. I'm here to help _____ .

EXERCISE 7 Fill in the blanks with an object or subject pronoun.

1. Victor is our friend. _____*We*_____ call him with questions. He answers _____*them*_____ .
                            a.   **b.**

2. We help each other. I am here to help you. _____ are here to help _____ .
                                          a.   **b.**

3. Dorota helps us. _____ are often confused and ask _____ questions.
                              a.   **b.**

4. Mr. Adams teaches Halina. _____ is her teacher. She likes _____ a lot.
                                  a.   **b.**

5. The questions are difficult. I don't understand _____ . They confuse _____ .
                                          a.   **b.**

6. Ali and I are new. Please don't ask _____ any questions. _____ don't know the answers.
                                        a.   **b.**

EXERCISE 8 Ali and Shafia are at home. Fill in the blanks in their conversation with an object or subject pronoun. Then listen and check your answers. 🎧 3.8

Ali: What's that?

Shafia: _____*It*_____'s a financial aid application. College is expensive in the United States.
                 1.

               We're immigrants. It's very expensive for _____ .
                                                                 2.

Ali: It's expensive for Americans, too. But it's easy for _____ to fill out the
                                                           3.

               application. It isn't easy for _____ . This question is hard. I'm confused
                                               4.

               about _____ . Let's call Dorota.
                              5.

Shafia: _____'s late. It's after 10 p.m. Maybe _____'s asleep.
              6.   **7.**

               Let's call _____ tomorrow.
                                   8.

Ali: Or call Simon.

Shafia: _____'s busy. His wife's father is sick. She's with _____ in the hospital.
              9.   **10.**

               Simon's with his kids. He's with _____ all day.
                                           11.

Ali: Let's read the application together. Maybe _____ can do _____ together.
                                                        12.   **13.**

Shafia: Yes, let's try! If we have problems, _____ can call Dorota in the morning.
                                                       14.

ABOUT YOU Complete the sentences about a friend. Write a name for item 1. Write subject or object pronouns for items 2–4.

_____ is my friend. I like _____ very much. _____ helps me,
          1.   **2.**   **3.**

and I help _____ .
                4.

SUMMARY OF UNIT 3

Imperatives—Affirmative

USE	EXAMPLES
To give instructions or suggestions	**Use** a pen.
To get someone's attention	**Look** at this.
Use *please* to be more polite.	**Help** me, please.

Imperatives—Negative

Don't worry.
Don't write *11/6* for *June 11.*
Don't be late.

Let's—Affirmative and Negative

AFFIRMATIVE	NEGATIVE
Let's go to the office.	**Let's not go** to the office.
Let's get an application.	**Let's not get** an application.
Let's call now.	**Let's not call** now.

Subject and Object Pronouns

SUBJECT PRONOUN	OBJECT PRONOUN	EXAMPLES
I	me	**I** am confused. Please help **me**. This question is about **me**.
you	you	**You** are not alone. I am here to help **you**. This application is for **you**.
he	him	**He** is at home. Call **him**.
she	her	**She** is at home. Call **her**.
it	it	**It** is your date of birth. Write **it**. I am finished with **it**.
we	us	**We** are busy. Don't bother **us**.
they	them	**They** are confused. Help **them**.

REVIEW

Choose the correct words to complete the conversation.

A: What's that?

B: It's an application for a passport. I'm a little confused. (*Please help/Don't help*) (*I/me*).
  1.   2.

A: Sure. (*Let's look/Please look*) at it together. . . . OK—(*write/let's write*) your name there.
  3.   4.

B: OK.

A: Wait—(*use/don't use*) a pen. (*Use/Don't use*) a pencil.
  5.   6.

B: Oh, right.

A: Then (*put/don't put*) your date of birth there. Use a number for the month.
  7.

B: OK, that's easy.

A: Good. Now (*fill out/fills out*) these lines for your address.
  8.

B: What about this line? (*I/Me*) don't know what to write there.
  9.

A: (*Don't see/Let's see*). Oh, what's your apartment number? (*Write/To write*) (*it/them*) on that line.
  10.   11.   12.

B: OK.

A: (*Forget/Don't forget*) to bring your ID with you. And (*make/forget*) a copy of your birth certificate.
  13.   14.

B: Thank you. You always help (*I/me*).
  15.

A: You're welcome. I'm happy to help (*you/us*).
  16.

B: Now (*go/let's go*) get some coffee!
  17.

FROM GRAMMAR TO WRITING

PART 1 Editing Advice

1. Use *not* after *let's* to make the negative.

             not
   Let's ~~don't~~ be late.

2. Don't use *to* after *don't*.

   Don't ~~to~~ write on this line.

3. Don't use *to* after *let's*.

   Let's ~~to~~ eat now.

4. Don't forget the apostrophe in *let's*.

        Let's
   ~~Lets~~ go home.

5. Use the subject pronoun before the verb.

       They
   ~~Them~~ are good students.

6. Use the object pronoun after the verb or preposition.

            him
   Don't bother ~~he~~.
         them
   Look at ~~they~~.

PART 2 Editing Practice

Some of the shaded words and phrases have mistakes. Find the mistakes and correct them. If the shaded words are correct, write *C*.

Peter: Let's ~~to~~ call Dorota for help with the application. She is always helpful to us.
           1.   *C* 2.   3.

Halina: Dorota is busy today. Her brother is sick. She's with he. Let's don't
                                             4.   5.

bother her now.

Peter: Maybe Simon is available. Let's call him.
                          6.   7.

Halina: Don't to call him now. Marta's father is still sick. She is with him at the hospital.
        8.   9.

Simon is with their kids. Dorota and Simon are both busy today.

Peter: You're right. Let's not to bother they.
                       10.   11.

Halina: Lets try to fill out the application together. The application is online.
        12.

Let's print her.
        13.

Peter: Make two copies, please. One is for you, and one is for I.
      14.   15.   16.

Halina: OK.

PART 3 Write

Rewrite the following paragraph. Change all the underlined nouns to object pronouns.

This is a financial aid application. Read <u>the financial aid application</u> carefully. Write your name and Social Security number on <u>the financial aid application</u>. Dashes are always in a Social Security number. Don't write <u>the dashes</u> on the application. Some questions are hard. Ask about <u>hard questions</u>. Dorota is helpful. Ask <u>Dorota</u> for help. The man at the financial aid office is helpful, too. Ask <u>the man</u> for help. <u>The man</u> helps people.

This is a financial aid application. Read it carefully....

PART 4 Learner's Log

1. These seven steps for how to get a Social Security card are out of order. Write the number of each step to put them in order. Then rewrite the steps in the correct order.

    _____ Find your original birth certificate.

    _____ Find another identity document.

    _____ Take or send all your documents to the Social Security office.

    _____ Don't forget to sign the form.

    _____ Get an application online or from the Social Security office.

    _____ Fill out all the necessary information.

    _____ Print the information.

2. Write one affirmative and one negative direction for each of these topics.
    - to fill out a Social Security card application.
    - to fill out a financial aid application.

3. Write any questions you still have about the topics above.

UNIT

4

The Simple Present
Frequency Words
Time Expressions

People paddleboarding in a harbor in
Massachusetts, U.S.

LIFESTYLES

Happiness is not a matter of intensity but of balance, order, rhythm, and harmony.

THOMAS MERTON

BEFORE YOU READ

1. What are your free-time activities?

2. What is your favorite summer activity?

READ

Read the following blog about free-time activities in the United States. Pay special attention to the simple present verbs and frequency words in bold. 🎧 4.1

Americans **work** hard. But they **have** fun, too. Americans **do** many different activities in their free time. They **often visit** each other. A visitor **usually needs** an invitation. Or the visitor **calls** first.

People **sometimes invite** their friends to their homes. **Sometimes**, they **eat** dinner together. Other times, they **watch** sports on TV together. Baseball, basketball, and football are popular sports to watch. Millions of Americans **watch** a football game called the Super Bowl each year. The two best football teams in the United States **play** in the Super Bowl in January or February.

Americans **like** the movies. They **often go** to the movies on weekends. Theaters **sell** popcorn and other snacks. People **buy** these treats at a concession stand[1].

Americans also **enjoy** museums. Families **spend** time at the exhibits. Museums **have** interesting activities, too. A list of activities is **usually** on a museum's website.

City parks **have** many fun activities, too. In the summer, many city parks **have** free outdoor concerts. People **sometimes have** picnics. They **cook** on a grill and **eat** outside. They **call** this kind of food "barbecue." It's very popular.

Americans **enjoy** their free time.

___

[1] Theaters and stadiums have *concession stands*. They sell drinks and snacks.

DID YOU **KNOW?**

Many theaters have cheaper tickets before 3 p.m. Senior citizens, children, and students may also get a discount.

COMPREHENSION Based on the reading, write T for *true* or F for *false*.

1. _____ Millions of Americans play football at the Super Bowl.

2. _____ Museums are popular for families.

3. _____ People invite their friends to their homes for concerts.

have fun	I **have fun** at the museum. I am happy there.
activity	City parks often have free **activities**, or things to do.
free time	Dorota works in the daytime. She has **free time** at night.
visit (v.) visitor (n.)	Simon's friends often **visit** him. They come to his house. They are **visitors**.
each other	We visit **each other**. I visit you, and you visit me.
invitation (n.) invite (v.)	Americans ask their friends to visit. This is an **invitation**. Do you want to **invite** your friend to the house?
popular	Many people like football. It's a **popular** sport.
best	This book is better than those books. It's the **best**.
team	One football **team** has many players. They play together.
enjoy	Simon and Victor like football. They **enjoy** the Super Bowl.
spend time	Tina **spends** a lot of **time** with her friends. They are always together.
exhibit	The museum has a new art **exhibit**.
outdoor concert	I like **outdoor concerts**. I listen to music in the park.
cook	My father often **cooks** on a grill in the summer.

LISTEN

Listen to the sentences about the blog. Circle *True* or *False*. 🎧 4.3

1. (True)   False
2. True   False
3. True   False
4. True   False

5. True   False
6. True   False
7. True   False
8. True   False

4.1 The Simple Present—Affirmative Statements

A simple present verb has two forms: the base form and the *-s* form.

SUBJECT	VERB (BASE FORM)	
I	**like**	concerts.
You	**have**	a grill.
We	**watch**	football games.
Americans	**enjoy**	movies.
They	**buy**	popcorn at the movies.

continued

SUBJECT	VERB (-S FORM)	
Simon	**enjoys**	the Super Bowl.
He	**likes**	sports.
Lisa	**has**	a lot of friends.
She	**visits**	them on weekends.
My family	**spends**	a lot of time in the park.
Our team	**plays**	every Saturday.
It	**has**	good players.

Notes:

1. *Have* is an irregular verb. The *-s* form is *has*.
2. *Family* and *team* are singular nouns. We use the *-s* form of the verb with these nouns.

EXERCISE 1 Fill in the blanks with the correct form of the simple present. Use the verb given.

1. Simon _____*enjoys*_____ movies on the weekends.
   enjoy

2. His kids _____ activities in parks.
   like

3. Simon's family _____ fun together.
   have

4. His daughter often _____ her friends to play.
   invite

5. We _____ time with our friends.
   spend

6. Americans _____ before a visit to a friend's house.
   call

7. I _____ museums with my friends.
   visit

8. The best teams _____ in the Super Bowl.
   play

4.2 Spelling of the -s Form

BASE FORM	-S FORM	EXPLANATION
visit like see	visit**s** like**s** see**s**	We add -s to most verbs to make the -s form.
kiss wash watch fix	kiss**es** wash**es** watch**es** fix**es**	We add -es to base forms with *ss*, *sh*, *ch*, or *x* at the end.
do go	do**es** go**es**	We add -es to *do* and *go*.
worry try	worr**ies** tr**ies**	If the base form ends in a consonant + *y*, we change the *y* to an *i* and add -es.
pay play	pay**s** play**s**	If the base form ends in a vowel + *y*, we do not change the *y*. We just add -s.

Pronunciation Note:

When we add -es to base forms with *ss, sh, ch,* or *x* at the end, we pronounce the extra syllable.

   She washes (/waˈʃəz/) her car every week.

*For a list of vowel and consonant sounds in English, see Appendix F.

EXERCISE 2 Fill in the blanks with the -s form of the verb given.

1. The team _____plays_____ football.
            play

2. Each football team _____ hard.
                          try

3. Simon's son, Ed, _____ football on TV.
                        watch

4. He _____ football games.
      like

5. He sometimes _____ to football games.
                    go

6. A football player sometimes _____ before a big game.
                                  worry

7. Simon _____ the grill after a barbecue.
           clean

8. He _____ a lot of time outside in the summer.
       spend

9. Simon _____ his car. He _____ it in his free time.
            a. love   b. wash

10. Simon _____ a lot of things with his family.
              do

4.3 The Simple Present—Use

EXAMPLES	EXPLANATION
American movie theaters **sell** popcorn. Americans **like** the movies.	We use the simple present for facts.
We **go** to the movies once a month. Every week we **visit** our friends.	We use the simple present for repeated actions.

EXERCISE 3 Write a sentence with the correct form of the verb in the simple present. Use the ideas from the blog on page 64. Answers will vary.

1. Americans/like

   _Americans like outdoor concerts._____

2. American museums/have

   _____

3. a city park/have

   _____

continued

4. people/invite

_____

5. a movie theater/sell

_____

6. American families/enjoy/on weekends

_____

4.4 Frequency Words

FREQUENCY	FREQUENCY WORD	EXAMPLES
100%	**always**	Simon **always** cleans his grill.
	usually	Americans **usually** call before a visit.
	often	Dorota **often** goes to the movies with friends.
	sometimes	Simon and Marta **sometimes** watch football games.
	rarely	Americans **rarely** visit friends without an invitation.
	hardly ever	My brothers **hardly ever** have free time.
0%	**never**	I **never** cook outside in January.

Notes:

1. Frequency words go before most verbs. _Usually_ and _sometimes_ can also go at the beginning of a sentence.

    Sometimes _we go to the movies._
    Usually _Dorota has free time on Sundays._

2. Frequency words follow the verb _be_.

    Simon **is always** on time.
    He **is never** late.

ABOUT YOU Write a sentence with the words given. Add a frequency word from Chart 4.4.

1. go to the movies

   I hardly ever go to the movies. _____

2. cook dinner at home

_____

3. watch TV in the evening

_____

4. invite my friends to my home

_____

5. play sports

_____

6. spend time at museums

_____

7. work on Saturdays

_____

8. have free time

_____

9. go to the city park

_____

10. be on time

_____

EXERCISE 4 Complete the sentences in Dorota's email about American customs. Use the words given and put them in the correct order. Use the correct form of the verb.

Hi Halina,

_____Newcomers always ask_____ me about dinner invitations.
      1. always/newcomers/ask

_____ each other to dinner at their homes.
    2. often/invite/Americans

_____ a guest for a specific day and time. "Let's have dinner
   3. an American/invite/usually

sometime." is not an invitation. _____ on time. It isn't polite
       4. always/a dinner guest/arrive

to be more than fifteen minutes late. _____
        5. bring/usually/guests

something for the host or hostess.

_____ flowers.
    6. they/bring/sometimes

At dinner, _____
       7. often/guests/say

something nice about the food.

_____ for more
   8. ask/guests/sometimes

food. This is not polite in some countries. But it's

OK here.

    Dorota

host

hostess

guests

EXERCISE 5 Fill in the blanks in Simon's conversation with Victor. Use the verbs from the box. Some verbs can be used more than once. Then listen and check your answers. 🎧 4.4

| pays | have | sells | likes | play | has | need | enjoy |

Simon: Are you and Lisa busy tonight?

Victor: No, why?

Simon: The city always _____ *has* _____ concerts in the park every Thursday evening.
1.
Let's all go tonight.

Victor: Sure. That's a great idea.

Simon: Bring Maya. Kids _____ outdoor concerts.
2.

Victor: Are the concerts expensive?

Simon: No. The city _____ for them. They're free for all of us.
3.

Victor: Where are the concerts?

Simon: At Logan Park on Central Street. Different bands _____ there from
4.
7 to 9 p.m. The kids _____ fun with their friends. A little store in the park
5.
_____ popcorn and ice cream. Amy _____ ice cream in
6.   7.
the summer. Marta and I _____ the different kinds of music.
8.

Victor: We _____ chairs, right?
9.

Simon: Yes, but I _____ some chairs for outside. Don't worry about that. Be at our
10.
house at about 6:30.

Victor: Thanks, Simon. See you tonight!

An outdoor concert in Colorado, USA

BEFORE YOU READ

1. What's a good job?

2. What's a hard job?

READ

Read the following blog. Pay special attention to the negative forms of the simple present, time expressions, and infinitives in bold. 4.5

Work is very important to Americans. They often ask each other about their jobs. But they **don't ask** each other, "How much money do you make?" They **don't talk** about their wages or salaries.

Americans usually work **five days a week**. Many people get paid **every two weeks**. Most office workers and teachers **don't work on Saturdays and Sundays**. But many people have other days off. Workers in stores and restaurants hardly ever have days off **on weekends**. Stores and restaurants are very busy **on Saturdays and Sundays**.

Full-time work is usually **eight hours a day**, or **forty hours a week**, but many Americans work more. Some people complain about their hours. They **don't like to work** so much. But others want **to make** more money. People with hourly wages get extra money for each hour of overtime work.

Sometimes a day off **doesn't mean** free time. Many people **don't relax** on their days off. Some people get part-time jobs on these days. High school and college students often have part-time jobs.

Today, the average American worker **doesn't expect to keep** the same job for a long time. Young people change jobs often. Older people **don't like to change** jobs as often. The typical worker **doesn't stay** at one job for more than five years, but people over sixty stay at their jobs for around ten years.

DID YOU KNOW?

The federal minimum wage is $7.25 per hour. But in some states and cities, the minimum wage is more than $13 per hour.

COMPREHENSION Based on the reading, write T for *true* or F for *false*.

1. _____ Many Americans have weekends off.

2. _____ Students often work part-time.

3. _____ Young people stay at the same job for many years.

WORDS TO KNOW 🎧 4.6

job/work	I like my **job**. The **work** is interesting.
make money	She **makes** a lot of **money**. She **makes** $75,000 a year.
wage	My **wages** are $8 an hour.
salary	His **salary** is $40,000 a year.
get paid	I **get paid** on Friday. I use direct deposit at my bank.
day off	Tuesday is my **day off**. I don't work on Tuesdays.
full-time	Simon has a **full-time** job. He works forty hours a week.
complain	She doesn't like her job. She **complains** about it a lot.
extra/overtime	For **extra** work, I get **extra** pay. I like to work **overtime**.
mean	*Weekend* **means** Saturday and Sunday.
relax	We **relax** on Sundays. We don't work. We go to the park.
part-time	Tina has a **part-time** job. She works after school.
average	The **average** American worker changes jobs often.
expect	He **expects** to keep his job for five years.
keep	I have a good job. I want to **keep** my job for a long time.

LISTEN

Listen to the sentences about the blog. Circle *True* or *False*. 🎧 4.7

1. (True)   False
2. True   False
3. True   False

4. True   False
5. True   False
6. True   False

7. True   False
8. True   False

4.5 The Simple Present—Negative Statements

We use *don't* or *doesn't* + the base form for the negative. *Don't* is the contraction for *do not*. *Doesn't* is the contraction for *does not*.

SUBJECT	DO + NOT	VERB (BASE FORM)	
I	**don't**	**work**	on Saturdays.
You	**don't**	**live**	near your work.
Tina	**doesn't**	**have**	a full-time job.
She	**doesn't**	**like**	her job.
Simon	**doesn't**	**relax**	on Fridays.
He	**doesn't**	**have**	Fridays off.
We	**don't**	**enjoy**	overtime work.
Some workers	**don't**	**make**	much money.
They	**don't**	**have**	good jobs.

Compare affirmative and negative statements.

AFFIRMATIVE	NEGATIVE
Tina has a part-time job.	She doesn't have a full-time job.
She works on Saturday.	She doesn't work on Friday.
Simon and Victor get a wage.	They don't get a salary.

> **GRAMMAR IN USE**
>
> We do not use the frequency words *hardly ever*, *never*, and *rarely* with negative verbs.
>
> We **hardly ever** <u>have</u> any days off.
>
> I **never** <u>work</u> on weekends.

EXERCISE 6 Fill in the blanks with the negative form of the verb given. Use contractions.

1. Tina _____ *doesn't have* _____ a full-time job.

have

2. Young people _____ one job for a long time.

keep

3. Dorota _____ about her job.

complain

4. Some workers _____ a lot of money.

make

5. You and I _____ the same days off.

have

6. Simon _____ about his salary.

talk

7. A day off _____ free time for Ali. He's always busy.

mean

8. I _____ on the weekend. I work part-time at a restaurant.

relax

EXERCISE 7 Write a negative sentence with the words given. Use contractions.

1. Simon works on Saturday.

   Simon doesn't work on Wednesday.

on Wednesday

2. Simon works on Sunday.

   Many Americans don't work on Sunday.

many Americans

3. Simon gets paid every two weeks.

   _____

every week

4. *Salary* means money for a year of work.

   _____

money for an hour of work

continued

5. Many people complain about long work hours.

_____
Dorota and Simon

6. I get Mondays and Tuesdays off.

_____
weekends off

7. Halina works part-time.

_____
forty hours a week

8. Some Americans work overtime.

_____
you and I

4.6 Time Expressions with the Simple Present

SUBJECT	VERB		TIME EXPRESSION
My sister She	works doesn't work		**eight hours a day.** **five days a week.** **every day.** **on the weekends.**
My friend and I We	have don't have	a day off	**twice a week.** **once a month.** **on Tuesdays.**
Those workers They	get paid don't get paid		**every two weeks.** **once a week.** **every Friday.**

Note:

Time expressions with two or more words usually go at the end of the
sentence. They don't go after the subject.

> He works **four days a week**.
>
> NOT: **Four days a week** he works.
>
> NOT: He **four days a week** works.

GRAMMAR IN USE

We use various phrases to talk about weekends:

> _on weekends_
>
> _on the weekends_
>
> _on the weekend_

We do not use the article _the_ to talk about the days of the week.

> _on Monday; on Tuesday; on Saturday_

ABOUT YOU Write sentences about you or someone you know. Use the simple present, affirmative or negative, and an expression of time. Add extra information where possible.

1. take the bus

   I take the bus twice a day. OR My sister doesn't take the bus.

   She drives to work every day.

2. relax

   _____

3. work

   _____

4. have a day off

   _____

5. drive

   _____

6. complain about work

   _____

7. go to class

   _____

4.7 Infinitives with Simple Present Verbs

We often use the infinitive (*to* + the base form) after simple present verbs. The form of the infinitive is always the same. We can use infinitives after the following verbs: *like, want, expect, try,* and *need.*

SUBJECT	VERB	INFINITIVE	
I	like don't like	**to relax**	on the weekends.
You	want don't want	**to take**	a day off.
She	expects doesn't expect	**to have**	a day off.
We	try don't try	**to do**	good work.
They	need don't need	**to work**	on Saturday.

EXERCISE 8 Fill in the blanks with the simple present, affirmative or negative, and the infinitive. Use the words given.

1. Americans _____*don't like to talk*_____ about their salaries.
   not/like/talk

2. I _____*expect to get*_____ extra money for overtime work.
   expect/get

3. Some people _____ about their jobs.
   like/complain

4. Simon _____ his job.
   not/want/leave

5. We _____ a day off this week.
   need/take

6. Americans _____ every day.
   not/expect/work

7. Dorota _____ on Sundays.
   not/like/work

8. Ali always _____ a good job.
   try/do

9. Halina _____ a new job.
   need/find

10. You _____ a lot of overtime.
    not/try/work

EXERCISE 9 Rewrite each sentence. Add the verb given.

1. Victor takes a day off on Sunday.

   Victor wants to take a day off on Sunday.
   want

2. He doesn't take a day off on Friday.

   He doesn't want to take a day off on Friday.
   want

3. Many Americans get a second job.

   _____
   try

4. The workers don't work on Sundays.

   _____
   expect

5. Sometimes I take Friday nights off.

   _____
   try

6. Simon doesn't work overtime.

   _____
   need

EXERCISE 10 Fill in the blanks with the simple present. Use the negative form of the verbs given. Then listen and check your answers. 🎧 4.8

Dorota: We have a day off tomorrow. Let's go to the museum.

Halina: I'm sorry, but I _____ don't have _____ time. I need to look for a new job.
                                    1. have

Dorota: You have a job.

Halina: I know, but I _____ it. I _____ enough hours.
                                 2. like   3. work

       And the job _____ enough money. My boss
                                   4. pay

       _____ my work. It's not a good job for me.
                5. like

Dorota: There's a job at my company. But it's only part-time. I _____ we have
                                            6. think

       any full-time jobs.

Halina: Thanks, Dorota, but I _____ part-time. I need a full-time job.
                          7. want/work

Dorota: The Internet is one place to look. But many people _____ their jobs on
                                          8. find

       websites. They hear about them from other people. So ask all of your friends.

ABOUT YOU Write true sentences about work in your hometown or country. Use the simple present of the verbs given, affirmative or negative. Read your sentences to the class.

1. The average worker in my hometown _____ doesn't work _____ every day.
                                      work

2. A worker _____ two days off every week.
                     get

3. Most people _____ more than eight hours a day at work.
                     spend

4. A company _____ extra money for overtime work.
                     pay

5. People _____ overtime.
                like/work

6. Workers _____ low wages.
                get

7. Companies _____ wages in cash.
                pay

8. The average worker _____ a part-time job on days off.
                take

9. Workers _____ four weeks off each year with pay.
                expect/get

10. People _____ on vacation on their weeks off.
                go

11. The average worker _____ jobs often.
                change

12. The average worker _____ the same job for a long time.
                keep

13. Teachers _____ a lot of money.
                make

14. Most people in my hometown _____ more than one job.
                work

BEFORE YOU READ

Circle *Yes* or *No*.

1. I like American food.   Yes   No
2. I eat in restaurants often.   Yes   No

READ

Read the following conversation. Pay special attention to the *yes/no* questions in the simple present in bold. 🎧 4.9

Simon and Peter are at a restaurant.

Peter: It's 1:30. It's early. **Do Americans usually have lunch at this time?**

Simon: One-thirty is late. Americans usually eat lunch around noon. Some have an hour for lunch, and others have thirty minutes. **Do you want to order a sandwich?**

Peter: Yes, I do. I'm hungry. Look. That man has a very big salad.

Simon: Yes, some people eat a salad for lunch.

Peter: **Do people eat salads instead of sandwiches?**

Simon: Yes, sometimes. Or they have a small sandwich with a small salad or cup of soup.

Peter: **Do Americans often eat in restaurants?**

Simon: Yes, they do. They're very busy. They don't always have time to cook every meal. Sometimes they go out to restaurants. Sometimes they order their food from restaurants.

Peter: **Do restaurants deliver food to your home?**

Simon: Yes, some do. And many restaurants have "takeout" food. They prepare the food for you. You take it home to eat. Supermarkets sell prepared food, too. Usually it's in the deli section. They have hot and cold food. Some supermarkets have tables, and people eat there. But most people take the prepared meals home. Prepared food is very popular because you don't have to cook.

Peter: **Does prepared food cost more?**

Simon: Yes, it does. But it's very convenient.

DID YOU KNOW?

61 percent of Americans eat at a restaurant at least once a week. 16 percent eat out three or more times a week, and 4 percent eat out more than three times a week.

A salad bar at a supermarket

COMPREHENSION Based on the reading, write T for *true* or F for *false*.

1. _____ Americans often eat in restaurants.

2. _____ People cook their own takeout food.

3. _____ Prepared food costs less than home-cooked food.

WORDS TO KNOW 🎧 4.10

order	Peter wants to **order** a sandwich. He asks the waiter for a tuna sandwich.
hungry	He's **hungry**. He wants to eat.
meal	I eat three **meals** a day. They are breakfast, lunch, and dinner.
deliver	That restaurant **delivers** pizza. Someone brings it to your house.
takeout	Let's order **takeout**. We can take the food home to eat.
prepared food	**Prepared food** is very popular. It's ready to eat.
deli	Let's go to the **deli** section. They have sandwiches there.
convenient	Prepared food is **convenient**. It's fast and easy.

LISTEN

Listen to the sentences about the conversation. Circle *True* or *False*. 🎧 4.11

1. (True)   False   5. True   False

2. True   False   6. True   False

3. True   False   7. True   False

4. True   False   8. True   False

4.8 The Simple Present—*Yes/No* Questions

DO	SUBJECT	VERB (BASE FORM)		SHORT ANSWER
Do	you	**like**	American food?	Yes, I do.
Does	Peter	**go**	to a restaurant for lunch?	Yes, he does.
Does	Simon	**eat**	lunch at 2 p.m.?	No, he doesn't.
Does	this restaurant	**have**	takeout food?	Yes, it does.
Do	the Japanese	**eat**	a lot of cheese?	No, they don't.
Do	we	**have**	time to cook?	No, we don't.
Do	they	**enjoy**	salad?	Yes, they do.

EXERCISE 11 Fill in the blanks with *do* or *does*. Then write a short answer to each question based on the conversation on page 78.

1. ___Does___ the man in the restaurant have a salad? _____Yes, he does._____
   a.   b.

2. _____ a sandwich have bread? _____
   a.   b.

3. _____ Peter want to order a salad for lunch? _____
   a.   b.

4. _____ many Americans eat lunch in restaurants? _____
   a.   b.

5. _____ American workers have two hours for lunch? _____
   a.   b.

6. _____ some restaurants deliver to your home? _____
   a.   b.

7. _____ the deli section have hot and cold food? _____
   a.   b.

8. _____ supermarkets often have prepared food? _____
   a.   b.

EXERCISE 12 Complete the conversation between Victor and Simon with the correct question from the box.

Do you work Monday through Friday?	Do you deliver the pizzas?✓	Does the job pay well?
Does Joe's Pizza have vegetarian pizza?	Do you like your new job?	Do you use your car?

Victor: I have a new part-time job. I work for Joe's Pizza.

Simon: _Do you deliver the pizzas?_____
                                                    1.

Victor: Yes, I do. I deliver them all over the city.

Simon: _____
                                    2.

Victor: No, I don't. I work on the weekends.

Simon: _____
                                    3.

Victor: No, I use the restaurant's car. It has a "Joe's Pizza" sign.

Simon: _____
                                    4.

Victor: No, it doesn't. But people often give me extra money for the delivery.

   We call that money a *tip*.

Simon: _____
                                    5.

Victor: Yes, it does. Many people order a pizza with no meat.

Simon: _____
                                    6.

Victor: Yes, I do! It's a great job.

EXERCISE 13 Complete each short conversation with a *yes/no* question in the simple present. Use the words given.

1. **A:** Many Americans eat lunch outside the home.

   B: _Do they eat lunch in restaurants?_
   eat in restaurants

2. **A:** Victor likes meat.

   B: _____
   like salads

3. **A:** Ali buys food at a supermarket.

   B: _____
   buy prepared food

4. **A:** That restaurant has takeout food.

   B: _____
   have vegetarian food

5. **A:** I go to lunch early.

   B: _____
   go before noon

6. **A:** Halina and Peter want to order some lunch.

   B: _____
   want to order sandwiches

7. **A:** This restaurant delivers pizza.

   B: _____
   deliver sandwiches

8. **A:** Americans eat prepared food.

   B: _____
   eat in the supermarket

ABOUT YOU Find a partner. Ask and answer *yes/no* questions with the words given. Your partner adds more information where possible. Then tell the class about your partner's answers.

1. you/like to eat in restaurants

   A: Do you like to eat in restaurants?

   B: Yes, I do. I like to eat in Chinese restaurants.

   A: Maria likes to eat in Chinese restaurants.

2. you/like pizza

3. you/like to cook

4. you/eat dinner with your family

5. you/eat lunch at home

6. you and your friends/sometimes order takeout food

continued

7. someone/cook for you

8. restaurants in your country/deliver

9. supermarkets in your country/have deli sections

10. most people in your country/eat meat

EXERCISE 14 Shafia and Ali are at Halina and Peter's house. Fill in the blanks to make *yes/no* questions in the simple present. Use the words given. Then listen and check your answers. 🎧 **4.12**

Shafia: Halina, this is a delicious meal. ___Do you and Peter cook___ like this every day?
   1. you and Peter/cook

   _____ time?
      2. you/have

Halina: No, this is a special meal for you.

   _____ good? Maybe
      3. the food/taste

   it's too different?

Ali: The soup is very good. _____
            4. it/have

   tomatoes in it?

Halina: Yes, it does.

Shafia: I like the carrots. _____ lemon on them?
                  5. they/have

Halina: Yes, they do.

Ali: _____ , Peter?
         6. you/like/cook

Peter: Yes, I do. But sometimes Halina and I are too busy. Then we buy prepared food at the

   supermarket.

Ali: _____ hot food like this?
            7. the supermarket/prepare

Peter: Yes, it does.

Shafia: _____ prepared food often?
               8. you and Halina/eat

Peter: No, we don't. But sometimes it's very convenient.

GRAMMAR IN USE

Sometimes in informal speaking, you can answer a *yes/no* question with a frequency word.

   A: *Do you eat takout food for lunch?*

   B: *Sometimes.*

BEFORE YOU READ

1. Do you exercise every day?

2. What kind of exercise do you do?

READ

Read the following conversation. Pay special attention to the *wh-* questions in the simple present in bold. 🎧 4.13

Dorota and Halina are on a walk.

Halina: Look at that woman in a business suit. **Why does** she **have** sneakers on?

Dorota: That's Louisa. She walks during her lunch hour. She wears sneakers on her walks. Some Americans exercise during their lunch hour.

Halina: **Where does** she **walk** in the winter?

Dorota: Maybe she goes to a gym nearby. There are many gyms in the city. Or maybe she goes to a gym in her office.

Halina: In her office? **What do** you **mean**?

Dorota: Some office buildings have gyms for their workers. They're free.

Halina: That's very interesting. I see a lot of people on bicycles here, too. Look! **Who rides** a bicycle in traffic downtown?

Dorota: She's a bike messenger. She works on her bicycle. She rides her bike and takes mail from one office to another in the city. Bike messengers always ride fast. They get a lot of exercise every day!

Halina: Do all Americans exercise every day?

Dorota: Some Americans don't exercise at all. They have desk jobs. They sit all day. But many people try to exercise a little every day. I do, too.

Halina: **What kind of exercise do** you **do**?

Dorota: I walk. It's great exercise. I stay healthy this way.

Halina: **Where do** you **walk**? In a gym?

Dorota: No. A gym costs money. I go to a park near my house.

Halina: **How often do** you **exercise**?

Dorota: I try to walk five days a week. But I don't always have time.

DID YOU KNOW?
It's good to walk quickly for thirty minutes a day. It is good for your health!

COMPREHENSION Based on the reading, write T for *true* or F for *false*.

1. _____ Some people have a gym at work.

2. _____ Bike messengers have desk jobs.

3. _____ Dorota walks every day.

WORDS TO KNOW 🎧 4.14

business suit	A **suit** is a kind of formal clothing. For some jobs, people wear **business suits** to work.
sneakers	I wear **sneakers** when I exercise. They are comfortable.
during	She often walks **during** her lunch hour.
wear	I **wear** a t-shirt in the summer. I **wear** a jacket in the winter.
exercise (n.) exercise (v.)	Louisa walks for **exercise**. Some Americans don't **exercise** a lot.
gym	I go to a **gym**. I exercise there.
nearby	My office is **nearby**. It is very close.
messenger	A **messenger** takes information from place to place.
ride a bicycle/bike	I **ride** my **bicycle** (**bike**) to work.
at all	My father has no vacation time. He doesn't travel **at all**.
desk job	He has a **desk job**. He works at a desk all day.
stay healthy	Dorota exercises a lot and eats well. She **stays healthy** that way.
cost	The gym is expensive. It **costs** a lot of money each month.

LISTEN

Listen to the sentences about the conversation. Circle *True* or *False*. 🎧 4.15

1. True   (False)

2. True   False

3. True   False

4. True   False

5. True   False

6. True   False

7. True   False

8. True   False

A bike messenger in traffic

4.9 The Simple Present—*Wh-* Questions

QUESTION WORD(S)	DO	SUBJECT	VERB (BASE FORM)		ANSWER
How much	**do**	I	**owe**	you?	Five dollars.
How much	**does**	that bike	**cost?**		It costs about $200.
How many days	**does**	Dorota	**exercise**	outside?	Five days a week.
How often	**do**	you	**ride**	your bike?	Three times a week.
Who	**do**	you	**see**	at the gym?	All my friends.
What kind of exercise	**does**	Marta	**do**	normally?	She rides a bike.
What	**does**	"bike"	**mean?**		It means "bicycle."
Why	**do**	we	**exercise?**		Because we want to stay healthy.
Where	**do**	they	**work?**		Near the gym.
When	**do**	Simon and Marta	**walk?**		In the morning.
What	**do**	they	**do**	for exercise?	They walk.

Notes:

1. When we ask *how often*, we want to know a number of times.

2. We use *because* with answers to *why* questions.

Compare statements and *wh-* questions.

STATEMENT	WH- QUESTION
Marta **rides** her bike.	How often **does** Marta **ride** her bike?
You **walk** fast.	Why **do** you **walk** fast?

EXERCISE 15 Fill in the correct question word in each short conversation. Use *what, who, when, where, how, why, what kind(s) of, how many, how much,* or *how often*. The underlined words are the answers to the questions.

1. **A:** _____How often_____ does she ride her bike?

   B: She rides her bike <u>every day</u>.

2. **A:** _____ does "healthy" mean?

   B: It means "<u>not sick</u>."

3. **A:** _____ do they walk every day?

   B: <u>Because it's good exercise</u>.

4. **A:** _____ hours do they walk every day?

   B: They walk <u>for one hour</u> every day.

continued

5. **A:** _____ shoes does Louisa have?

   B: She has <u>sneakers</u>.

6. **A:** _____ do good sneakers cost?

   B: They cost <u>about $100</u>.

7. **A:** _____ do some people get to work?

   B: <u>They ride their bicycles</u>.

8. **A:** _____ does he exercise?

   B: He exercises <u>in a gym</u>.

9. **A:** _____ does Louisa exercise?

   B: She exercises <u>during her lunch hour</u>.

10. **A:** _____ do you work with?

    B: I work with <u>Tina and Joe</u>.

EXERCISE 16 Write questions with the words given. Write an answer to each question. Use the ideas from the conversation on page 83.

1. what/Halina/ask Dorota

   A: <u>What does Halina ask Dorota about?</u>

   B: <u>She asks Dorota about exercise in the United States.</u>

2. what kind of exercise/Dorota/do

   A: _____

   B: _____

3. where/Dorota/exercise

   A: _____

   B: _____

4. when/Louisa/exercise

   A: _____

   B: _____

5. how often/Dorota/exercise

A: _____

B: _____

6. why/people/need to exercise

A: _____

B: _____

7. what/bike messengers/do

A: _____

B: _____

EXERCISE 17 Complete the question in each short conversation.

1. A: Dorota walks for exercise.

   B: How often *does she walk?* _____

2. A: She wears sneakers to work.

   B: Why _____

3. A: Lisa has a day off each week.

   B: When _____

4. A: I have some new shoes.

   B: What kind of _____

5. A: She goes to the gym in the winter.

   B: How often _____

6. A: Peter sees some bikes in the street.

   B: How many _____

7. A: Bike messengers ride fast.

   B: Why _____

8. A: Shafia and Ali like to run.

   B: Where _____

4.10 The Simple Present—Subject Questions

We do not use *do/does* when the question word is the subject.

QUESTION WORD(S)	VERB (BASE FORM OR *-S* FORM)		SHORT ANSWER
Who	**wants**	a new bike?	Tina does.
Who	**works**	in that company?	We do.
What kind of people	**exercise**	here?	Office workers do.
Which company	**has**	a gym for workers?	My company does.
How many people	**wear**	sneakers to exercise?	Everybody does.
Whose friend	**exercises**	at lunch time?	Dorota's friend does.
What	**happens**	at the gym?	People exercise.

Notes:

1. *Who* questions are singular. Answers can be singular or plural.

2. *What kind of* can be plural:

   A: **What kinds of** *events happen in the park?*

   B: *Free concerts and farmers' markets.*

3. *How many* questions are plural. Answers can be singular or plural.

EXERCISE 18 Write a question about each statement. Use the question words given as subjects.

1. Somebody needs a job.

   <u>Who needs a job?</u>

                                 who

2. Somebody wants to exercise.

   _____
                                 who

3. Some jobs pay well.

   _____
                           what kinds of

4. Some people ride their bicycles to work.

   _____
                             how many

5. Some workers exercise during their lunch hour.

   _____
                             which

6. Some people in my company exercise before work.

   _____
                             how many

7. Someone's company has a gym for the workers.

_____
whose

8. Something happens after lunch.

_____
what

EXERCISE 19 Write a *wh-* or subject question to complete each short conversation below. The underlined words are the answers. Some questions may vary.

1. A: What kinds of clothes do people wear at the gym?

   B: People wear <u>workout clothes at the gym</u>.

2. A: _____

   B: <u>Because they want to stay healthy</u>.

3. A: _____

   B: <u>Dorota's friend</u> does.

4. A: _____

   B: Some office workers exercise <u>after work in the evening</u>.

5. A: _____

   B: A bike messenger <u>takes mail from one office to another</u>.

6. A: _____

   B: <u>That bike costs over $500</u>.

7. A: _____

   B: Louisa exercises <u>five days a week</u>.

8. A: _____

   B: <u>A bike messenger</u> works on a bicycle.

FUN WITH GRAMMAR

Play in groups of 3–5 students. Write the question words from Charts 4.9 and 4.10 on slips of paper. Put all the slips in a bag. Take turns. Take a slip of paper out of the bag. Make a *yes/no, wh-,* or subject question, using the word on the paper. See if anyone in the group can answer the question. Each correctly-worded question and each correctly worded answer is worth 1 point. The person with the most points wins.

SUMMARY OF UNIT 4

The Simple Present—Statements

SUBJECT	VERB		TIME EXPRESSION
I	like	concerts.	
Americans	watch	football games.	
She	washes	the dishes	every day.
James	goes	to work	five days a week.
He	worries	about work.	
Katie	doesn't work		on the weekends.
My friend and I	don't have	a day off	twice a week.
		INFINITIVE	
I	like	to relax	on the weekends.
She	doesn't need	to work	on Saturday.
They	don't want	to relax.	

The Simple Present—*Yes/No* and *Wh-* Questions

QUESTION WORD(S)	*DO*	SUBJECT	VERB (BASE FORM)		ANSWER
	Do	you	like	American food?	Yes, I do.
	Does	Peter	eat	lunch at 2 p.m.?	No, he doesn't.
How much	do	I	owe	you?	Five dollars.
How often	do	you	ride	your bike?	Three times a week.
Why	do	we	exercise?		To stay healthy.
Who	does	Marta	see	at the gym?	Her friends.
Where	does	she	work?		Near the gym.

The Simple Present—Subject Questions

QUESTION WORD(S)	VERB (BASE FORM OR –S FORM)		SHORT ANSWER
Who	wants	a new bike?	Tina does.
What kind of people	exercise	here?	Office workers do.
Which company	has	a gym for workers?	My company does.
Whose friend	exercises	at lunch time?	Dorota's friend does.
What	happens	at the gym?	People exercise.

FREQUENCY	0% ⟵⟶ 100%						
FREQUENCY WORDS	never	hardly ever	rarely	sometimes	often	usually	always

REVIEW

Fill in the blanks. Use the correct form of the words given.

A: _____ part-time, Anna?
         _{1. you/work}

B: No, _____ . I _____ a full-time job. I _____ at a restaurant.
       _{2.}   _{3. have}   _{4. work}

A: _____ your job?
     _{5. you/like}

B: Yes, _____ . I _____ to work at 3:00. I usually _____ home
        _{6.}   _{7. go}   _{8. come}

    at 11:00.

A: Oh, that's late!

B: Yes, but I _____ in the morning. So my daughter and I _____ time together.
          _{9. not work}   _{10. spend}

A: _____ to school in the morning?
      _{11. she/go}

B: No. _____ to school. She's only three.
     _{12. she/not go}

A: _____ together?
      _{13. what/you and your daughter/do}

B: We like _____ in the park.
       _{14. walk}

A: Nice. _____ to the park?
         _{15. how often/you/go}

B: _____ to go every day. Then _____ home for lunch.
     _{16. we/try}   _{17. we/go}

A: _____ ?
      _{18. what kind of food/your daughter/eat}

B: _____ different kinds of food. She _____ peanut butter, though.
     _{19. she/like}   _{20. not like}

A: _____ peanut butter? My son _____ it. _____ a peanut
    _{21. who/not like}   _{22. love}   _{23. he/take}

    butter sandwich to school every day.

B: _____ to school?
       _{24. where/your son/go}

A: _____ to Maple Street School.
     _{25. he/go}

B: _____ it?
     _{26. he/enjoy}

A: Yes, _____ . _____ a lot of friends there. _____ to leave his
        _{27.}   _{28. he/have}   _{29. he/not like}

    friends at the end of the day.

B: _____ ?
      _{30. how much/the school/cost}

A: Oh, it doesn't cost anything. It's free. It's a public school.

B: _____ to the school?
    _{31. how many/children/go}

A: One hundred and fifty children _____ there. It's a small school.
                _{32. go}

FROM GRAMMAR TO WRITING

PART 1 Editing Advice

1. Use the -s form in the affirmative with *he*, *she*, *it*, and singular subjects.

   Dorota ~~work~~ **works** in an office.

   She ~~have~~ **has** a good job.

2. Don't use the -s form after *does* or *doesn't*.

   She doesn't ~~has~~ **have** a new job.

   Where does she ~~works~~ **work**?

3. Don't use *do* or *does* in questions about the subject.

   Who ~~does want~~ **wants** to go to the gym?

4. Use the correct word order in questions.

   Where does ⟨work⟩ your friend?

5. Use the correct question word order with *mean* and *cost*.

   What ~~means *bike*~~ **does bike mean**?

   How much ~~costs that bike~~ **does that bike cost**?

6. Don't separate the subject and verb with time expressions of two or more words.

   He ⟨three days a week⟩ goes to the gym.

7. Use the correct word order with frequency words.

   He goes ⟨always⟩ to the gym.

   He ⟨usually⟩ is tired.

PART 2 Editing Practice

Some of the shaded words and phrases have mistakes. Find the mistakes and correct them. If the shaded words are correct, write *C*.

Simon: Look at that fast bike messenger.

Victor: ~~What means *bike messenger*?~~ **What does bike messenger mean?**
   1.

Simon: A bike messenger delivers things. **C**
   2.

Victor: What does a bike messenger delivers?
   3.

Simon: A bicycle messenger deliver packages to offices downtown.
   4.

Victor: Who does work as a bicycle messenger?
   5.

Simon: Usually young, healthy people do this job. But the job is not always safe.
6.

Victor: Not safe? Why? What does happen to them?
7.

Simon: People don't always watch for the messengers. They open sometimes their car doors,
8.

and a messenger hits them. And sometimes bike messengers don't stop at red lights.
9.

They ride always very fast.
10.

Victor: Does a messenger make a lot of money?
11.

Simon: Not a lot. Messengers make between $10 and $20 an hour. And they ride often thirty to forty
12.   13.

miles a day. More work mean more money. But there is a problem. Now companies send
14.

documents by email. There is less work.

Victor: Do they work in bad weather, too?
15.

Simon: Yes. And they don't complain. It's part of their job.
16.

Victor: There is one good thing: they get a lot of exercise. Never they need go to a gym!
17.   18.

PART 3 Write

Rewrite the following paragraph. Change *I* to *Nina* or *she*. Make necessary changes to the verbs.

I live in Chicago. I like the city. Why do I like it? Because it's wonderful in the summer! I often go to a big park downtown. It has concerts every Thursday evening. I don't pay for these concerts. They're free. I like to visit Lake Michigan. It has many free beaches. But the water is often cold. I don't swim in June or July. I swim only in August. I also visit a beautiful park on the lake. Sometimes I have dinner at a restaurant near the lake. I don't do that often. It's expensive. I sometimes invite friends to visit Chicago.

Nina lives in Chicago....

PART 4 Learner's Log

1. Write one sentence about each of these topics:
   • free-time activities in the United States
   • work in the United States
   • eating customs in the United States
   • exercise in the United States

2. Write any questions you still have about the topics above.

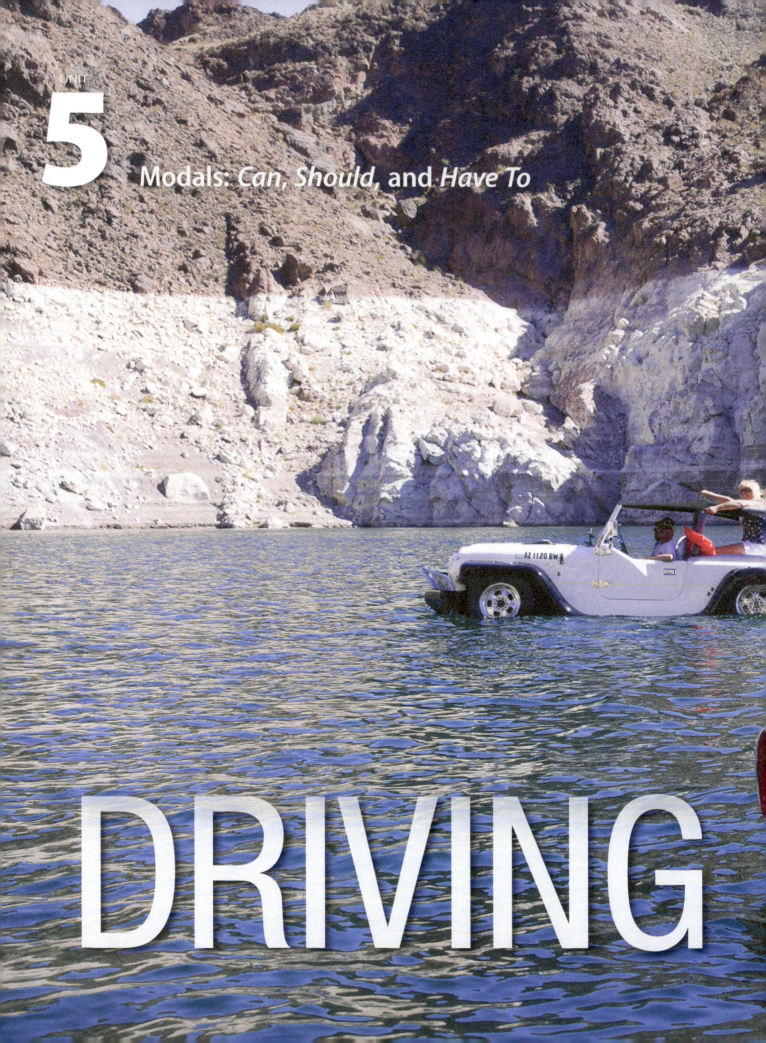

Modals: *Can, Should,* and *Have To*

DRIVING

Two cars in the first Amphicar Swim-in on Lake Mead near Las Vegas, Nevada, U.S., October, 2015

Baseball is like driving. It's the *who gets home safely* that counts.

TOMMY LASORDA

BEFORE YOU READ

Circle *Yes* or *No*.

1. Do you know how to drive?   Yes   No
2. Do you have a driver's license from this state?   Yes   No

READ

Read the following conversation. Pay special attention to the affirmative and negative forms of *can*, *should*, and *have to* in bold. 🎧 5.1

Simon's son, Ed, wants to learn to drive. He is fifteen years old.

Ed: Dad, I want to get my driver's license.

Simon: You **have to get** a learner's permit first.

Ed: How do I get that?

Simon: I **can help** you with the rules. But in this state, drivers under the age of eighteen **have to take** a driver's education class at school. It's the law. You **have to study** thirty hours in the classroom.

Ed: A class takes a long time. I **can learn** faster with you.

Simon: No, you **can't**. It takes a long time to learn to drive. You **shouldn't be** in a hurry. First, you **have to pass** two tests: a driving test and a written test. The written test is about the traffic laws.

Ed: And then I **can get** my license?

Simon: No. You **can get** a learner's permit. Then you **have to practice** in the car. In this state, you **have to practice** at least fifty hours, but you **should practice** much more. And you **have to wait** three months. Then you **can take** the driving test.

Ed: And I **can get** my license. I **can drive** with my friends.

Simon: Not exactly. You **can have** only one other teenager in the car. And after 9 p.m., you **can drive** home from work, but that's all. You **can't drive** alone at night for other reasons. Here, drivers under eighteen **have to drive** with an adult driver at night. The adult **has to be** over twenty-one.

Ed: I don't like that. Are you sure?

Simon: Yes, I am. You **can go** online and check the state's traffic laws.

DID YOU KNOW?

Car crashes are the number-one cause of death for people aged fifteen to nineteen. Many states have laws to protect younger drivers.

COMPREHENSION Based on the reading, write T for *true* or F for *false*.

1. _____ Ed needs a learner's permit.

2. _____ It is easy to get a driver's license.

3. _____ Drivers under 18 can always drive alone at night.

WORDS TO KNOW 🎧 5.2

learner's permit	A new driver practices with a **learner's permit**.
rule	Teenagers can't drive between 11 p.m. and 6 a.m. That's the **rule**.
under/over	Ed is fifteen years old. He's **under** age sixteen. Tina is seventeen years old. She's **over** age sixteen.
law	You have to stop at all stop signs and red lights. It's the **law**.
take time	It **takes** a long **time** to be a good driver. You must practice a lot.
in a hurry	Ed wants his license now. He's **in a hurry.**
pass a test	When you **pass** the **tests**, you can get your learner's permit.
written test	We use a pencil and paper for **written tests**.
practice (v.) practice (n.)	Ed's new at driving. He has to **practice**. Ed isn't a good driver yet. He needs a lot of **practice**.
at least	He has to practice **at least** fifty hours. He can practice more than fifty hours.
experience	Simon drives every day. He has a lot of **experience** driving.
adult/teenager	Simon is an **adult**. He is forty years old. Ed is a **teenager**. He is fifteen years old.
safety (n.) save (v.)	The laws are for your **safety**. They keep you safe. Seat belts **save** many lives each year.

LISTEN

Listen to the sentences about the conversation. Circle *True* or *False*. 🎧 5.3

1. True   (False)   5. True   False

2. True   False   6. True   False

3. True   False   7. True   False

4. True   False   8. True   False

5.1 Modal: *Can*—Affirmative and Negative

We use *can* to show ability, permission, or possibility.

SUBJECT	CAN	VERB (BASE FORM)	
I She Simon It We You They	**can** **cannot** **can't**	help	him.

Notes:

1. We write the negative of *can* as one word: *cannot*. The contraction for *cannot* is *can't*.

2. The main verb does not have an *-s* ending after *can*.

Pronunciation Note:

In affirmative statements, we usually pronounce *can* /kən/. In negative statements, we pronounce *can't* /kænt/. It is hard to hear the final *t*, so we use the vowel sound and stress to tell the difference between *can* and *can't*. Listen to your teacher pronounce these sentences:

      *I can **go**.* (stress on *go*)   *I **can't** go.* (stress on *can't*)

GRAMMAR IN USE

We often use *can't* with rules or laws.

    *You **can't park** at a bus stop.*

EXERCISE 1 Fill in the blanks with *can* or *can't*. Use the ideas from the conversation on page 96.

1. Ed _____*can't*_____ drive now.

2. Simon _____ help Ed with the rules.

3. Ed _____ get his driver's license now.

4. People _____ find the laws and safe driving practices on the state website.

5. Ed _____ take the driver's education class now.

6. Simon _____ help Ed practice in the car now.

7. Ed _____ get a learner's permit without a driver's education class.

8. Teenagers under eighteen _____ drive alone at night in Ed's state.

9. Teenagers under eighteen _____ have one other teenager in the car.

10. Teenagers under eighteen _____ drive home from work after 9 p.m.

5.2 Modal: *Should*—Affirmative and Negative

We use *should* when we give advice or make a suggestion.

SUBJECT	*SHOULD*	VERB (BASE FORM)	
I He She We You They	should should not shouldn't	take	the test today.

EXERCISE 2 Complete the conversations with *should* or *shouldn't* and the words given.

1. **A:** I have my written test tomorrow.

   B: _____ You should read _____ the driver's handbook again tonight.

you/read

2. **A:** My car is dirty.

   B: _____ it today!

you/wash

3. **A:** Ed wants to learn to drive.

   B: _____ in a hurry.

he/be

4. **A:** Ed wants to be a safe driver.

   B: _____ a lot with a good driver.

he/practice

5. **A:** I'm very tired today, and I have driving practice.

   B: _____ today. Wait until tomorrow.

you/drive

6. **A:** Ed doesn't know the driving laws in his state.

   B: _____ them before the written test.

he/learn

7. **A:** Many cars are on the roads from 4 p.m. to 7 p.m.

   B: _____ during those hours.

new drivers/drive

8. **A:** I don't have the driver's handbook, and I need to study it tonight.

   B: _____ online. The information is on the state website.

you/look

   You can download a copy of the handbook, too.

5.3 *Have To*—Affirmative and Negative

Have to shows necessity.

SUBJECT	*HAVE TO*	VERB (BASE FORM)	
I You We They	**have to** **do not have to** **don't have to**	pass	the test now.
She He Ed	**has to** **does not have to** **doesn't have to**		

Notes:

1. In the affirmative, *have to* shows laws or strong necessity.

   *Ed **has to** get a learner's permit.*

2. In the negative, *have to* means "not necessary".

   *Simon **doesn't have to** work on Saturday.*

Pronunciation Note:

In normal speech, we pronounce *have to* /hæftə/. We pronounce *has to* /hæstə/.
Listen to your teacher pronounce the following sentences in normal speech:

   *We **have to** take the test.*   *She **has to** drive to work.*

EXERCISE 3 Fill in the blanks with the affirmative or negative form of *have to* and the verbs given. Use the ideas from the conversation on page 96.

1. Ed _____ has to take _____ a driver's education class.

        take

2. Simon _____ a learner's permit.

        get

3. All drivers _____ the written test and driving test.

        pass

4. Ed _____ at least fifty hours before the driving test.

        practice

5. People over age eighteen _____ a driver's education class.

        take

6. Drivers over age eighteen _____ with an adult driver at night.

        be

7. All drivers _____ a driver's license or permit.

        have

8. Simon _____ Ed the traffic laws. Ed can learn them at school.

        teach

ABOUT YOU Complete the sentences about driving so they are true about your country. Fill in the blanks with the affirmative or negative form of *have to* and the verbs given.

1. We _____*have to get*_____ a permit before the driving test.

get

2. We _____*don't have to finish*_____ high school to get a driver's license.

finish

3. Drivers _____ eighteen years old to get a driver's license.

be

4. Drivers under age eighteen _____ a driver's education class.

take

5. New drivers _____ a vision test.

pass

6. Young drivers _____ with an adult driver.

practice

7. New drivers _____ all the answers right on the written test.

get

8. New drivers _____ at least three months before the driving test.

wait

EXERCISE 4 Look at the road signs. Write two sentences about each road sign. Use the affirmative and negative of *can*, *should*, or *have to*.

1. *Drivers can't go over 65 miles per hour.*

   Drivers have to go at least 45 miles per hour.

2. _____

   _____

3. _____

   _____

4. _____

   _____

continued

5. _____

6. _____

7. _____

8. _____

9. _____

ABOUT YOU Complete the sentences about drivers in your country. Answers will vary.

1. They can _learn to drive at age fifteen._

2. They can't _drive without a permit._

3. They can _____

4. They can't _____

5. They should _____

6. They shouldn't _____

7. They have to _____

8. They don't have to _____

EXERCISE 5 Complete the conversations with the affirmative or negative form of *can*, *should*, or *have to* and the verb given. Some answers may vary.

1. **A:** I don't have a car.

   B: Don't worry. You _____*can use*_____ my car today.

   _{use}

2. **A:** I don't like to drive.

   B: That's OK. You _____ the bus.

   _{take}

3. **A:** Where are your car keys?

   B: They're in the car.

   A: You _____ your keys in the car.

   _{leave}

4. **A:** Today is a holiday. Do you want to go to a movie?

   B: No, I'm sorry. I _____ the traffic laws for my test on Friday.

   _{a. study}

   A: You _____ it today. It's Monday. You have three more days before the test.

   _{b. do}

5. **A:** Your car is very dirty. You _____ it.

   _{a. wash}

   B: I know, but I _____ it today. I'm too busy.

   _{b. wash}

6. **A:** Let's walk to work today.

   B: We don't have time. We _____ at work in thirty minutes.

   _{be}

7. **A:** My son wants to get his driver's license. But he's only fifteen.

   B: Then he _____ a driver's education class first. But don't worry.

   _{a. take}

   He _____ for it. He _____ the class free in school.

   _{b. pay}   _{c. take}

8. **A:** My written test is tomorrow, and I don't know the rules of the road.

   B: You _____ to study until the night before the test.

   _{a. wait}

   You _____ all the laws in one night. It's not possible.

   _{b. learn}

9. **A:** There's a good program on TV now about driving safety.

   B: We _____ it.

   _{watch}

10. **A:** My daughter wants to learn to drive, but she's only fourteen.

    B: She _____ until she's a little older.

    _{wait}

EXERCISE 6 Complete the conversations with the correct verbs from the box. Then listen and check your answers. 🎧 5.4

CONVERSATION A: Ed asks Marta about his friend from Mexico.

doesn't have to get	should study	can drive
has to take	has to get	can use ✓

Ed: Mom, one of my friends is from Mexico and has an international driver's license.

He _____ can use _____ it to drive in this state, right?
1.

Marta: Yes, he can. But he _____ with an international license for only three
2.

months. Then he _____ a new driver's license in this state.
3.

Ed: What about a learner's permit?

Marta: He _____ a learner's permit. But he _____ the
4.   5.

rules of the road for this state. Then he _____ the written and driving
6.

tests. The laws here are very different from the laws in Mexico.

CONVERSATION B: The driving teacher talks to students in a driver's education class.

have to wear	can't see	shouldn't worry	can take

Mr. Brown: Today's class is about the tests for your learner's permit. Does anyone have a question? Karl?

Karl: I'm worried about the vision test. I _____ very well.
7.

Mr. Brown: You _____ . You _____ the test with your
8.   9.

glasses on. But then you _____ your glasses in the car, too.
10.

It's the law.

FUN WITH GRAMMAR

Play Bingo. Your teacher will give you a blank Bingo card. Write *can, can't, should, shouldn't, have to*, or *don't have to* in each square. Some squares will have the same words. Put the words or phrases in any order. Your teacher will call out a word or phrase. Find a square with that word or phrase and write a sentence in the square, using that word or phrase. To win the game, you have to get sentences in four squares in a row, either horizontally (➞), vertically (↓), or diagonally (↗). The first person to get four correctly written sentences in a row says, "Bingo!" and wins the game.

1. Where should children sit in a car?

2. Do you have a child in your family? If so, what kind of car seat does the child use?

READ

Read the following conversation. Pay special attention to the *yes/no* questions and *wh-* questions with *can*, *should*, and *have to* in bold. 🎧 5.5

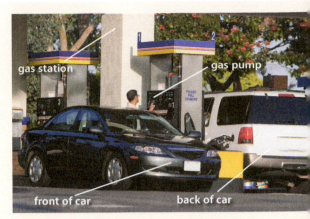

gas station   gas pump

front of car   back of car

Dorota and Halina are on the way to an outlet mall. Halina asks Dorota about car seats for her daughter, Anna.

Halina: This is my first trip to an outlet mall. **Can I get** a new car seat for Anna there? She's too big for her old infant seat now. And she's still too small for a seat belt.

Dorota: Sure. And things aren't so expensive at the outlet mall.

Halina: **What kind** of car seat **should I get**?

Dorota: Well, she's two now. Seats for toddlers are different. We can look in several stores.

Halina: **How long does** Anna **have to use** a car seat?

Dorota: In this state, children have to use a car seat until age eight, eighty pounds, or fifty-seven inches tall.

Halina: **Where should** I **put** Anna's seat? **Can I put** it in the front passenger seat?

Dorota: No. Anna shouldn't be in the front seat. The air bag can hurt children. They have to sit in the back seat until age twelve.

(five minutes later)

Dorota: I have to stop for gas. Here's a gas station.

Halina: I can pay. **Do** we **have to pay** first?

Dorota: Yes, the sign says, "Pay First." But don't worry. I can put it on my credit card. I can pay right here at the pump.

Halina: **Should** I **wash** the windows?

Dorota: OK. You can wash the windows. And I can pump the gas.

Halina: **Can I buy** water here? I'm thirsty.

Dorota: Yes, you can. This gas station has a store.

> **DID YOU KNOW?**
> You can get a ticket if your child is not in a car seat. The ticket can be between $10 and $500.

COMPREHENSION Based on the reading, write T for *true* or F for *false*.

1. _____ Anna cannot sit in her old car seat.

2. _____ The outlet mall is expensive.

3. _____ Children under eight years old should sit in the front seat of a car.

WORDS TO KNOW  5.6

on the way	They are in the car. They are **on the way** to the mall.
outlet mall	**Outlet malls** have many stores and good prices.
trip	We are in the car. We're on a **trip** out of town.
infant	That baby is only three months old. She's an **infant**.
seat belt	Everyone has to wear a **seat belt** in a car. It keeps you safe.
toddler	A child between the ages of one and three is often called a **toddler**.
several	We can look in **several** stores. I know three good stores.
until	Children sit in the back seat **until** age twelve. Then they can sit in the front seat.
passenger	A **passenger** sits next to the driver or in the back seat.
air bag	In an accident, **air bags** keep the driver and passengers safe.
hurt	Air bags can **hurt** small children. They can be dangerous.
pump (v.) pump (n.)	We have to **pump** our own gas. We fill the tank. We can pay at the **pump** with a credit card.

LISTEN

Listen to the sentences about the conversation. Circle *True* or *False*. 5.7

1. (True)   False   5. True   False
2. True   False   6. True   False
3. True   False   7. True   False
4. True   False   8. True   False

An air bag

5.4 *Can*, *Should*, and *Have To—Yes/No* Questions

We put *can* or *should* before the subject to make a question.

MODAL	SUBJECT	VERB (BASE FORM)		SHORT ANSWER
Can	I	get	some water?	Yes, you can.
	young children	sit	in the front seat?	No, they can't.
Should	Halina	buy	an infant seat?	No, she shouldn't.
	Halina	get	a new car seat for Anna?	Yes, she should.

We use *do* or *does* to make questions with *have to*.

DO	SUBJECT	*HAVE TO*	VERB (BASE FORM)		SHORT ANSWER
Does	Dorota		get	gas now?	Yes, she does.
	a teenager	**have to**	sit	in the back?	No, he/she doesn't.
Do	I		pump	the gas?	Yes, you do.
	we		pay	inside?	No, we don't.

106   Unit 5

We use *can* to ask about ability.

   Can you **swim**?   Yes, I can.

We also use *can* to ask for permission.

   Can I **borrow** your book?   Sure.

We also use *can* to make an offer.

   Can I **help** you?   No, thank you.

EXERCISE 7 Write a short answer for each question. Use the ideas from the conversation on page 105.

1. Does Dorota have to get gas? _Yes, she does._____

2. Can Anna sit in the front seat? _No, she can't._____

3. Should Halina put Anna's car seat in the front passenger seat? _____

4. Can air bags hurt small children? _____

5. Does Dorota have to pay in cash for her gas? _____

6. Can people pump their own gas at the gas station? _____

7. Do children over age eight have to use a car seat? _____

8. Do young children have to sit in the back seat of the car? _____

EXERCISE 8 Match the parts of the sentences to make *yes/no* questions.

1. Can I pay ___c___

2. Can we go _____

3. Should I wash _____

4. Should we buy _____

5. Can I put _____

6. Does Anna have to sit _____

7. Does everyone have to use _____

8. Do we have to stop _____

a. to the outlet mall?

b. a new car?

c. with a credit card? ✓

d. the car seat in the front?

e. in the back seat?

f. the windows for you?

g. for gas?

h. a seat belt?

EXERCISE 9 Complete the *yes/no* question with *can*, *should*, or *have to* and the words given.

1. **A:** It's a beautiful day. _____Can we go_____ for a walk in the park?
   <u>we/go</u>

   B: Yes, we can.

2. **A:** It takes two hours to drive to the mall. _____ gas first?
   <u>we/get</u>

   B: Yes, we do.

3. **A:** Gas in this station is expensive. _____ another station?
   <u>we/try</u>

   B: Yes, we should.

4. **A:** Your car windows are dirty. _____ them for you?
   <u>I/wash</u>

   B: Yes, you can. Thank you.

5. **A:** I have a new car seat for my son. _____ in the back seat?
   <u>he/sit</u>

   B: Yes, he does.

6. **A:** I'm in the back seat. _____ a seat belt?
   <u>I/use</u>

   B: Yes, you do.

ABOUT YOU Put the words given in the correct order to form a question. Write a short answer about people and customs in your country. Then share your answers with a partner.

1. Can people buy food and drinks at a gas station? Yes, they can. _____
   food and drinks/at a gas station/people/can/buy

2. _____
   have to/young children/in a car seat/sit

3. _____
   in the front seat/sit/can/children

4. _____
   pump/their own gas/have to/people

5. _____
   adults/wear/have to/seat belts

6. _____
   most people/drive/to work/have to

5.5 Can, Should, and Have To—Wh- Questions

Can/Should

QUESTION WORD(S)	MODAL	SUBJECT	VERB (BASE FORM)		ANSWER
Where	can	Halina	get	a car seat?	At the outlet mall.
How		parents	keep	their children safe in a car?	They can put them in a car seat.
Why	should	we	go	to the outlet mall?	To get a good price.
Which car seat		I	buy	for Anna?	This one is good.

Have To

QUESTION WORD(S)	DO	SUBJECT	HAVE TO	VERB (BASE FORM)		ANSWER
Where	does	Anna	have to	sit?		In the back seat.
How much	do	we		spend	for a car seat?	Between $50 and $250.

EXERCISE 10 Answer each question. Use the ideas from the conversation on page 105.

1. How can people pay for gas?

   They can pay with a credit card or cash.

2. When can a child sit in the front passenger seat?

   _____

3. Why does a small child have to sit in the back seat?

   _____

4. Where can people pay for gas at the gas station?

   _____

5. Why does Halina have to get a new car seat for Anna?

   _____

6. Where can Halina buy water?

   _____

7. What kind of seat should Halina buy?

   _____

continued

8. Why does Dorota have to stop at a gas station?

   _____

9. How can children ride safely in a car?

   _____

10. Why should Halina buy a car seat at the outlet mall?

    _____

EXERCISE 11 Ask a question about each statement, using the question word(s) given.

1. Anna has to sit in the back seat.

   Why _does Anna have to sit in the back seat?_____

2. They have to stop for gas on their trip.

   How often _____

3. Everyone should drive carefully.

   Why _____

4. An air bag can hurt small children.

   How _____

5. Halina has to buy some things for Anna.

   What _____

6. Anna can't sit in the front seat right now.

   Where _____

7. You should get a new car seat for your daughter.

   Why _____

8. You have to pay a lot for this car seat.

   How much _____

EXERCISE 12 Complete each short conversation with a question. Use the words given.

1. **A:** Please get in the car.

   B: _Where should we sit?_____
   where/we/should/sit

2. A: There's child safety information online.

B: _____
which website/I/should/check

3. A: Halina doesn't have a good car seat for Anna.

B: _____
where/she/can/buy a good one

4. A: Anna is two years old.

B: _____
what kind of car seat/Halina/have to buy for her

5. A: Car seats have different prices.

B: _____
how much/I/should/spend

6. A: My son is two years old. Do I need a car seat?

B: Yes. Toddlers have to sit in car seats.

A: _____
why/they/have to sit in car seats

B: Because they can get hurt in an accident.

7. A: You should buy a new car seat for your son when he's bigger. He's still very small.

B: _____
when/I/should/buy a new one

8. A: Drivers under age eighteen have to drive with an adult at night.

B: _____
why/they/have to drive with an adult

5.6 *Can, Should,* and *Have To*—Subject Questions

Can/Should

QUESTION WORD(S)	MODAL	VERB (BASE FORM)		ANSWER
What	**can**	happen	to the baby in the front seat?	The air bag can hurt her.
How many people	**can**	sit	in the back seat?	Three can.
Who	**should**	pay	for the gas?	Dorota should.

Have To

QUESTION WORD(S)	*HAVE TO*	VERB (BASE FORM)		ANSWER
Who	**has to**	stop	for gas?	Dorota does.
Which children	**have to**	sit	in the back seat?	All small children do.

EXERCISE 13 Complete each short conversation with a question. Use the following question words as subjects: *who, which, how many,* or *what.* The underlined words are the answer.

1. **A:** Who has to buy a car seat?

   B: Halina has to buy a car seat.

2. **A:** _____

   B: Amy should use a car seat. It will keep her safe.

3. **A:** _____

   B: The gas station on my street can give us the best price for gas.

4. **A:** _____

   B: Young children should sit in the back seat.

5. **A:** _____

   B: Two people have to travel today.

6. **A:** _____

   B: Air bags can hurt children in a car.

7. **A:** _____

   B: Drivers under age eighteen have to drive with an adult at night.

8. **A:** _____

   B: Halina should buy some water.

9. **A:** _____

   B: <u>This car seat</u> is very popular.

10. **A:** _____

   B: <u>Everyone</u> has to wear a seat belt.

EXERCISE 14 Marta and Simon talk about Ed's driving practice. Fill in each blank in their conversation with a phrase from the box. Then listen and check your answers.  5.8

When does he have to take	Can you put	I have to take	Ed should learn
Do you have to use ✓	We can stop	He should practice	he can learn a lot

Marta: ___*Do you have to use*___ the car today?
1.

Simon: Yes.

Marta: _____ some gas in the car for me? It's almost empty.
2.

Simon: Sure. _____ Ed out for driving practice later this afternoon.
3.

   _____ at the gas station. _____
4.   5.

   how to pump gas, too.

Marta: _____ the driving test?
6.

Simon: In just three weeks!

Marta: _____ a lot. He doesn't have much time.
7.

Simon: I know. But _____ in three weeks.
8.

Old gas station on Route 66, Hackberry, Arizona, U.S.

SUMMARY OF UNIT 5

Can, Should, Have To—Affirmative and Negative Statements

SUBJECT	MODAL/*HAVE TO*	VERB (BASE FORM)	
I You She He It Simon We They	can cannot can't should should not shouldn't	take	the test today.
I You We They	have to do not have to don't have to	pass	the test now.
She He It Ed	has to does not have to doesn't have to		

Can and *Should*—Questions

QUESTION WORD	MODAL	SUBJECT	VERB (BASE FORM)		ANSWER
	Can	I	get	some water?	Yes, you can.
	Should	they	buy	an infant seat?	No, they shouldn't.
Where	can	Halina	get	a car seat?	At the outlet mall.
Why	should	we	go	to the mall?	To buy a car seat.

Have To—Questions

QUESTION WORD	*DO*	SUBJECT	*HAVE TO*	VERB (BASE FORM)		ANSWER
	Does	she		get	gas?	Yes, she does.
	Do	I	have to	pump	the gas?	No, you don't.
Where	does	Anna		sit?		In the back seat.
How much	do	we		spend?		About $100.

REVIEW

A. Choose the correct words to complete the conversation.

A: I (*have to/can*) buy a new car seat for my son.
  1.

B: (*Why do you have to/Why can you*) buy a new car seat?
  2.

A: Because he's too big for his old one. Where (*I should/should I*) shop for one?
  3.

B: Well, (*you can/can you*) buy a car seat online. But (*you should/should you*) go to the outlet mall first.
  4.   5.

A: Why (*I should/should I*) go to the outlet mall first?
  6.

B: Because things aren't as expensive there.

A: OK. (*I have to/Do I have to*) put the car seat in the back seat?
  7.

B: Yes. (*You can't/Can't you*) put it in the front seat. It can be dangerous.
  8.

A: Why (*it can/can it*) be dangerous?
  9.

B: The airbags (*can/should*) hurt him.
  10.

A: Oh. I'm glad I asked.

B. Fill in the blanks with *can*, *should*, or *have to* and the words given. For questions, use a question word if needed. The underlined words are the answer.

A: _____ about driving in this country?
  1. I/know

B: Well, you should know <u>the rules of the road</u>. Do you have a driver's license?

A: No, I don't.

B: OK. _____ a driver's license in order to drive.
  2. you/have

A: _____ a driver's license?
  3. I/get

B: You can get a license <u>at the Department of Motor Vehicles</u>.

A: _____ there now?
  4. I/go

B: <u>No, you shouldn't.</u> _____ a license yet. First, you have to take a driver's education class.
  5. you/not get

A: _____ a class?
  6. I/take

B: <u>To learn the rules of the road.</u> Then _____ driving at least fifty hours.
  7. you/practice

A: Fifty hours? That's a lot. Do I really have to practice fifty hours?

B: Yes. But _____ you.
  8. I/help

A: Oh, that's great. Thank you. _____ right now?
  9. we/start

B: <u>No, we can't.</u> First _____ the class. Then _____ your learner's permit.
  10. you/take   11. you/get

FROM GRAMMAR TO WRITING

PART 1 Editing Advice

1. Always use the base form after *can*, *should*, and *have to*.

   She can ~~drives~~ <u>drive</u> the car.

2. Don't use *to* after *can* and *should*.

   The child can't ~~to~~ sit in the front seat.

3. Use the correct word order in a question.

   Why <u>you</u> can't drive?

4. Don't forget to use *do* or *does* with *have to* in questions.

   Why <u>do</u> you have to take a vision test?

5. Don't use *do* or *does* with subject questions.

   Who ~~does have~~ <u>has</u> to sit in the back? The baby does.

PART 2 Editing Practice

Some of the shaded words and phrases have mistakes. Find the mistakes and correct them.
If the shaded words are correct, write *C*.

This is a conversation between Ed and his driving teacher after the first class.

Ed:	How many pages <u>do</u> we have to study in the driver's handbook for tomorrow? **1.**
Mr. Brown:	You <u>should learn</u> the laws in the first twenty pages. **2.** <u>C</u>
Ed:	Tell me about licenses in this state. When <u>I can drive</u> with my friends? **3.**
Mr. Brown:	You're only sixteen. In this state, you <u>can to have</u> only one passenger in the car **4.** under age twenty-one. And you still <u>has to have</u> an adult in the car between 10 p.m. **5.** and 6 a.m. for the first six months.
Ed:	How many hours <u>we have to practice</u> before the driving test? **6.**
Mr. Brown:	Fifty hours. But <u>you should to practice</u> more. And you have to practice ten hours at night. **7.**
Ed:	How <u>we can do</u> that? We <u>can't drive</u> at night. **8.** **9.**
Mr. Brown:	Sunday through Thursday, you can drive until 10 p.m., and then an adult driver <u>has to goes</u> with you. **10.**
Ed:	<u>Does the adult has to</u> be one of my parents? **11.**

Mr. Brown: No, but the adult has to be at least twenty-one years old. And the adult <u>has to have a</u>

12.

valid license.

Ed: Yes, I know. And we <u>have to wear</u> a seat belt, too.

13.

PART 3 Write

Write about what is wrong in each picture. Write one negative and one affirmative sentence about each picture. Use *can*, *should*, and *have to*.

A.

B.

C.

D.

A. The baby can't sit on the mother's lap. The baby has to be in an infant seat.

PART 4 Learner's Log

1. Use *can*, *should*, and *have to* (affirmative and/or negative) to write one sentence about each of these topics. Give advice, rules, or information.

   - rules about children's car seats
   - things you can do at a gas station
   - what you need for a driver's license

2. Write any questions you still have about the topics above.

A school is a building of four walls...
with tomorrow inside.

DAN VALENTINE

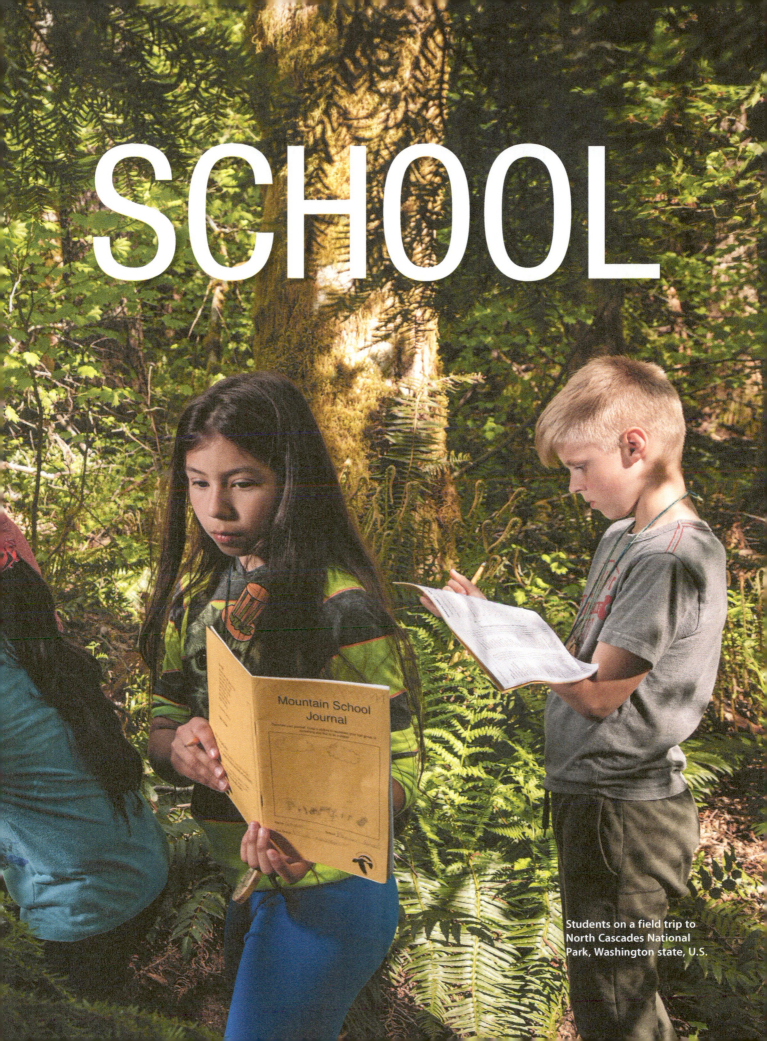

SCHOOL

Students on a field trip to North Cascades National Park, Washington state, U.S.

Circle *Yes* or *No*.

1. Are there guidelines for school lunches in your country? Yes   No

2. Do elementary schools in your country give free lunches to children? Yes   No

READ

Read the following article. Pay special attention to the affirmative and negative statements with *must* and *have to* in bold. 🎧 6.1

Children need good nutrition. The United States has the National School Lunch Program to give children well-balanced meals. Schools in this program **must follow** guidelines. They **must not serve** children a lot of fat, sugar, or salt. They **must serve** food from each of these five groups: protein (for example, meat, fish, or beans), vegetables, fruit, grains and bread, and milk.

A school lunch of a sandwich, milk, carrots, celery, nuts, and an apple

Some families don't make much money. These families **have to pay** a small amount (less than fifty cents per lunch). Children from very low-income families **don't have to pay** for a school lunch at all. Some families have enough money and **have to pay** the full price. But it isn't expensive. It's usually less than three dollars.

Parents **must fill out** an application to get free lunch for their children. They **must tell** the truth about their family income.

Children **don't have to eat** the school lunch. They can bring a lunch from home.

DID YOU **KNOW?**

In the United States, over 30 million children participate in the National School Lunch Program.

COMPREHENSION Based on the reading, write T for *true* or F for *false*.

1. _____ The National School Lunch Program helps students get good nutrition.

2. _____ School lunches cost the same amount for everyone.

3. _____ The National School Lunch Program pays for lunches that students bring from home.

nutrition	Children need good **nutrition**. They need to eat healthy food, such as fruits and vegetables.
balanced	A **balanced** lunch has items from each food group: protein, fruit, vegetables, grains, and milk.
guideline	The National School Lunch Program makes **guidelines**. They tell the schools what to serve.
serve	Schools give children lunch. They **serve** lunch every day.
fat	French fries and potato chips have a lot of **fat**. They are not good for you.
grain	We use **grains** to make bread.
tell the truth	**Tell the truth** on the application. Don't give false information.
income (n.) low-income (adj.)	Their **income** is $30,000 a year. They are a **low-income** family.
amount	Fifty cents is a small **amount** of money.
less than	The lunch costs $5.25. It's **less than** $6.00.

LISTEN

Listen to the sentences about the article. Circle *True* or *False*. ⬛6.3

1. (True)   False   5. True   False

2. True   False   6. True   False

3. True   False   7. True   False

4. True   False   8. True   False

6.1 Modal: *Must*—Affirmative and Negative Statements

EXAMPLES	EXPLANATION
Schools **must** serve milk to children. Parents **must** fill out an application for the free lunch program.	We use *must* to show rules or laws.
School lunches **must not** have a lot of sugar. School lunches **must not** have a lot of fat.	When the rule is "don't do this," we use *must not*.

EXERCISE 1 Fill in the blanks with one of the verbs from the box.

be	fill out	tell	sign	pay ✓	serve

1. The lunch is not free for everyone. Some families must _____pay_____.

2. The school must _____ a nutritious lunch with protein, vegetables, fruit, grains, and milk.

3. Parents must _____ an application for the school lunch program.

4. Parents must _____ the application.

5. Parents must _____ the truth about their family income.

6. School lunches must _____ well balanced.

EXERCISE 2 Read the application for the school lunch program below. Then change sentences 1–10 from imperative statements to statements with *must* or *must not*.

Application for Free and Reduced-Price Meals

To apply for free and reduced-price meals for your child(ren), you must fill out this form and sign it. Use a black or blue pen.

PART 1: List the name(s) of your child(ren) at school.

NAME(S) OF CHILD(REN) LAST NAME, FIRST NAME	AGE	SCHOOL	GRADE	CLASS
1.				
2.				
3.				

PART 2: List the names of all adult household members and their monthly incomes.

LAST NAME, FIRST NAME	MONTHLY INCOME
1.	
2.	
3.	

PART 3: Signature and Social Security Number. I certify that all the above information is true.

SIGNATURE OF PARENT OR GUARDIAN	MAILING ADDRESS

SOCIAL SECURITY NUMBER	PHONE NUMBER
_ _ _	( )

FOR SCHOOL USE ONLY   Date Received: _____   Date Approved: _____

1. Print your answers. / _You must print your answers._

2. Don't use a pencil. / _You must not use a pencil._

3. Fill out the application. / _____

4. Sign your name. / _____

5. Don't print your name in Part 3. / _____

6. Don't write in the last box. / _____

7. Write your monthly income. / _____

8. Don't use a red pen. / _____

9. Don't give false information. / _____

10. Write your Social Security number. / _____

6.2 *Must* and *Have To*

Must and *have to* have similar meanings.

EXAMPLES	EXPLANATION
You **must** write your family income. You **have to** write your family income. Schools **must** serve children milk. Schools **have to** serve children milk.	*Must* is very formal. We use *must* for rules and laws. We can also use *have to* for rules and laws. *Must* is stronger than *have to*.
Marta **has to** make lunch for her daughter. We **have to** buy more bread.	We use *have to* for personal necessity. We don't use *must* for personal necessity.

GRAMMAR IN USE

Have to is more common than *must* in questions.
Do I **have to** sign the application?   Do schools **have to** serve milk?

EXERCISE 3 Fill in the blanks with *must* + a verb to talk about rules. Use one of the verbs from the box. Answers will vary.

include	apply ✓	state	follow	sign	provide	serve

1. Students _____ must apply _____ for the school lunch program.

2. Schools _____ guidelines from the National School Lunch Program.

3. On an application, parents _____ their names.

4. On the school lunch application, parents _____ their family income.

5. School lunches _____ food from each of the five groups.

6. Schools _____ children milk with every lunch.

ABOUT YOU Fill in the blanks to talk about personal necessities. Use *have to* + a verb.

1. I _____ have to call my mom _____ every day.

2. In class, we _____.

3. The teacher _____.

4. My mother _____.

5. Children _____.

6. My classmates _____.

7. I _____ every week.

8. At work, we _____.

6.3 *Must Not* and *Don't Have To*

Must and *have to* have similar meanings. *Must not* and *don't have to* have different meanings.

EXAMPLES	EXPLANATION
School lunches **must not** have a lot of fat. You must tell the truth. You **must not** give false information.	*Must not* gives a rule.
Children **don't have to** eat the school lunch. They can bring a lunch from home. Children of low-income families **don't have to** pay for lunch. They can get a free lunch.	*Don't have to* shows that something is not necessary.

EXERCISE 4 Fill in the blanks with the negative of *must* or *have to*. Remember, they have different meanings.

1. Schools in the lunch program _____ must not _____ serve a lot of sugar.

2. Children _____ don't have to _____ be in the school lunch program.

3. Many families in the school lunch program _____ pay. Their children get free lunch.

4. Maya _____ eat at school. She can eat at home.

5. Parents _____ give false information on the application. They will get in trouble.

6. You _____ drink the milk. You can drink water.

7. Ed _____ study at home. He can study in the library.

8. You _____ talk loudly in the school library. It's a rule.

9. Children _____ come late to school. Everyone should be on time.

10. Schools _____ provide unhealthy lunches.

ABOUT YOU Work with a partner. Name three things you don't have to do on the weekends.

I don't have to work on Saturdays.

ABOUT YOU Work with a partner. Name three things students must not do at this school or in this class.

Students must not talk in the library.

College students study in the library.

1. What foods are good for children?

2. What are some foods children don't like to eat?

READ

Read the following blog. Pay special attention to the quantity expressions with count and noncount nouns in bold. 🎧 6.4

It's time for a new school year. Today's topic is school lunches for your kids! Your children have two choices: buy a lunch at school or bring a lunch from home.

School lunches can be inexpensive and convenient. They usually include **a piece of fruit**, **a carton of milk**, and a protein, such as **a piece of fish** or **meat**, or maybe **a slice of pizza** or a sandwich. Pizza is always a favorite choice with kids. Unfortunately, kids sometimes throw the fruit away. Sometimes, students want **a bottle of soda** or a **piece of candy**, but these are not healthy choices. Students shouldn't have **any candy** or **soda**.

Other students bring their lunches to school. They use a brown bag or a lunch box. Their parents help them pack lunches with sandwiches, fruit, vegetables, and maybe a healthy cookie or snack. Some parents still pack **a bag of chips** or a candy bar. These choices have **a lot of fat** or **sugar**, and aren't very healthy. Vegetables are very healthy. They don't have **much fat** or **sugar**. Fruit is also a better choice than a candy bar. **A bunch of grapes** is a perfect snack. If you and your child pack a lunch together, you can choose healthy options that he or she wants to eat.

DID YOU KNOW?

The U.S. government's *Smart Snacks in School* nutrition standards limit the calories, sodium, fat, and sugar in all foods and drinks sold at schools.

COMPREHENSION Based on the reading, write T for *true* or F for *false*.

1. _____ School lunches usually provide a bottle of soda.

2. _____ Some parents pack unhealthy snacks in their children's lunches.

3. _____ Grapes are a healthy snack.

WORDS TO KNOW 🎧 6.5

favorite	Maya loves pizza. Pizza is her **favorite** lunch.
unfortunately	We use the word "**unfortunately**" to introduce bad news.
throw away	Please **throw away** your lunch bag after you eat. Don't leave it on the table.
brown bag (n.)	A **brown bag** is a paper bag for lunches. You can carry your lunch in a **brown bag**.
lunch box	Some kids take their lunches to school in a **lunch box**.
better	Juice is good, but water is **better**.
bunch of	The kids sometimes get a small **bunch of** grapes with lunch.
option	Fruit is a better **option** than candy.

LISTEN

Listen to the sentences about the blog. Circle *True* or *False*. 🎧 6.6

1. True (False)   5. True   False

2. True False   6. True   False

3. True False   7. True   False

4. True False   8. True   False

6.4 Count and Noncount Nouns

Some nouns are count nouns. We can count them. Some nouns are noncount nouns.
We don't count them.

EXAMPLES	EXPLANATION
One **sandwich** has jelly. Two **sandwiches** have cheese. One **child** has a lunch box from home. Twenty **children** get free lunch.	A count noun has a singular and a plural form. We can use a number with a count noun.
You need **bread** for a sandwich. Victor drinks **coffee** every day. The school always serves **fruit**. You must eat **food** every day.	A noncount noun has no plural form. We don't use a number with a noncount noun.

Notes:

1. You sometimes see the plural of *fruit* and *food*. *Fruits* means different kinds of fruit. *Foods* means different kinds of food.

2. Some common noncount nouns are:

     LIQUIDS: *water, milk, cream, oil, tea, coffee, soup, juice*

     DAIRY: *milk, cream, cheese, ice cream, butter, yogurt*

     MEATS: *beef, chicken, pork, fish, seafood*

     SMALL THINGS: *salt, pepper, sugar, rice, candy, pasta, macaroni, corn, popcorn*

     BAKED GOODS: *pizza, cake, bread, pie*

     OTHER: *food, fruit, meat, fat*

ABOUT YOU Work with a partner. Tell how often you eat or drink each item. Practice count nouns and frequency words or time expressions.

1. potato(es)

   I eat potatoes at least once a week.

2. banana(s)

3. grape(s)

4. egg(s)

5. cracker(s)

6. orange(s)

7. avocado(es)

8. apple(s)

9. potato chip(s)

10. hamburger(s)

11. hot dog(s)

12. sandwich(es)

ABOUT YOU Write how often you eat or drink each item. Practice noncount nouns (no plural form) and frequency words or time expressions.

1. fruit _____ I eat fruit every day. _____

2. popcorn _____

3. coffee _____

4. milk _____

5. tea _____

6. butter _____

7. water _____

8. soda _____

9. juice _____

10. bread _____

11. rice _____

12. pizza _____

13. meat _____

14. chicken _____

15. fish _____

16. cheese _____

17. yogurt _____

18. candy _____

6.5 Quantity Expressions with Noncount Nouns

EXAMPLES	EXPLANATION
I eat **three pieces of fruit** a day. I drink **two cups of tea** a day. Children get **one carton of milk** with lunch.	To talk about quantity with a noncount noun, we use a unit of measurement that you can count: *cup of, bowl of, carton of, teaspoon of, piece of, slice of,* etc.

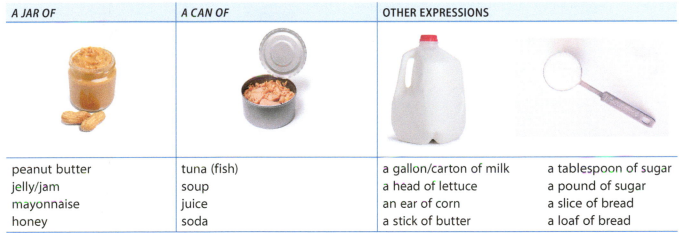

A BOTTLE OF	*A GLASS/CUP OF*	*A PIECE OF*	
oil juice soda water	milk coffee water tea	fruit cake candy chicken	fish meat bread pizza

A JAR OF	*A CAN OF*	*OTHER EXPRESSIONS*	
peanut butter jelly/jam mayonnaise honey	tuna (fish) soup juice soda	a gallon/carton of milk a head of lettuce an ear of corn a stick of butter	a tablespoon of sugar a pound of sugar a slice of bread a loaf of bread

EXERCISE 5 Complete the conversation with one of the words from the box. Then listen and check your answers. 🎧 6.7

can	jar	candy ✓	fruit	milk

Amy: I'm hungry. Can I have a piece of _____candy_____?
1.

Marta: You know it isn't good for you. Have a piece of _____.
2.

Amy: Can I have a peanut butter and jelly sandwich, too? Where's the peanut butter?

Marta: There's a _____ of peanut butter in the cabinet next to the refrigerator.
3.

Amy: I see a _____ of soda in the refrigerator. Can I have it?
4.

Marta: No. Soda has a lot of sugar. Drink a glass of _____ instead.
5.

EXERCISE 6 Victor is teaching Maya to make a tuna sandwich. Circle the correct quantity expression to complete the sentence. Then listen and check your answers. 🎧 6.8

Victor: There's a (*loaf/slice/can*) of bread on the table. Take two
1.

(*bunches/tablespoons/slices*) of bread and put them
2.

on a plate. Open a (*piece/glass/can*) of tuna and put
3.

the tuna in a bowl. There's a (*glass/jar/piece*) of
4.

mayonnaise in the refrigerator. Add two

(*bottles/jars/tablespoons*) of mayonnaise. Mix the tuna
5.

and mayonnaise. Spread the mixture on the bread.

You can also add a (*can/tablespoon/slice*) of tomato.
6.

Now you have a healthy lunch.

Maya: Can I have a (*stick/can/piece*) of soda with my
7.

sandwich, please?

Victor: No, sorry. But you can have a (*glass/jar/head*) of water. And you can have
8.

a (*piece/bottle/tablespoon*) of fruit after lunch. Do you want an apple or
9.

a(n) (*ear/piece/bunch*) of grapes?
10.

ABOUT YOU Add a quantity if you eat or drink these items. If you do not eat or drink an item, write, "I don't eat/drink…"

1. I eat _____ two slices _____ of bread a day.   OR I don't eat bread.

2. I drink _____ of water a day.

3. I eat _____ of fruit a day.

4. I drink _____ of coffee a day.

5. I drink _____ of milk a day.

6. I drink _____ of tea a day.

7. I drink _____ of juice a week.

8. I eat _____ of corn a month.

9. I eat _____ of candy a week.

10. I eat _____ of pizza a week.

6.6 A Lot Of/Much/A Little with Noncount Nouns

EXAMPLES	EXPLANATION
I eat **a lot of** cheese. I don't drink **a lot of** milk. I don't use **much** sugar.	We use *a lot of* with large quantities. In negatives, you can also use *much*.
He uses **a little** sugar. He drinks **a little** tea.	We use *a little* with small quantities.

GRAMMAR IN USE

We say *use* or *take*, not *eat*, with *sugar, salt, milk, cream,* and *butter* when we add these things to food.

> Do you **use** a lot of butter in your cooking?

> I **take** milk in my coffee.

ABOUT YOU Tell a partner if you eat, drink, or use these items. Use *a lot of* or *much*.

1. milk

    I drink a lot of milk.

2. meat

3. salt

4. cheese

5. popcorn

6. rice

7. candy

8. water

9. coffee

10. oil

11. sugar

12. butter

13. soup

14. fruit

EXERCISE 7 Complete the sentences. Fill in the blanks with *a little* and a word from the box.

meat	butter	milk	salt	popcorn	sugar	oil ✓

1. Use _____ a little oil _____ to cook.

2. Put _____ and _____ in the coffee.

    a.   b.

3. The pizza has _____ and a lot of cheese.

4. Put _____ on the bread.

5. Put _____ in the soup.

6. I eat _____ at the movies.

6.7 *Some/Any* with Noncount Nouns

EXAMPLES	EXPLANATION
A: Does the pizza have **any** meat? **B:** Yes. The pizza has **some** meat. **A:** Do kids get **any** soda with their lunches? **B:** No. They don't get **any** soda. **A:** Do you want **some** coffee? **B:** No. I don't want **any** coffee.	We use *any* or *some* in questions. We use *some* in affirmatives. We use *any* in negatives.

GRAMMAR IN USE

We use *some* and *any* when it is not easy or not important to say exactly how much/many we are thinking of.

*I want **some** milk.*

Do you have any sugar?

EXERCISE 8 Fill in the blanks with *some* or *any*. In some cases, both answers are possible.

1. The pizza has ____some____ meat.

2. I don't want _____ soda.

3. The school lunch doesn't have _____ candy.

4. Do you want _____ milk?

5. I want _____ juice.

6. The sandwich has _____ mayonnaise.

7. Does the soup have _____ salt?

8. She's a vegetarian. She doesn't eat _____ meat.

9. I can't buy my lunch today. I don't have _____ money.

10. You should eat _____ fruit every day.

1. What do children need for school?

2. Do you think school uniforms are a good idea? Why or why not?

READ

Read the following conversation. Pay special attention to the quantity expressions with count and noncount nouns in bold. 🎧 6.9

It's Maya's first day of school. She has a note for Victor.

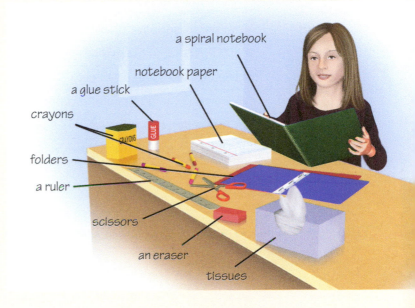

a spiral notebook
notebook paper
a glue stick
crayons
folders
a ruler
scissors
an eraser
tissues

Victor: What's this?

Maya: It's a note from school. It has **a lot of information** and a list of school supplies. I need **a lot of supplies**.

Victor: What do you need?

Maya: I need two erasers, one ruler, two spiral notebooks, ten pencils, one glue stick, one pair of scissors, one package of notebook paper, four folders, one box of tissues, and crayons.

Victor: **How many crayons** do you need?

Maya: One box of twenty-four.

Victor calls Simon for help.

Victor: I have **a few questions** about my daughter's school. I need **some advice**. Do you have **any time** now?

Simon: Yes, Victor. I have **a little time** now.

Victor: Oh thank you, Simon! Maya has a list of school supplies. Where can I buy them?

Simon: **Many stores** sell school supplies, but the office supply store near my house has a sale now. I have **a few coupons**. We can go together.

Victor: Do I have to buy **any books**? **How much money** do I need for books?

Simon: You don't have to buy **any books**. Public schools supply the books. Students return them at the end of the school year.

Victor: That's good. The note has **a lot of information** about homework. Do American kids get **a lot of homework**?

Simon: Yes, they do.

Victor: One more question. Do I have to buy a uniform for my daughter?

Simon: I don't know. Children in some schools need uniforms. Let me read the information from Maya's school.

DID YOU KNOW?

On average, a family spends $122 on school supplies per child every year.

COMPREHENSION Based on the reading, write T for *true* or F for *false*.

1. _____ Maya has a lot of supplies.

2. _____ Maya's school supplies her books.

3. _____ Victor has coupons for school supplies.

WORDS TO KNOW 🎧 6.10

note	The teacher sometimes writes a **note** to parents.
supplies (n.) supply (v.)	Children need school **supplies**. They need pencils, paper, rulers, and more. The school **supplies** students with books. The students use the school's books.
advice	Victor needs Simon's **advice** about school.
coupon	I like to save money. I can get fifty cents off with this **coupon** from the newspaper.
public school	Every child can go to **public school**. Public school is free.
return	Students don't keep the school's books. They **return** them to the school.
uniform	In some schools, all the children wear the same outfit, or clothing. This is a **uniform**.

LISTEN

Listen to the sentences about the conversation. Circle *True* or *False*. 🎧 6.11

1. (True)   False   5. True   False

2. True   False   6. True   False

3. True   False   7. True   False

4. True   False   8. True   False

6.8 *Some* vs. *Any*

EXAMPLES	EXPLANATION
Maya has **some** information from her teacher. Victor has **some** questions for Simon.	We use *some* with noncount nouns and plural count nouns.
Does she need **any/some** glue? Does she need **any/some** pencils?	We use *any* or *some* with both noncount nouns and plural count nouns in questions.
Maya doesn't have **any** homework today. Victor doesn't have **any** coupons.	We use *any* with both noncount nouns and plural count nouns in negatives.

Note:

Homework, *information*, and *advice* are noncount nouns. They have no plural form. To add a specific quantity, we can say *a homework assignment*, *a piece of information*, and *a piece of advice*.

EXERCISE 9 Fill in the blanks with *some* or *any*.

1. I need ____some____ paper for school.

2. Do you have _____ homework today?

3. We have _____ math homework.

4. I don't have _____ problems with my homework.

5. Maya needs _____ notebooks.

6. I don't need _____ paper for my gym class.

7. Do you need _____ erasers for school?

8. We need _____ crayons for school.

9. Victor needs _____ advice from Simon.

10. Does the school offer _____ after-school programs?

ABOUT YOU Answer the questions. Use *some* or *any* in your answers.

1. Do you have any time to watch TV?

   Yes. I have some time to watch TV after school.

2. Do you have any homework today?

   _____

3. Do you need any books for this course?

   _____

4. Does this class have any students from South Korea?

   _____

5. Do you need any paper to do this exercise?

   _____

6. Do you have any information about universities in the United States?

   _____

7. Do you have any advice for new students?

   _____

continued

8. Do you have any hobbies?

_____

9. Do you need any new supplies?

_____

10. Do you have any questions about this lesson?

_____

6.9 *A Lot Of* and *Many* vs. *Much*

EXAMPLES	EXPLANATION
Maya needs **a lot of/many** school supplies. Does she need **a lot of/many** pencils? She doesn't need **a lot of/many** notebooks.	We use *a lot of* or *many* with count nouns.
Does Victor have **a lot of/much** information about the school? He doesn't have **a lot of/much** money. Maya needs **a lot of** paper.	We use *a lot of* or *much* with noncount nouns in questions and negatives. In affirmative statements, we use *a lot of*, not *much*.

EXERCISE 10 Circle the correct answer to complete the sentence. In some cases, both answers are possible.

1. I have (*much*/*a lot of*) paper, but I don't have (*many*/*a lot of*) pencils.
      a.   b.

2. Some children drink (*much/a lot of*) juice, but they don't drink (*many/much*) water.
                          a.   b.

3. Maya eats (*a lot of/many*) fruit, but she doesn't eat (*much/many*) bananas.
            a.   b.

4. (*Many/Much*) stores have school supply sales in August.

5. I need (*a lot of/much*) information about schools in the United States.

6. Children need (*a lot of/much*) school supplies.

7. I have (*much/a lot of*) homework, but I don't have (*much/many*) time to do it.
            a.   b.

8. (*Many/A lot of*) children get a free lunch in the United States.

6.10 *A Few* vs. *A Little*

EXAMPLES	EXPLANATION
Maya needs **a few** erasers. She needs **a few** pencils.	We use *a few* with count nouns.
Victor spends **a little** time with Maya every day. School lunches cost **a little** money.	We use *a little* with noncount nouns.

GRAMMAR IN USE

To talk about a small quantity, make sure to use *a little*, not *little*.

   *I need **a little** advice.* NOT *I need little advice.*

EXERCISE 11 Fill in the blanks with *a few* or *a little*.

1. Maya drinks ___a little___ juice every day.

2. Victor has _____ time to help Maya with her homework.

3. Maya has _____ good friends at school.

4. Maya watches _____ TV programs on the weekend.

5. Victor needs _____ advice from Simon.

6. Maya needs _____ pencils for school.

7. Simon has _____ information for Victor.

8. Simon has _____ coupons.

ABOUT YOU Fill in the blanks.

1. I have a few _good friends_____.

2. I need a little _____.

3. I know a few _____.

4. I eat a little _____ every day.

5. I eat a few _____ every week.

6. I use a little _____.

7. I spend a little _____.

8. I have a little _____.

6.11 *How Many vs. How Much*

EXAMPLES	EXPLANATION
How many coupons do you have? **How many** pencils does Maya need for school?	We use *how many* with count nouns.
How much paper does she need? **How much** money do I need for books?	We use *how much* with noncount nouns.
How much does this book cost? **How much** is the school lunch?	We use *how much* to ask about cost.

ABOUT YOU Find a partner. Ask these questions about elementary schools in your partner's country. Write short answers.

1. How many days a week do kids go to school? _____ *five days a week* _____

2. How many months a year do kids go to school? _____

3. How many kids are in an average class? _____

4. How much time do kids spend on homework? _____

5. How many hours a day are kids in school? _____

6. How much time do kids have for vacation? _____

7. How much money do kids spend on books? _____

8. Do kids get school lunch? How much does it cost? _____

9. Do kids wear a uniform? How much does a uniform cost? _____

10. How many classes do most students have every day? _____

ABOUT YOU Fill in the blanks with *how much* or *how many*. Then answer the question.

1. ___*How many*___ lessons do we do a day? ___*We do one lesson a day.*___
       a.   b.

2. _____ classes do you have now? _____
       a.   b.

3. _____ money do you need to take one class? _____
       a.   b.

4. _____ paper do you need for your homework? _____
       a.   b.

5. _____ students in this class speak Spanish? _____
       a.   b.

6. _____ books do we need for this course? _____
       a.   b.

7. _____ time do you spend on your homework? _____
       a.   b.

8. _____ homework do you have today? _____
       a.   b.

EXERCISE 12 Circle the correct word to complete this conversation between a parent, Mrs. Murphy, and a school employee, Mr. Johnson. Then listen and check your answers. 🎧 6.12

Mrs. Murphy: I have (*a little/a few*) questions. I need (*a little/a few*) information.
1.   2.

Do you have (*any/many*) time to answer my questions?
3.

Mr. Johnson: Yes. I have (*a little/a few*) time right now.
4.

Mrs. Murphy: Can my kids get into the free lunch program?

Mr. Johnson: It depends on your income. If you don't make (*many/much*) money, they can probably
5.

get into the free lunch program.

Mrs. Murphy: I don't make (*many/a lot of*) money. What should I do?
6.

Mr. Johnson: You have to fill out a form. The form has (*many/much*) questions.
7.

Mrs. Murphy: (*How much/How many*) does a school lunch cost?
8.

Mr. Johnson: In this city, the full price is $3.25. That's not (*much/any*) money for a healthy lunch.
9.

Mrs. Murphy: I have (*a lot of/much*) kids in
10.

school, so for me, it's

(*much/a lot of*) money.
11.

Mr. Johnson: (*How much/How many*) kids
12.

do you have?

Mrs. Murphy: Six. Four are in school, so I

really need to learn about

the free lunch program.

Mr. Johnson: Of course. Let me get you

the form.

A school employee helps a parent with paperwork.

FUN WITH GRAMMAR

Play with a group. One student starts. Say one of the following words or phrases and the name of another student in the group. That student must say a sentence using the word or phrase and then a new word or phrase, plus the name of another student in the group. Continue playing. Each student creates a sentence and then gives a new student a word or phrase to use. If you can't think of a sentence, say *Pass*.

a lot of	*some*	*how much*	*a cup of*
a little	*any*	*a bottle of*	*a tablespoon of*
much	*a few*	*a glass of*	*a bunch of*
many	*how many*	*a piece of*	*a can of*

SUMMARY OF UNIT 6

Must and *Have To*

USE	EXAMPLES
For rules and laws	You **must** write your family income. School lunches **must not** have a lot of fat. Schools **have to** serve children milk.
For personal necessity	Marta **has to** make lunch for her daughter.
To show that something is not necessary	Children **don't have to** eat the school lunch.

Quantity Expressions with Noncount Nouns

a bottle of juice	**an ear of** corn
a glass of milk	**a stick of** butter
a cup of coffee	**a tablespoon of** sugar
a piece of fruit	**a pound of** sugar
a jar of peanut butter	**a slice of** bread
a can of soup	**a loaf of** bread
a carton of milk	**a head of** lettuce

Quantifiers

QUANTIFIER	USE	EXAMPLES
a lot of	with count nouns with noncount nouns	Maya needs **a lot of** school supplies. Does she need **a lot of** pencils? I eat **a lot of** cheese.
many	with count nouns	Maya needs **many** school supplies. She doesn't need **many** notebooks. Does she need **many** pencils?
much	with noncount nouns in negatives with noncount nouns in questions	I don't use **much** sugar. Does Victor have **much** information?
a little	with noncount nouns	He drinks **a little** tea.
a few	with count nouns	She needs **a few** pencils.
some	with noncount nouns with count nouns with count nouns in questions with noncount nouns in questions	Maya has **some** information. Victor has **some** questions. Does she need **some** pencils? Do you want **some** coffee?
any	with count nouns in questions with noncount nouns in questions with count nouns in negatives with noncount nouns in negatives	Does she need **any** pencils? Do you want **any** coffee? Victor doesn't have **any** coupons. I don't want **any** coffee.
How many	with count nouns	**How many** coupons do you have?
How much	with noncount nouns to ask about cost	**How much** paper does she need? **How much** does this book cost?

REVIEW

A. Choose the correct words to complete the conversation.

A: Hi, Lola. What are you looking at?

B: Hi, Tim. It's Eva's first week of school, and the school sent (*a lot of/much/many*) information home with
   _1._

   her. I (*have/have to/don't have to*) read a lot of papers.
   _2._

A: Do you need (*much/some/many*) help?
   _3._

B: I would love (*much/a little/many*) help!
   _4._

A: OK, let's see. Well, here's a list of school supplies. You (*must to/have to/don't have to*) buy
   _5._

   everything on the list—just (*a little/some/much*) things.
   _6._

B: OK. (*How much/How many/Many*) things does she need?
   _7._

A: She needs (*some/any/a little*) notebooks and pencils. And (*a little/a few/many*) glue sticks.
   _8._   _9._

   And (*much/a lot of/a little*) crayons . . .
   _10._

B: Great. And what about this form?

A: That's the application for reduced-price lunch. First, you (*have to/must not/don't have to*) write
   _11._

   Eva's name. Then you (*have/must/must not*) write your income there. You (*must/must not/don't have to*)
   _12._   _13._

   write in that box—only the school can write there.

B: OK. (*How many/How much/Much*) does the school lunch cost?
   _14._

A: It's not (*many/much/a lot*) money. Don't worry. Now, let's go to the office supply store!
   _15._

B. Complete the conversation with words from the box.

any	a lot of	some	a loaf of	a bottle of
a jar of	a carton of	cans of		

A: I'm going to the store. What do we need?

B: We need _____ milk. And _____ peanut butter. And
   _1._   _2._

   _____ apples, please. I love apples.
   _3._

A: OK. I'll get _____ oranges, too.
   _4._

B: Great. Oh, can you get three _____ tuna and _____ bread, too?
   _5._   _6._

A: Sure. Do we need _____ juice?
   _7._

B: Actually, we're out of juice. Please get _____ juice, too!
   _8._

FROM GRAMMAR TO WRITING

PART 1 Editing Advice

1. Don't use *to* after *must*.

   Schools ~~must to~~ serve a healthy lunch.
   <small>have to/must</small>

2. Don't put *a* or *an* before a noncount noun.

   I like to eat ~~a~~ rice.

3. Use *of* with a unit of measure.

   I want a cup ^of^ coffee.

4. Don't forget *of* with *a lot of*.

   I don't have a lot ^of^ homework today.

5. Don't confuse *much* and *many*, or *a little* and *a few*.

   He doesn't have ~~much~~ friends.
   <small>many</small>

   Maya doesn't have ~~many~~ homework today.
   <small>much</small>

   I eat a ~~little~~ grapes every day.
   <small>few</small>

   Put a ~~few~~ salt in the soup.
   <small>little</small>

6. Don't use *much* in affirmative statements.

   He drinks ~~much~~ tea.
   <small>a lot of</small>

7. Don't use *no* after a negative verb.

   I don't have ~~no~~ money.
   <small>any</small>

8. Don't use the plural form with noncount nouns.

   Victor gets a lot of ~~informations~~ from Simon.
   <small>information</small>

PART 2 Editing Practice

Some of the shaded words and phrases have mistakes. Find the mistakes and correct them.
If the shaded words are correct, write *C*.

Maya is home with Victor after school.

Maya: Can I have ~~a little~~ grapes? And can I have some milk, too?
<small>a few</small>   <small>C</small>
          1.   2.

Victor: I'm sorry. We don't have no milk today. Do you want a glass water?
                    3.   4.

Maya: I don't like to drink a water. Do we have any juice?
                    5.   6.

Victor: Yes, but you can have just a little. Juice contains much sugar.
                              7.   8.

Maya: Soda contains a lot sugar.
                    9.

About eighty percent of the food on shelves of supermarkets today didn't exist 100 years ago.

DR. LARRY MCCLEARY

A man who sells fish entertains customers at a fish market in Seattle, Washington, U.S.

Victor: That's why we don't drink any soda. It's not very healthy.
10.

Maya: Oh. Can I watch TV now?

Victor: Do you have any homework today? Do your homework first, please. Then you can watch TV.
11.

Maya: OK. I just have a homework for math. And I have a form for a school trip. You must to sign it.
12.   13.

Victor: I have to read it first. Hmmm. I don't understand something here. I have to call Simon
14.

for some advices.
15.

PART 3 Write

1. Use information from the first exercise on page 138 to write a short paragraph of five or six sentences about schools in your partner's country.

   Akio is from Japan. In Japan, kids go to school five days a week....

2. Rewrite the following paragraph. Add a quantity word or expression before the underlined words.

   I buy healthy food for my family. And I try to be a good example for my family. Here are

examples. I drink water before each meal. Then I'm not so hungry. I don't drink soda. Sometimes

I drink tea after a meal. I have cereal or eggs for breakfast. I have salad with soup for lunch. I eat

fruit every day, too. I don't eat red meat. I try to eat fish or chicken every week. I also try to eat

beans for protein. I always eat vegetables with dinner. Friends ask me about food for their kids.

I always give them advice: "A parent has to be a good example."

   I buy a lot of healthy food for my family....

PART 4 Learner's Log

1. Write one sentence about each of these topics:
   - rules for school lunch programs
   - foods in school lunch programs
   - healthy foods
   - school supplies

2. Write any questions you still have about the topics above.

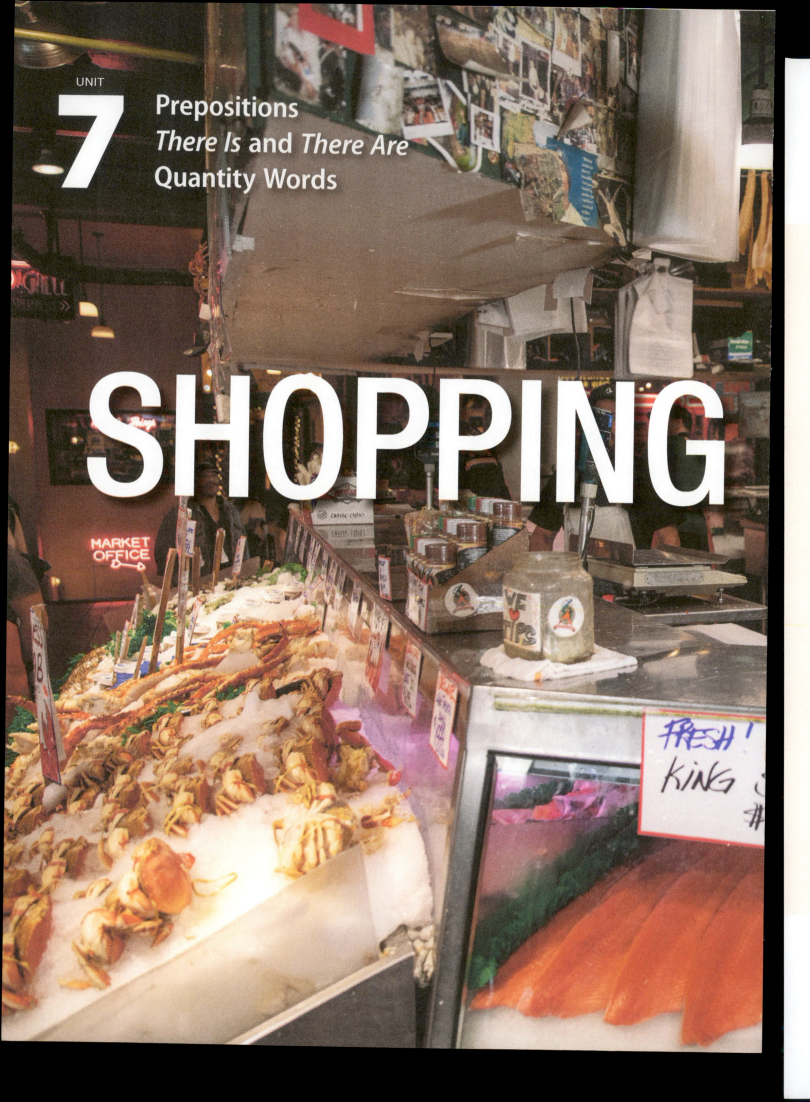

SHOPPING

BEFORE YOU READ

1. What stores do you like? Why?

2. Do you shop late at night? Why or why not?

READ

Read the following conversation between Sue and Rick, an American couple. Pay special attention to the prepositions in bold. 📷 7.1

Sue: Look. We're **out of** coffee. We need coffee **for** tomorrow morning. Can you go out and buy some?

Rick: Now? It's late. It's **after** 9:30. We can get it **in** the morning. I always wake up early. I can go shopping **before** breakfast.

Sue: Tomorrow is Saturday. The store is always crowded **on** Saturdays. I don't like to shop **on** the weekend. Anyway, we like to drink coffee **in** the morning.

Rick: But the supermarket is closed **at** night.

Sue: You're right. But the convenience store is open. It's open **24/7**.

Rick: My news program is **on** TV **at** 10 p.m. I don't have time **before** the news. It starts **in** twenty minutes.

Sue: You can go **after** the news. Or you can watch the news online.

(15 minutes later)

Rick: Hello?

Sue: Hi. Are you **at** the convenience store now?

Rick: I'm still **in** the car. I'm **in** the parking lot.

Sue: Can you go **to** the pharmacy, too, and get some aspirin? I have a headache.

Rick: Can I get the aspirin **at** the convenience store?

Sue: You can, but aspirin is **on** sale this week **at** the pharmacy—two bottles **for** $8.00. It costs $8.00 **for** one bottle **at** the convenience store.

Rick: Which pharmacy?

Sue: The pharmacy **near** the convenience store. It's **on** the corner. It's **next to** the gas station.

Rick: Is the pharmacy open late, too?

Sue: Yes, it's open **24/7**.

> **DID YOU KNOW?**
>
> Prices at a convenience store are sometimes high. You are paying for the convenience of a store that is open when other stores are closed. Some are open 24 hours a day, seven days a week (24/7).

COMPREHENSION Based on the reading, write T for *true* or F for *false*.

1. _____ The convenience store is always open.

2. _____ The convenience store doesn't sell aspirin.

3. _____ The pharmacy is closed on Sundays.

wake up	Rick **wakes up** early. He has to go to work.
go shopping	I like to **go shopping** early. There aren't many other customers at the stores.
shop	I like to **shop** at night.
convenience store	A **convenience store** is a small supermarket. It's open late, often 24/7.
program	TV has many **programs**. Every hour you can see a different show.
news	The **news** tells us about local, national, and international events.
still	Rick's not at the store yet. He's **still** in his car.
aspirin	My back hurts sometimes. Then I take **aspirin** to feel better.
headache	My head hurts. I have a terrible **headache**.
pharmacy	You can buy aspirin and other medicine in a **pharmacy**.
corner	The store is on the **corner** of Main Street and Willow Street.

LISTEN

Listen to the sentences about the conversation. Circle *True* or *False*. 🎧 **7.3**

1. (True)   False   4. True   False   7. True   False

2. True   False   5. True   False   8. True   False

3. True   False   6. True   False   9. True   False

7.1 Time Expressions with Prepositions

Prepositions are connecting words. We can use prepositions with time expressions.

The store is open	**in** the morning.
	in the daytime.
	in the afternoon.
	in the evening.
	at night.
The movie starts	**at** 10 p.m.
	in twenty minutes.
You can go out	**after** 9:30.
	after dinner.
	after work.
Sue goes to sleep	**before** 10:30.
The stores are crowded	**on** Saturdays.
	on the weekend.

Note:

A sentence can have more than one time expression.

> Rick goes to work **at** 7 **in** the morning.

> He wakes up **at** 8 a.m. **on** the weekend.

EXERCISE 1 Fill in the blanks with the correct preposition of time: *in, on, after, before,* or *at.*

1. Sue and Rick don't work _____ *at* _____ night.

2. They work _____ Mondays.

3. Lisa doesn't work _____ the evening.

4. Simon doesn't work _____ the weekend.

5. They can buy coffee _____ the morning.

6. Many stores open _____ 9 a.m.

7. The convenience store is open _____ night.

8. It's 5:37 now. It's _____ 5:30.

9. We go shopping _____ the afternoon.

10. The supermarket closes at 10 p.m. Go there _____ 10.

ABOUT YOU Work with a partner. Ask a question with *when do you* and the words given. Your partner will answer.

1. watch TV

   A: *When do you watch TV?*

   B: *I watch TV at night.*

2. drink coffee

3. relax

4. go to sleep

5. wake up

6. go shopping

7. listen to OR watch the news

8. wash your clothes

9. eat lunch

10. read blogs

11. see your friends

12. do your homework

13. take an aspirin

14. work

7.2 Time Expressions without Prepositions

In some cases, we don't use a preposition with a time expression.

The store is open	24 hours a day.
	seven days a week.
We shop	three times a month.
They buy milk	once a week.
We cook	every day.
The convenience store is open	24/7.
	all day and all night.

ABOUT YOU Fill in the blanks. Share your answers with a partner.

1. I _____visit my parents_____ once a month.

2. I _____ five days a week.

3. I _____ twice a day.

4. I _____ four times a month.

5. I _____ all day.

6. I _____ every day.

ABOUT YOU Fill in the blanks with a time expression. Tell about the people and places in your country. Share your answers with a partner.

1. People usually watch the news _____every day_____.

2. Most people use the Internet _____.

3. Pharmacies are usually open _____.

4. Supermarkets in big cities are open _____.

5. Convenience stores are open _____.

6. Most banks are open _____.

7. Most people shop for food _____.

8. Students go to school _____.

ABOUT YOU Work with a partner. Ask a question with *how many* and the words given. Your partner will answer.

1. days a week/work

   A: *How many days a week do you work?*

   B: *I work five days a week.*

2. hours a day/talk on the phone

3. hours a day/spend online

4. times a month/go to the library

5. hours a night/sleep

6. times a day/cook

7. days a week/shop for food

8. minutes a day/exercise

7.3 Prepositions of Place

We can use prepositions with a place.

PREPOSITION	EXAMPLES
in	Rick is **in** the car. He is **in** the parking lot.
near	The pharmacy is **near** the convenience store.
next to	The pharmacy is **next to** the gas station.
on	The convenience store is **on** the corner.
at	Rick is **at** the convenience store now. Sue and Rick are **at** home in the evening. They are **at** work in the daytime.
to	Go **to** the pharmacy.

Note:

Compare the following sentences:

*I'm **in** the store.* (I'm not outside the store.)

*I'm **at** the store.* (I may be inside or in the parking lot, ready to go in.)

EXERCISE 2 Victor and Lisa are on the telephone. Fill in the blanks with the correct preposition: *in*, *on*, *at*, *to*, *near*, or *next to*. Then listen and check your answers. 🎧 7.4

Victor: Hello?

Lisa: Hi, Victor. Where are you now?

Victor: I'm _____*at*_____ school. Where are you?
1.

Lisa: I'm _____ home. Are you _____ class?
2.   3.

Victor: No. I'm _____ the parking lot. I'm _____ my car.
4.   5.

My class starts in ten minutes.

Lisa: Can you go _____ the store on your way home? We need milk. There's a sale
6.

_____ Tom's Market.
7.

Victor: Where's Tom's Market?

Lisa: It's _____ the school. It's not far. It's _____ the corner. It's _____
8.   9.   10.

the laundromat.

Victor: My class is over _____ 9. Is the market still open at 9?
11.

Lisa: Yes, it is. It closes at 9:30. Go _____ the store right after class, please.
12.

7.4 Prepositions in Common Expressions

We can use prepositions in many common expressions.

PREPOSITION	EXAMPLES
on	Rick is **on the phone**.
	The news program is **on** TV.
	You can hear the news **on the radio**.
	Aspirin is **on sale**.
	Please buy some milk **on** your **way** home.
for	Aspirin is on sale this week, two bottles **for $8.00**.
out of	We don't have any coffee. We're **out of coffee**.

GRAMMAR IN USE

It's important to remember which expressions use the article *the* and which do not.

   *on **the** phone*   *on **the** radio*

   BUT: *on TV*

EXERCISE 3 Fill in the blanks in this conversation with the correct preposition: *on, at, next to, after, out of,* or *for*. Then listen and check your answers. 🎧 7.5

Simon: I'm going to the store ___*after*___ work. Eggs are on sale—two dozen _____ $6.49.
                                                    1.   2.

Marta: Buy bananas, too. They're _____ sale—one pound _____ 49 cents.
                                                          3.   4.

Simon: Anything else?

Marta: Oh, yes. Buy coffee, too.

Simon: Are we _____ coffee? So soon?
                                    5.

15 minutes later

Simon: I'm at the market now. Do we need anything else?

Marta: Yes. Buy some tea. The tea is _____ the coffee. Then come home right away.
                                                              6.

We're eating dinner early tonight.

EXERCISE 4 Fill in the blanks in this phone conversation with the correct preposition: *in, on, at, to,* or *after*. Then listen and check your answers. 🎧 7.6

Sue: Hi, Rick. I'm _____*on*_____ my cell phone.
  1.

Rick: Are you _____ the car?
  2.

Sue: No. I'm still _____ work. My shift ends in a few minutes, but I can't come home right now.
  3.

  _____ work, I have to make a few stops. I can be home _____ about an hour and a half.
  4.   5.

Rick: Where do you need to go?

Sue: First, I need to buy gas. Then I have to go _____ the supermarket.
  6.

Rick: Can you come home after that?

Sue: No. Then I have to go to the post office. The post office closes _____ 5 p.m.
  7.

Rick: Do you have to do all of this now? I'm making dinner. And it's almost ready.

Sue: Oh, that's great, Rick. I can go to the supermarket _____ dinner. And then you can get
  8.

  gas _____ your way to work.
  9.

Rick: Good. Then just stop _____ the post office. And try to get home soon.
  10.

FUN WITH GRAMMAR

Play Bingo. Your teacher will give you a blank Bingo card. Write the prepositions *in, on, at, to, after, before, near, next to, for,* or *out of* in each square. Some squares will have the same words. Put the prepositions in any order. Your teacher will call out a preposition. Find a square with that preposition and write a sentence in the square, using that preposition. To win the game, you have to have sentences in four squares in a row, either horizontally (→), vertically (↓), or diagonally (↗). The first person to get four correct sentences in a row says, "Bingo!" and wins the game.

BEFORE YOU READ

1. How do clerks in a store help customers?

2. Do you like to shop in big stores or small stores? Why?

READ

Read the following conversations. Pay special attention to the affirmative and negative forms of *there is* and *there are* and the quantity words in bold. 🎧 7.7

CONVERSATION A: At a big home supply store

Sue: You know I don't like to shop at the big home supply store on Saturdays. **There are a lot of** shoppers, and **there's no** place to park.

Rick: Look. **There's** a space over there.

(in the store)

Sue: **There are no** shopping carts.

Rick: We can take a basket. We only need a package of lightbulbs. We need one for the lamp in the living room.

Sue: **There are** so **many** things in this store. It's hard to find anything.

Rick: **There's** a clerk over there. Let's ask him. Excuse me, sir. I need to find lightbulbs.

Clerk: Lightbulbs are in aisle[1] 3. **There's** a clerk there. He can help you.

Two minutes later

Sue: **There's no** clerk in aisle 3 now. Can you please help us?

Clerk: Sorry. I don't work in aisle 3. That's not my department.

Sue: *(To Rick)* The service here is terrible. **There aren't enough** clerks in this store. No one wants to help us.

Rick: But the prices are good here. And **there are** always coupons for this store in the newspaper. I have a coupon for a package of six lightbulbs for $10. That's 20% off!

CONVERSATION B: In a small hardware store

Clerk: Can I help you?

Peter: Yes. I need lightbulbs.

Clerk: Lightbulbs are downstairs, but **there isn't** an elevator in this store. I can get the lightbulbs for you. Do you want some coffee? **There's** a coffee machine over there. It's free for customers.

Peter: Thanks for your help. *(Thinking)* I prefer small stores to big stores. **There's** good service here. **There are** helpful clerks here, too. And **there's** free coffee at this store.

---

[1] The pronunciation of *aisle* is /aɪl/. We don't pronounce the *s*.

COMPREHENSION Based on the reading, write T for *true* or F for *false*.

1. _____ Sue and Rick need to buy a lot of things.

2. _____ The clerk in the large store helps Sue and Rick.

3. _____ The clerk in the small store helps Peter.

WORDS TO KNOW 🎧 7.8

home supply store/ hardware store	A **home supply store** and a **hardware store** sell many things for the home: tools, lightbulbs, paint, etc.
shopping cart	We use a **shopping cart** for our items in a store. We push the **cart** down the aisles.
basket	We can use a **basket** for a few items in a store. We carry the basket.
lightbulb	The lamp isn't working. Rick needs to buy a new **lightbulb** for the lamp.
lamp	Sue needs light to read the newspaper. She turns on the **lamp**.
clerk	**Clerks** work in stores. They help customers.
aisle	The lightbulbs are in aisle 3.
service	Peter likes good **service**. He likes help in a store.
enough	There are a lot of shoppers, but there aren't **enough** clerks.
% (percent) off	The coupon says 40% **(percent) off**. The lightbulbs are usually $5. But they're $3 with the coupon.
downstairs	My bedroom is on the second floor, but the kitchen is **downstairs**.
elevator	This store doesn't have an **elevator** to the second floor.
prefer	Peter doesn't like big stores. He **prefers** small stores.

LISTEN

Listen to the sentences about the conversations. Circle *True* or *False*. 🎧 7.9

1. (True)   False   5. True   False

2. True   False   6. True   False

3. True   False   7. True   False

4. True   False   8. True   False

7.5 *There Is* and *There Are*—Affirmative Statements

Sometimes we use *there is* or *there are* to introduce the subject.

Singular Nouns

THERE	IS	A/AN/ONE	SINGULAR NOUN	PREPOSITIONAL PHRASE
There	is	a	parking lot	at the store.
		an	elevator	in the hardware store.
		one	clerk	in aisle 4.

Noncount Nouns

THERE	IS	QUANTITY WORD	NONCOUNT NOUN	PREPOSITIONAL PHRASE
There	is		free coffee	for the customers.
		some	milk	near the coffee machine.
		a lot of	sugar	in your coffee.

Plural Nouns

THERE	ARE	QUANTITY WORD	PLURAL NOUN	PREPOSITIONAL PHRASE
There	are		coupons	in the newspaper.
		two	clerks	in aisle 6.
		a lot of	cars	in the parking lot.

Notes:
1. The contraction for *there is* is **there's.**
2. *There are* does not have a contraction.

EXERCISE 5 Fill in the blanks with *there is* or *there are*. Use contractions when possible.

1. _____There are_____ a lot of items in the big store.

2. _____ a sale on lightbulbs this week.

3. _____ a lot of lightbulbs in aisle 3.

4. _____ two elevators in the big store.

5. _____ many shoppers in the big store.

6. _____ a sign near the entrance.

7. _____ coffee for the customers in the small store.

8. _____ good service in the small store.

EXERCISE 6 This is a phone conversation between Simon and Victor. Fill in the blanks with *there is* or *there are*. Use contractions when possible. Then listen and check your answers. 🎧 7.10

Simon: Hello?

Victor: Hi, Simon. It's Victor.

Simon: Are you at home?

Victor: No, I'm not. I'm at the department store with my wife. _____There's_____ a big sale
1.

at this store—50 percent off all winter items. We love sales. We like to save money. Lisa wants to

buy a winter coat. _____ a lot of people in the coat department,
2.

but _____ only one clerk. Where are you?
3.

Simon: I'm at home. _____ a football game on TV.
4.

Victor: I know. And now _____ a long line at the register. I have to wait.
5.

Simon: That's too bad. It's a great game.

Victor: I know. _____ a TV in the store, and _____
6.   7.

some nice chairs in front of the TV. So I can watch the game, too.

Simon: _____ two games today. Let's watch the next game together.
8.

Victor: OK. Sounds great!

7.6 *There Is* and *There Are*—Negative Statements

We can use *there is* and *there are* in negative statements.

Singular Count Nouns

THERE	IS	NO	SINGULAR COUNT NOUN	PREPOSITIONAL PHRASE
There	is	no	coffee machine	in the big store.
			elevator	in the hardware store.
			clerk	in aisle 3.

Noncount Nouns

THERE	ISN'T	ANY	NONCOUNT NOUN	PREPOSITIONAL PHRASE
There	isn't	any	space	in the parking lot.
			coffee	in the big store.
			time	for shopping now.
THERE	IS	NO	NONCOUNT NOUN	PREPOSITIONAL PHRASE
There	is	no	space	in the parking lot.
			coffee	in the big store.
			time	for shopping now.

Plural Nouns

THERE	AREN'T	ANY	PLURAL NOUN	PREPOSITIONAL PHRASE
There	aren't	any	lightbulbs	in this aisle.
			shopping carts	in the small store.
THERE	ARE	NO	PLURAL NOUN	PREPOSITIONAL PHRASE
There	are	no	lightbulbs	in this aisle.
			shopping carts	in the small store.

GRAMMAR IN USE

Remember to use *any* with *There isn't/There aren't*.

There **isn't any** space.   Not: *There isn't no space.*

Remember to use *no* with *There is/There are*.

There **are no** lightbulbs.   Not: *There are not lightbulbs.*

EXERCISE 7 Read the affirmative statement. Complete the negative statement.

1. There's a small hardware store near my house. __There aren't any/There are no__ big stores near

   my house.

2. There are coupons for the big store. _____ coupons for the small store.

3. There are lightbulbs in a hardware store. _____ lightbulbs in a shoe store.

4. There's usually a clerk in aisle 3. _____ clerk in aisle 3 now.

5. There's an elevator in the department store. _____ elevator in the

   convenience store.

6. There's free coffee in the small store. _____ free coffee in the big store.

7.7 Quantity Words

QUANTITY	EXAMPLES
xxxxxxxx	There are **many/a lot of** cars in the parking lot.
xxx	There are **some** lamps in aisle 3.
xx (You need xxxx.)	There aren't **enough** clerks in the big store.
x	There is **one/an** elevator in the big store.
0	There aren't **any** lightbulbs in aisle 5.
	There are **no** lightbulbs in aisle 5.

ABOUT YOU Use *there's* or *there are* and the words given to tell about your class and your school. Use quantity words from the chart above. You may have to change the noun to the plural form.

1. copy machine

   There's a copy machine in the library.

2. book

3. desk for all students

4. Indian students

5. computer

6. young student

7. telephone

8. elevator

9. teacher

ABOUT YOU Fill in the blanks to tell about the place where you live.

1. There aren't enough _____ windows _____ in my bedroom.

2. There are no _____ in my neighborhood.

3. There's no _____ in my city.

4. There aren't many _____ in my neighborhood.

5. There are a lot of _____ in my home.

6. There are some _____ in my home.

7. There aren't enough _____ in my bedroom.

8. There's a(n) _____ in my kitchen.

9. There aren't any _____ in my bathroom.

EXERCISE 8 Fill in the blanks with *any*, *some*, *a lot of*, *enough*, *one*, or *no* to complete this conversation. In some cases, more than one answer is possible. Then listen and check your answers. 7.11

Sue: Where are the batteries? I need _____*some*_____ batteries for the flashlight.
         1.

Rick: Look in the closet.

Sue: There aren't _____ batteries in the closet.
         2.

Rick: Look in the kitchen. There are _____ batteries there, I think.
         3.

Sue: There's only _____ battery here. This flashlight needs two batteries.
         4.

         We need to go to the hardware store and get more batteries.

Rick: Let's go to the home supply store.

Sue: Not again. You know I prefer the small store. In the big store, there aren't

         _____ clerks to help you. Sometimes I have questions, but there are
         5.

         _____ clerks to answer them. Or I find a clerk and he says, "That's not
         6.

         my department."

Rick: I don't have _____ questions about batteries. A battery is a battery.
         7.

         Look at this section of the newspaper. There are _____ things on sale at
         8.

         the big store—hundreds of things.

Sue: We don't need hundreds of things. We just need batteries.

Hardware stores like this one in Staunton, Virginia, are common in towns across the U.S.

EXERCISE 9 Fill in the blanks with the missing words from the box below. You can combine two words to fill in some blanks. Use contractions when possible. Then listen and check your answers. 🎧 7.12

there	they	is	are	it	not	isn't

Rick: Let's go to the hardware store today. _____There's_____ a sale on plants.
                        1.

_____ really cheap today.
        2.

Sue: Let's go to the bookstore, too. _____ a sale on all travel books.
                 3.

_____ 50 percent off. Let's go to the bookstore first and then to the
        4.

hardware store.

Rick: _____ enough time. It's almost 4:00. The hardware store closes at 5:30.
        5.

_____ Saturday, and the hardware store _____
        6.   7.

open late on Saturday.

Sue: The small hardware store _____ open late, but the home supply store is
                 8.

open. You know, I don't really want to go to the hardware store with you.

_____ always too crowded. I have an idea. You can go to the hardware
        9.

store, and I can go to the bookstore. I need something to read.

Rick: Need or want? You have a lot of books.

Sue: _____ all old. I need new books.
        10.

Rick: And I need some plants.

BEFORE YOU READ

1. Is it easy to make choices in a store? Why or why not?

2. Do you compare prices when you shop? Why or why not?

READ

Read the following conversation. Pay special attention to the *yes/no* questions and *wh-* questions using *there is* and *there are* in bold. 🎧 7.13

Halina and her husband, Peter, are in the supermarket.

Peter: There are many brands of shampoo. **Why are there** so many brands? Do people need so many choices?

Halina: I don't think so. **Is there** a difference between this shampoo for $3.99 and that shampoo for $10.99?

Peter: I don't know. Let's buy the cheap one.

Halina: OK. There's probably no difference.

Peter: **Are there** any other items on the shopping list?

Halina: Just two. We need sugar. The sugar is in aisle 6.

(one minute later)

Halina: This sign says 25 ounces for $1.75. That one says five pounds for $2.25. Which one is a better buy?

Peter: I don't know. What's an ounce?

Halina: It's part of a pound. There are sixteen ounces in a pound.

Peter: **Is there** a calculator on your phone?

Halina: Yes, but we don't need it. Look. There's a small sign under the sugar. The five-pound bag is about 2.8¢ an ounce. The 25-ounce bag is about 7¢ an ounce. The big bag is a better buy.

Peter: You're a smart shopper. Are we finished? **Is there** anything else on the list?

Halina: Yes. There's one more thing—dog food.

Peter: Wow! Look. There are over twenty kinds of dog food.

Halina: Dogs have choices, too.

DID YOU **KNOW?**
One pound = .45 kilograms
One ounce = 28.35 grams

COMPREHENSION Based on the reading, write T for *true* or F for *false*.

1. _____ There are two brands of shampoo in the store.

2. _____ An ounce is smaller than a pound.

3. _____ Halina and Peter have a dog.

WORDS TO KNOW 🎧 7.14

brand	Many companies make soap. There are a lot of different **brands**.
shampoo	I need to buy **shampoo** so I can wash my hair.
choice	There are twenty kinds of dog food, so there are many **choices**. We have to pick one.
difference between	What's the **difference between** the cheap shampoo and the expensive one?
ounce	An **ounce** is a unit of measure. Sixteen **ounces** is equal to one pound.
calculator	I have a **calculator** on my phone. It helps me do math.
better buy	The large bag of sugar is a **better buy**. We can save money.

LISTEN

Listen to the sentences about the conversation. Circle *True* or *False*. 🎧 7.15

1. (True)   False

2. True   False

3. True   False

4. True   False

5. True   False

6. True   False

7. True   False

8. True   False

7.8 *There Is* and *There Are*—*Yes/No* Questions

Compare statements and questions with *there is* and *there are*.

STATEMENT	QUESTION	SHORT ANSWER
There's a shampoo aisle.	**Is there** a hardware aisle in this store?	No, there isn't.
There are large bags of sugar.	**Are there** any small bags of sugar?	Yes, there are.
There's dog food in this aisle.	**Is there** any cat food in this aisle?	Yes, there is.

Notes:

1. We often use *any* in questions with noncount and plural count nouns.

2. We don't make a contraction in an affirmative short answer.

     Yes, there is.   NOT: *Yes, there's.*

EXERCISE 10 Complete the short answers.

1. Are there any clerks in the store? Yes, _____ *there are* _____.

2. Is there a price on the shampoo bottles? No, _____.

3. Are there a lot of shoppers in the store? Yes, _____.

4. Is there any dog food on sale this week? No, _____.

5. Are there a lot of choices of dog food? Yes, _____.

6. Is there a coupon for sugar? Yes, _____.

7. Are there any shopping carts in this store? No, _____.

EXERCISE 11 Complete the questions.

1. _____ *Is there* _____ good service in a small store?

2. _____ any shoppers in the checkout line?

3. _____ a clerk in the cereal aisle?

4. _____ any space in the parking lot?

5. _____ any coupons for shampoo in the newspaper?

6. _____ an elevator in the supermarket?

7. _____ a lot of shoppers today?

EXERCISE 12 Work with a partner. Ask a question with *is there* or *are there any* and the words given. Your partner will answer.

1. an elevator/in this building
   A: *Is there an elevator in this building?*
   B: *No, there isn't.*

2. Mexican students/in this class

3. new words/in this lesson

4. photos/on this page

5. a verb chart/in your dictionary

6. hard exercises/in this lesson

7. a computer lab/at this school

8. restrooms/on this floor

9. a gym/at this school

10. a library/in your town

7.9 *There Is* and *There Are*—*Wh-* Questions

How much, *how many*, and *why* are common question words with *is there* and *are there*. Notice question word order with *be* before *there*.

QUESTION WORD(S)	BE	THERE	PHRASE	ANSWER
How much sugar	is		in the bag?	One pound.
How many ounces	are	there	in a pound?	Sixteen.
Why	are		twenty different kinds of shampoo?	I don't know.

Compare *yes/no* questions and *wh-* questions.

YES/NO QUESTION	WH- QUESTION
Are there ten items on the list?	How many items **are there** on the list?
Are there different kinds of shampoo?	Why **are there** different kinds of shampoo?
Are there many kinds of dog food?	How many kinds of dog food **are there**?
Is there a difference between this shampoo and that shampoo?	Why **is there** a difference in price?

EXERCISE 13 Read the statements. Write *wh-* questions with the words given.

1. There are ten kinds of shampoo.

   How many <u>kinds of shampoo are there?</u>

2. There are a lot of people in this line.

   Why _____

3. There are 16 ounces in a pound.

   How many _____

4. There are a few items on the list.

   How many _____

5. There are many brands of dog food.

   Why _____

6. There's some sugar in this bag.

   How much _____

7. There is a pharmacy in the store.

   Why _____

8. There's a lot of time.

   How much _____

EXERCISE 14 Work with a partner. Use the following words to ask and answer questions about your class or school. Use *how much* or *how many* in your questions.

1. desks/in this room
   A: *How many desks are there in this room?*
   B: *There are twenty desks in this room.*

2. students/in this class

3. windows/in this room

4. paper/on the floor

5. phones/in this room

6. men's restrooms/on this floor

7. floors/in this building

8. pages/in this book

9. new vocabulary/on this page

10. photos/this unit

EXERCISE 15 Write two questions and answers for the items below.

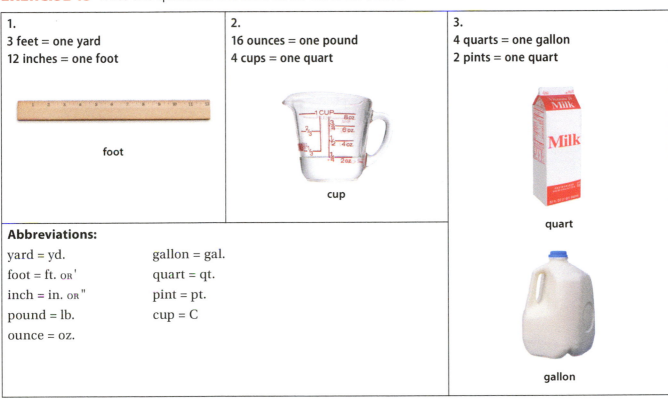

1.
3 feet = one yard
12 inches = one foot

foot

2.
16 ounces = one pound
4 cups = one quart

cup

3.
4 quarts = one gallon
2 pints = one quart

quart

gallon

Abbreviations:

yard = yd.	gallon = gal.
foot = ft. OR '	quart = qt.
inch = in. OR "	pint = pt.
pound = lb.	cup = C
ounce = oz.	

1. a. How many feet are there in a yard?

   There are 3 feet in a yard.

   b. _____

   _____

2. a. _____

   _____

   b. _____

   _____

continued

3. a. _____

   _____

   b. _____

   _____

EXERCISE 16 Fill in the blanks with words from the box. You can use some items more than once. Use contractions when possible. Then listen and check your answers. 🎧 7.16

| there is | there are | is there | are there | how many |

Ali: I'm going for a walk.

Shafia: Wait. I need a few things at the supermarket. Let me look at my shopping list.

Ali: How many items _____ are there _____?
                                        1.

Shafia: About ten. Also go to the office supply store, please. We need some pens.

Ali: Where's the office supply store?

Shafia: _____ a few office supply stores near here.
                        2.

              _____ one next to the supermarket on Elm Street.
                        3.

Ali: _____ pens _____ in a box?
                        4.   5.

Shafia: You can buy a box of twenty.

Ali: _____ anything else on your list?
                        6.

Shafia: Yes, _____. We need paper for the printer, too. Please buy two packs
                        7.

              of paper.

Ali: _____ sheets of paper _____ in one pack?
                        8.   9.

Shafia: Five hundred, I think.

Ali: What about printer ink? _____ enough ink in the printer?
                                            10.

Shafia: I don't think so. Please get some ink, too.

EXERCISE 17 Fill in the blanks to complete the conversation. Use *there is*, *there are*, *is there*, or *are there*. Use contractions when possible. Then listen and check your answers. 7.17

Marta: The kids need new coats. Let's go shopping today. _____There's_____ a twelve-hour
 1.

sale at Baker's Department Store—today only.

Simon: _____ a sale on men's coats, too?
 2.

Marta: Yes, _____ . _____ a lot of great things on sale:
 3.   4.

winter coats, sweaters, boots, gloves, and more.

Simon: How do you always know about all the sales in town?

Marta: _____ an ad in the store window. It says, "End of winter sale.
 5.

All winter items 50% off."

Simon: Why _____ a sale on winter things? It's still winter.
 6.

Marta: Spring is almost here.

Simon: It's only January. It's so cold. _____ two or three more months of winter.
 7.

Marta: You're right! But stores need space for new things for the spring.

Simon: Well, that's good for us. _____ winter sales in other stores, too?
 8.

Marta: Yes. _____ an ad in the window of the shoe store, too.
 9.

Simon: Great. We can look at boots at both stores and choose the best deal.

_____ anything you need?
 10.

Marta: Maybe some warm gloves. Let's go!

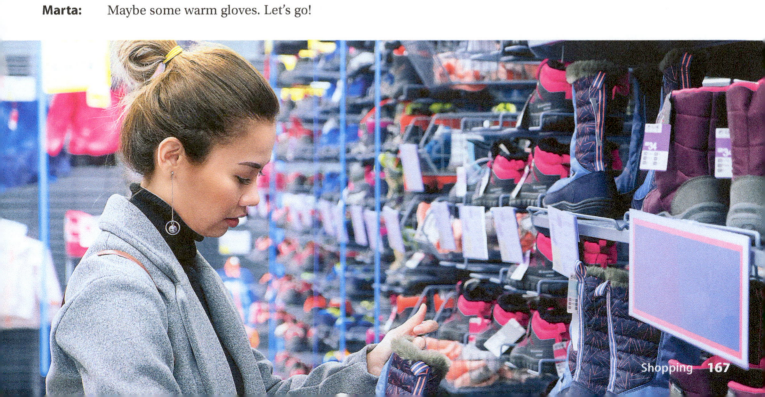

SUMMARY OF UNIT 7

Time Expressions

in the morning **in** twenty minutes	three times a month
at night **at** 10 p.m.	once a week
on Saturdays	every day
after 9:30	24 hours a day
before 10:30	24/7

Prepositions of Place and Prepositions in Common Expressions

in	Rick is **in** the car.	
near	The pharmacy is **near** the supermarket.	
next to	The pharmacy is **next to** the gas station.	
on	The store is **on** the corner. Rick is **on** the phone.	The program is **on** TV. Toothpaste is **on** sale.
at	Rick is **at** the store.	
to	Go **to** the pharmacy.	
for	Aspirin is on sale—two bottles **for** $8.00.	
out of	We're **out of** coffee.	

There Is and *There Are*—Affirmative Statements

THERE	BE	A/AN OR QUANTITY WORD	NOUN	PREPOSITIONAL PHRASE
	is	an	elevator	in the store.
There	**is**	some	milk	in the fridge.
	are	two	clerks	in aisle 6.

There Is and *There Are*—Negative Statements

THERE	BE	NO OR ANY	NOUN	PREPOSITIONAL PHRASE
	is	**no**	elevator	in the store.
There	**are**		lightbulbs	in this aisle.
	isn't	**any**	coffee	in the big store.
	aren't		lightbulbs	in this aisle.

There Is and *There Are*—Questions

YES/NO QUESTION	WH- QUESTION
Are there ten items on the list?	**How many** items **are there** on the list?
Are there different kinds of shampoo?	**Why are there** different kinds of shampoo?
Is there any sugar?	**How much** sugar **is there**?
Is there a difference between this shampoo and that shampoo?	**Why is there** a difference in price?

REVIEW

Choose the correct words to complete the conversation.

A: Hello?

B: Hi, Tim. Are you still (*on/at/near*) work?
1.

A: Yes, I am. I'm coming home (*on/after/in*) a few minutes, though.
2.

B: Can you please go (*at/in/to*) the supermarket (*on/in/to*) your way home? We're (*after/out of/for*) milk.
3. 4. 5.

And (*there's/are there/there are*) (*some/one/any*) other things we need, too.
6. 7.

A: Sure. Is the supermarket open (*after/in/at*) the evening?
8.

B: Yes. It's open late (*on/in/at*) Thursdays.
9.

A: OK. The supermarket (*near/next to/on*) the corner of 5th Street and Oak Street, right?
10.

B: No. That one isn't open (*in/at/on*) night. (*There's/There are/There's no*) a supermarket
11. 12.

(*on/before/next to*) the hardware store. Go (*to/near/for*) that one.
13. 14.

A: OK, got it.

(30 minutes later)

A: Hi, Kate. I'm (*on/at/to*) the store. How many items (*there are/is there/are there*) on your list?
15. 16.

B: Not too many. (*There's/There are/There is*) ten items, but you don't have to get everything.
17.

A: Oranges are (*on/in/for*) sale. Five (*on/for/out of*) a dollar. That's a good price.
18. 19.

B: Yes, it is. Please get oranges. (*There are/There aren't/There are no*) any oranges in the fridge.
20.

(*There are/There aren't/There is*) no apples, either. Please get apples, too.
21.

A: OK. Where's the dairy section? I don't see it.

B: (*There's/There are/Is there*) two dairy aisles in that store, actually. (*There's/There are/Is there*) one
22. 23.

(*next to/out of/for*) the fruit . . .
24.

A: Oh, yes. I see it.

B: (*Is there/Are there/How much is there*) any milk in that aisle?
25.

A: Hmm. No, (*there is/there isn't/there aren't*).
26.

B: OK. (*There's/Is there/There are*) another dairy aisle. It's (*on/in/near*) the meat section.
27. 28.

A: OK . . . Oh, there's (*any/many/a lot of*) milk here!
29.

B: Great. And can you please buy coffee? There isn't (*some/no/enough*) here.
30.

A: Sure. I'll be home soon!

FROM GRAMMAR TO WRITING

PART 1 Editing Advice

1. Use the correct preposition.

   Sue likes to shop ~~in~~ *at* night.

   Your favorite program begins ~~after~~ *in* twenty minutes.

2. Don't use prepositions with certain time expressions.

   Simon works five days ~~in~~ a week.

3. Don't use *to* after *near*.

   There's a convenience store near ~~to~~ my house.

4. Don't write a contraction for *there are*.

   ~~There're~~ *There are* fifteen students in the class.

5. Don't use *a* after *there are*.

   There are ~~a~~ good sales this week.

6. Don't use two negatives together.

   There aren't ~~no~~ *any* lightbulbs in this aisle.

7. Use correct word order.

   How many batteries ~~there are~~ *are there* in the flashlight?

PART 2 Editing Practice

Some of the shaded words and phrases have mistakes. Find the mistakes and correct them. If the shaded words are correct, write *C*.

Ali: I need a lightbulb for this lamp. Are there *C* any extra lightbulbs?
                                                                              1.

Shafia: No, there isn't *aren't*. We need to buy more.
                           2.

Ali: Let's go in the hardware store. Is it open now?
                          3.

Shafia: No. It's late. The hardware store isn't open in the night. It closes in 6:00 p.m. But the big store
                                                         4.   **5.**

             near to the bank is open very late.
             6.

Ali: There are a lot of things in sale at that store this week. Let's make a list.
                  7.   **8.**   **9.**

Shafia: We don't need a lot of things. We only need lightbulbs.

Ali: What about batteries? Are there a batteries in the house?
                                    10.   **11.**

Shafia: There're some AA batteries.
            12.

Ali: But we need C batteries for the radio.

Shafia: There aren't no C batteries in the house.
            13.

Ali: Do you want to go to the store with me?
            14.

Shafia: My favorite show starts after five minutes. Can you go alone?
            15.

Ali: OK.

Shafia: There's no rice in the house. Can you get some rice, too?
            16.

Ali: There isn't any rice at the hardware store.
            17.

Shafia: Of course not. But the hardware store is next the supermarket. In fact, you don't need to go to
            18.

the hardware store at all. There are a lightbulbs and batteries at the supermarket, too.
            19.   **20.**

Ali: OK. Good. There's no need to go to two stores. Is this supermarket open at night?
            21.   **22.**

Shafia: Yes. It's open seven days in a week. And it's open all night.
            23.   **24.**

PART 3 Write

Write five or six sentences to describe each photo. You can write affirmative statements, negative statements, or questions.

In photo A, a woman is with a sales person at a

hardware store.

PART 4 Learner's Log

1. Write one sentence about each of these topics:
   - shopping in the United States
   - different types of stores
   - getting a good price

2. Write any questions you still have about shopping in the United States.

ERRANDS

What you do today can improve all
your tomorrows.

RALPH MARSTON

Divers mail plastic letters in a post box on the bottom of the sea off the coast of Ito, Japan.

1. What services does the U.S. post office have? What does it sell?

2. Do you ever send packages? Why or why not?

READ

Lisa is at the post office. She's writing an email to a friend on her phone as she waits. Read her email. Pay special attention to the present continuous in bold. 🎧 8.1

clerk

customer

package

Hi Rosa,

It's Friday morning and I'm **practicing** my English. People **are doing** errands. I'm at the post office. Many things **are happening** at the post office. The clerks are very busy. Many people **are waiting** in line. They**'re not getting** fast service today. But they **aren't complaining**.

A customer at the counter has two packages. There is a clerk behind the counter. The clerk **is weighing** one package. He**'s using** a scale. The customer **is holding** the second package. He **isn't paying** for the postage in cash. He**'s using** his credit card.

My friend Marta **is picking up** a package. Her daughter, Amy, is with her. Amy **is holding** Marta's hand. Marta **is giving** her identification (ID) to the clerk.

A customer **is using** the automated postal center. He **isn't waiting** in line. He's **mailing** a package, and he**'s weighing** the package on the scale. He**'s paying** by credit card. The machine **is printing** the postage label. Self-service is fast.

A customer **is buying** stamps from a stamp machine. He**'s paying** in cash. He**'s not using** coins. He**'s putting** a ten-dollar bill in the stamp machine. Stamp machines in the post office give coins for change. This man **is getting** some one-dollar coins in change. Nobody **is buying** mailing supplies today.

DID YOU **KNOW?**

People in the United States send about 146 billion pieces of mail each year. The United States Postal Service handles about 47 percent of the world's mail.

COMPREHENSION Based on the reading, write T for *true* or F for *false*.

1. _____ The post office is crowded today.

2. _____ There's no self-service center at the post office.

3. _____ Some people are buying mailing supplies.

WORDS TO KNOW 🎧 8.2

do errands	Marta has to **do errands** today. She's going to the post office and the bank.
wait in line	The **line** is long. The customers have to **wait in line**.
complain	The customers aren't happy. They are **complaining**.
customer	There are many **customers** in the post office.
counter	The clerks work behind the **counter** at the post office.
package	One customer is sending a **package**. It is a present for his mother's birthday.
weigh	The clerk is **weighing** a customer's package. The package **weighs** two pounds.
scale	We use a **scale** to weigh things.
hold	A customer is **holding** a package. He has the package in his hands.
postage	When we mail a package, we have to pay **postage**.
pick up	Marta is **picking up** her mail.
automated postal center	We can pay for postage at the **automated postal center**. We don't need a clerk.
print	In the automated postal center, a machine weighs a package. It also **prints** the postage.
self-service	You don't need a clerk to buy stamps. You can use a machine. It's **self-service**.
stamp	When we mail a letter, we put a **stamp** on it. A **stamp** shows the postage.
mailing supplies	**Mailing supplies** are boxes and envelopes.

LISTEN

Listen to the sentences about the activities in the post office. Circle *True* or *False*. 🎧 8.3

1. (True)   False
2. True   False
3. True   False
4. True   False
5. True   False

6. True   False
7. True   False
8. True   False
9. True   False
10. True   False

A self-service station in a post office

8.1 The Present Continuous—Affirmative Statements

We form the present continuous with a form of *be* + verb *-ing*.

SUBJECT	BE	VERB *-ING*	
I	am	mailing	a letter.
Dorota	is	waiting	in line.
Nobody	is	buying	mailing supplies.
We	are	using	the stamp machine.
You	are	picking up	a package.
The clerks	are	standing	behind the counter.

Notes:

1. We can make contractions with a pronoun + *be*.

    I'm mailing a letter.
    She's waiting in line.
    We're using the stamp machine.

2. We can make contractions with a singular noun + *is*.

    Lisa's writing an email.

3. We cannot make a contraction with a plural noun + *are*.

EXERCISE 1 Fill in the blanks with the present continuous. Use contractions when possible. Use the ideas from the reading and the verbs from the box. Answers may vary.

pick	give	weigh	help	pay	hold	stand	buy ✓	wait	do

1. One customer <u>'s buying</u> some stamps.

2. Amy _____ next to Marta.

3. Many people _____ in line.

4. Marta _____ her ID to the postal clerk.

5. Marta _____ up a package.

6. The clerks _____ the customers.

7. A customer _____ a package at the automated postal center.

8. A lot of people _____ errands today.

9. Some customers _____ in cash.

10. Marta _____ Amy's hand.

8.2 Spelling Rules of the *-ing* Form

VERB	*-ING* FORM	RULE
go eat look	go**ing** eat**ing** look**ing**	In most cases, we add *-ing* to the base form.
sit plan	sit**ting** plan**ning**	If a one-syllable verb ends in consonant + vowel + consonant, we double the last consonant. Then we add *-ing*.
give write	giv**ing** writ**ing**	If the verb ends in a consonant + *e*, we drop the *e*. Then we add *-ing*. NOT: giveing Do not double the last consonant after you drop the *e*. NOT: writting
show fix pay	show**ing** fix**ing** pay**ing**	We don't double final *w*, *x*, or *y*. We just add *-ing*. NOT: showwing, fixxing, payying

---

GRAMMAR IN USE

We do not usually use *like* in the present continuous.

> *I like this bank.* NOT: *I'm liking this bank.*

EXERCISE 2 Fill in the blanks with the present continuous of the verb given. Spell the *-ing* form correctly. Use contractions when possible.

1. Marta <u>'s picking</u> up a package.
   pick

2. A few customers _____ some stamps from a machine.
   get

3. Amy _____ with Marta.
   wait

4. The clerk _____ a customer's credit card.
   take

5. Marta and Amy _____ in line.
   stand

6. They _____ at the people in the post office.
   look

7. Two customers _____ machines.
   use

8. A man _____ money in the stamp machine.
   put

9. One customer _____ a package.
   weigh

10. Nobody _____ to buy mailing supplies.
    plan

11. Marta _____ her ID to a clerk.
    give

12. Lisa _____ an email now.
    write

8.3 The Present Continuous—Use

EXAMPLES	EXPLANATION
People **are buying** stamps now.	The action is happening now, at this time.
Halina**'s standing** near the counter. Marta and Amy **are holding** hands. Nobody**'s sleeping** now.	The verbs *stand, sleep, sit, wear, hold,* and *wait* have no action. We use the present continuous to describe a present situation.
I**'m working** overtime this week. Lisa**'s learning** some new words today.	The action is happening during a specific present time period.

Note:

Some common time expressions with the present continuous are: *now, right now, at the moment, at this time, today, all day, this week,* and *this month.*

EXERCISE 3 Write two sentences about each picture with verbs from the box. Answers will vary.

stand	wait	wear	play	hold ✓	give	write
pick up	go ✓	buy	put	mail	get	sit

1. This man is going into the post office.

   He's holding some envelopes.

2. _____

   _____

3. _____

   _____

4. _____

   _____

5. _____

   _____

6. _____

_____

8.4 The Present Continuous—Negative Statements

SUBJECT	BE + NOT	VERB -ING	
I	**am not**	**getting**	mailing supplies.
You	**are not**	**buying**	stamps.
Marta	**is not**	**going**	to the bank.
Halina and Dorota	**are not**	**talking**	to the clerk.

Note:

We can make negative contractions with _be_.

**I'm not** waiting in line. (There's only one contraction for _am not_.)

Marta's **not** using the stamp machine.   _She **isn't** mailing a letter._

We're **not** buying supplies.   _We **aren't** mailing a package._

EXERCISE 4 Read the first sentence. Then write a negative sentence with the words given. Use contractions when possible.

1. Marta is picking up a package.

   She's not talking to Amy now. OR She isn't talking to Amy now.
   talk to Amy now

2. A customer is buying stamps.

   _____
   use his credit card

3. Many people are waiting in line.

   _____
   complain about the service

4. Halina and Dorota are waiting for service.

   _____
   use self-service

5. Lisa is writing in her journal.

   _____
   mail a package

6. Halina is doing errands alone today.

   _____
   shop with Peter

ABOUT YOU Use the words given to write true sentences about your activities at the present time. Make an affirmative or negative statement. If you write a negative statement, write a true affirmative statement also. Use contractions when possible.

1. I/do errands now

   I'm not doing errands now. I'm doing an exercise in English.

2. We/use pencils now

   We're using pencils now.

3. I/write an email

   _____

4. The teacher/wear sneakers

   _____

5. We/use a dictionary

   _____

6. The teacher/look at my ID

   _____

7. We/talk about the supermarket

   _____

8. The students/complain about this exercise

   _____

9. I/try to learn all the new words

   _____

10. The teacher/help me now

    _____

11. My classmates/have fun now

    _____

12. I/feel tired now

    _____

EXERCISE 5 Marta has her package now. She's leaving the post office. She sees Dorota and Halina. Read their conversation. Then write five or six sentences about the conversation. Use the present continuous, affirmative and/or negative.

Marta: Hi, Dorota. It's nice to see you, Halina. How are you?

Halina: I'm fine, thanks. It's good to see you, too, Marta.

Dorota: Hi, Marta. I'm mailing this package to my son. He's in college now. He's living in Canada this year. As usual, this line isn't moving very fast.

Marta: Did you know the post office has services online now? The website has prices for all packages. You can print the postage, and you can pay for it online with your credit card. Then you can give the package to your mail carrier the next day. It costs the same. And it's fast!

Dorota: I know. But I can't weigh the package at home. I don't have a scale. I need to send this package today. My son's waiting for his winter clothes.

Marta: The post office has a new automated postal center. You can weigh the package and pay for postage from a machine now. It's over there. And nobody's waiting.

Dorota: That's OK. It's my turn now.

Marta: Amy and I are going to lunch now. Do you both want to come with us?

Halina: I'm sorry. We can't. Peter's waiting for us outside in the car. But thanks for asking.

Dorota is waiting in line.

_____

_____

_____

EXERCISE 6 Complete the short conversations with the affirmative or negative of the verb given in the present continuous. Use contractions when possible.

1. **A:** Can I use your computer?

   B: Sorry, I 'm using _____ it at the moment. Can you wait?

use

2. **A:** Can you mail this letter for me?

   B: Sorry, I _____ home today. I _____ to the post office.

a. stay   b. go

3. **A:** Why can't Dorota do these errands with you now?

   B: Her friend _____ her today.

visit

4. **A:** I need help at the post office.

   B: Victor _____ today. He can go with you.

work

5. **A:** Why can't I use the phone right now?

   B: Because I _____ to make an important call.

plan

6. **A:** What's wrong with this stamp machine?

   B: I don't know. But it _____ right today. Let's wait in line for a clerk.

work

7. **A:** This post office is very busy right now.

   B: Yes. A lot of people _____ in line.

wait

8. **A:** Look at the line at the counter. It's too long.

   B: But nobody _____ the automated postal center. Let's use that.

use

9. **A:** I _____ the directions correctly. But it _____ the postage

a. follow   b. print

   label. What's wrong?

   B: I don't know. Let's ask the clerk.

10. **A:** I _____ anything right now. Do you want to go for a walk with me?

a. do

    B: I'm sorry. I can't. I _____ right now.

b. study

BEFORE YOU READ

1. Are there any drive-throughs in your neighborhood? What are they for?

2. Which drive-throughs do you use?

READ

Read the following conversation. Pay special attention to the *yes/no* questions and *wh-* questions using the present continuous in bold. 🎧 8.4

Amy: **Are we going** home now, Mommy?

Marta: Not yet. I still have a few errands.

Amy: **Where are we going** now?

Marta: To the bank. I need to get some cash.

Amy: **Why are you turning** here? The bank's over there.

Marta: I'm using the drive-through ATM, and it's right here.

Amy: There's someone ahead of us. **What's she doing? Is she getting** cash, too?

Marta: I don't know. Perhaps she's getting money. Or maybe she's depositing a check.

Amy: Do you always use the ATM?

Marta: No. Sometimes I go inside the bank. Then a bank teller helps me.

Amy: **What's that man doing** over there?

Marta: He's making a deposit. He's depositing money into his account.

Amy: **Why is he getting** out of his car?

Marta: His car isn't close enough to the ATM.

Amy: **What's he holding**?

Marta: It's his bank card. You have to use a bank card in the ATM.

Amy: **Is he putting** money in the machine now?

Marta: Not yet. First, he has to put in his PIN. He has to type four or six numbers to use his bank card. The PIN is secret. Only he knows the numbers.

Amy: What's a PIN?

Marta: It's short for *personal identification number*. It keeps your account safe.

COMPREHENSION Based on the reading, write T for *true* or F for *false*.

1. _____ Marta is making a deposit.

2. _____ Marta doesn't always use the ATM.

3. _____ Marta has a bank card.

WORDS TO KNOW 🎧 8.5

drive-through	Marta and Amy are using a **drive-through**. They don't have to get out of the car for service.
turn	They are **turning** into the drive-through.
ahead of	Three people are **ahead of** us in line. We have to wait.
maybe	She's at the bank. **Maybe** she needs to take out money. I'm not sure.
cash a check	The woman has a check. She needs **cash**. She's **cashing** her **check** at the bank.
teller	A **teller** is helping a customer at the bank.
deposit (v.) deposit (n.)	We put money in the bank. We **deposit** money. The man is making a **deposit** in the bank.
bank card	You use your **bank card** to make deposits or take out money.

LISTEN

Listen to the questions about the conversation. Circle *True* or *False*. 🎧 8.6

1. (True)   False   5. True   False

2. True   False   6. True   False

3. True   False   7. True   False

4. True   False   8. True   False

8.5 The Present Continuous—*Yes/No* Questions

BE	SUBJECT	VERB -*ING*		SHORT ANSWER
Am	I	**using**	the right envelope?	Yes, you are.
Are	you	**talking**	to the teller?	Yes, I am.
Is	Halina	**going**	into the bank?	No, she isn't.
Are	we	**turning**	here?	No, we're not.
Are	they	**waiting**	in their cars?	Yes, they are.

EXERCISE 7 Write a *yes/no* question with the words given. Answer the question with a short answer. Use the ideas from the conversation on page 183.

1. Amy/talk to her mother

   Is Amy talking to her mother? Yes, she is.

2. Marta and Amy/use the drive-through

   _____

184 Unit 8

3. Marta/cash a check

_____

4. Marta and Amy/wait in the car

_____

5. Marta/answer Amy's questions

_____

6. the teller/help Marta now

_____

7. the man/hold a bank card

_____

8. the man/getting cash

_____

ABOUT YOU   Use the words given to ask a partner questions about what he or she is doing. Your partner will answer with a short answer first and then add information. Write the questions and answers for practice.

1. you/speak English

A: Are you speaking English now? _____

B: Yes, I am. I'm using the present continuous. _____

2. you/ask for help

A: _____

B: _____

3. someone/help you

A: _____

B: _____

4. your teacher/grade your work

A: _____

B: _____

continued

5. you/write in your book

A: _____

B: _____

6. your teacher/stand in front of the class

A: _____

B: _____

7. you/learn a lot of new words today

A: _____

B: _____

8. you/wait for something

A: _____

B: _____

9. you/sit at a desk

A: _____

B: _____

10. your classmates/complain about something

A: _____

B: _____

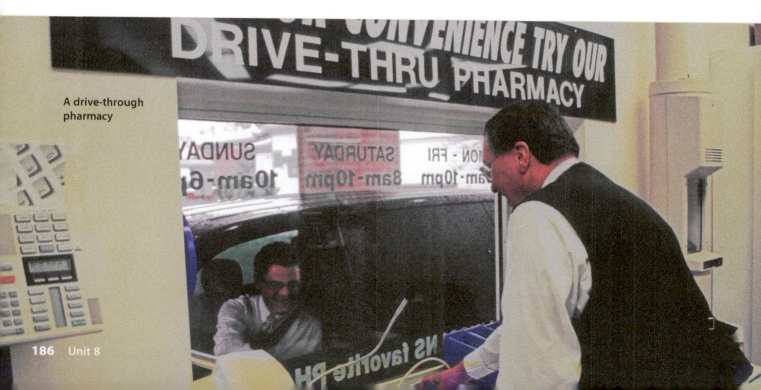

A drive-through pharmacy

8.6 The Present Continuous—*Wh-* Questions

QUESTION WORD(S)	BE	SUBJECT	VERB *-ING*		SHORT ANSWER
What	**are**	you	**doing?**		Waiting for service.
Where	**is**	he	**going?**		To the drive-through.
How many people	**is**	the teller	**helping?**		Two.
Who	**is**	the teller	**helping?**		A man and a woman.
How	**are**	some customers	**making**	a deposit?	At the ATM.
Why	**are**	people	**using**	the drive-through?	Because it's easy and fast.

Notes:

1. Sometimes a preposition (*about, to,* etc.) comes at the end of a question.
   *What is he waiting **for**?*

2. Remember, we can make a contraction with some question words and *is*.
   What's** Amy asking **about?

EXERCISE 8 Complete each of the short conversations. Write a question in the present continuous for each answer given. Use the question words *who, what, where, why, how many,* and *how.* The underlined phrase is the answer.

1. **A:** <u>What is Amy asking Marta about?</u>

   B: Amy's asking Marta <u>about the drive-through</u>.

2. **A:** _____

   B: Two customers are waiting in line <u>at the drive-through pharmacy</u>.

3. **A:** _____

   B: Marta is waiting for <u>some cash</u> at the bank.

4. **A:** _____

   B: She is expecting to get <u>five</u> $20 bills.

5. **A:** _____

   B: The customer is putting a deposit <u>in the ATM</u>.

6. **A:** _____

   B: Halina and Peter are learning <u>how to use the machine</u>.

7. **A:** _____

   B: <u>Because we have a test tomorrow</u>.

continued

8. A: _____

B: The teller is helping <u>one</u> customer at the moment.

9. A: _____

B: Simon and Victor are talking about <u>their children</u>.

10. A: _____

B: <u>Because it's easy and convenient to use the drive-through</u>.

EXERCISE 9 Complete the conversation between Marta and Amy at the fast-food restaurant drive-through. Use the words and expressions from the box. Then listen and check your answers. 🎧 8.7

| are waiting   he's asking   is putting   what are you ordering   why are we going   how is it doing ✓ |

Amy: Mommy, the sign is talking. _____How is it doing_____ that?

　　　　　　　　　　　　　　　　　　　　　　1.

Marta: It's not the sign. It's the clerk. Look. He's over there behind the window.

　　　　　_____ for our order.
　　　　　　　　　2.

Amy: _____ ?
　　　　　　3.

Marta: A chicken sandwich and a salad. And some milk, too. What about you?

Amy: Ummmmmm.

Marta: Hurry, Amy. The clerk's waiting. And customers _____ behind us.
　　　　　　　　　　　　　　　　　　　　　　　　　　　　　　　　4.

Amy: Ummmm. I want a grilled cheese!

Marta: (*speaking to the clerk*) One chicken sandwich, one grilled cheese, one salad, and

　　　　　two cartons of milk, please.

Clerk: That's $15.79. Please go to the next window.

Amy: _____ there?
　　　　　　5.

Marta: To pay and to pick up our food. Look. The

　　　　　clerk _____ our
　　　　　　　　　　6.

　　　　　lunch in a bag.

Clerk: Your change is $4.21. Thank you. Have

　　　　　a good day.

8.7 The Present Continuous—Subject Questions

QUESTION WORD(S)	BE	VERB -ING		ANSWER
Who	is	talking?		Amy and Marta are.
What	is	happening	at the bank?	Customers are doing business.
Which customer	is	waiting	in line?	Marta is.
How many customers	are	getting	cash now?	One customer is.

Notes:
1. We use a plural verb (*are*) after *how many*, even if the answer is singular.
2. We use a singular verb (*is*) after *who*, even if the answer is plural.
3. We use a noun after *which* and *how many/much*.

EXERCISE 10 Write a question for each answer given. Use the question words *who*, *which*, *what*, and *how many* as subjects. The underlined word or phrase is the answer.

1. Which customer is using the ATM? OR Who is using the ATM?

    A man is using the ATM.

2. _____

    The teller is counting the money.

3. _____

    One customer is making a deposit.

4. _____

    A man and a woman are getting help now.

5. _____

    Something is happening at the bank.

6. _____

    Three customers are using the drive-through.

FUN WITH GRAMMAR

Play with a partner. Look out the window. Write five questions about what is happening outside, using the present continuous. (If your classroom doesn't have a window, go to a place in the school where there are people, like the cafeteria.) Exchange questions with your partner. Answer your partner's questions, using the present continuous.

SUMMARY OF UNIT 8

The Present Continuous—Affirmative and Negative Statements

AFFIRMATIVE	NEGATIVE
I **am mailing** a letter.	I **am not getting** supplies.
You **are picking up** a package.	You **are not buying** stamps.
Marta **is waiting** in line.	She **is not going** to the bank.
We **are using** the ATM.	We **are not making** a deposit.
They **are standing** behind the counter.	They **are not helping** customers.

The Present Continuous—*Yes/No* Questions

BE	SUBJECT	VERB *-ING*		SHORT ANSWER
Am	I	**using**	the right envelope?	Yes, you are.
Are	you	**talking**	to the teller?	Yes, I am.
Is	Halina	**going**	into the bank?	No, she isn't.
Are	we	**turning**	here?	No, we're not.
Are	they	**waiting**	in their cars?	Yes, they are.

The Present Continuous—*Wh-* Questions

QUESTION WORD(S)	*BE*	SUBJECT	VERB *-ING*		SHORT ANSWER
What	**are**	you	**doing**?		Waiting for service.
Where	**is**	he	**going**?		To the drive-through.
How many people	**is**	the teller	**helping**?		Two.
Who	**is**	the teller	**helping**?		A man and a woman.
How	**are**	some customers	**making**	a deposit?	At the ATM.
Why	**are**	people	**using**	the drive-through?	Because it's easy and fast.

The Present Continuous—Subject Questions

QUESTION WORD(S)	*BE*	VERB *-ING*		ANSWER
Who	**is**	**talking**?		Amy and Marta are.
What	**is**	**happening**	at the bank?	Customers are doing business.
Which customer	**is**	**waiting**	in line?	Marta is.
How many customers	**are**	**getting**	cash now?	One customer is.

REVIEW

Fill in the blanks with the present continuous of the words given. Use contractions when possible.

A: Hello?

B: Hi, Magda. _____?
                    1. what/do

A: I _____ in line at the post office. Why?
         2. wait

B: I _____ lunch in the park. Do you want to join me?
        3. eat

A: Hmm. I _____ a package right now. Then I have to go to the bank.
             4. mail

B: Go to the bank later. It's so nice in the park right now. A lot of people _____
                                                     5. take

the day off. They _____ in the sun.
                6. relax

A: Well, we _____ here at the post office. We _____
            7. not relax   **8. not get**

very fast service today.

B: _____ ?
     9. people/complain

A: No, _____. One woman _____ the automated
          10.   **11. use**

postal center. She _____ by credit card. But most people
                   12. pay

_____ in line for the clerks.
     13. wait

B: _____ ?
  14. how many/clerks/work

A: Only two. _____ in the park now?
        15. what/happen

B: Well, some people _____ soccer. I _____
             16. play   **17. watch**

them. One man _____ on a grill. Some other people
              18. cook

_____ to an outdoor concert. We _____
     19. listen   **20. have**

a wonderful time.

A: That sounds good. OK. I'm finally finished at the post office. I _____ to the
                                                           21. not/go

bank. I _____ to the park!
        22. walk

B: Great!

A: _____ ?
      23. where/you/sit

B: I _____ near the soccer field. Under a big tree.
        24. sit

A: _____ a big hat?
       25. you/wear

B: No, I'm not. Oh, I see the woman with the big hat. I'm near her. Do you see me?

I _____ my hands.
        26. wave

A: Yes!

FROM GRAMMAR TO WRITING

PART 1 Editing Advice

1. Always use a form of *be* with the present continuous.

       is
   He working at that store.

2. Don't forget to use the *-ing* form with present continuous verbs.

       are waiting
   Marta and Amy ~~are wait~~ at the drive-through.

3. Use the correct word order in a question.

       is he
   What ~~he is~~ doing there?

4. Don't use the present continuous for usual or customary actions.

       works
   Sometimes Simon ~~is working~~ on Saturdays.

5. Follow the spelling rules for the *-ing* form.

       taking
   A clerk is ~~takeing~~ a customer's order.

       showing
   Maya is ~~showwing~~ Lisa her art project.

PART 2 Editing Practice

Some of the shaded words and phrases have mistakes. Find the mistakes and correct them.
If the shaded words are correct, write *C*.

Amy: Why ~~you are~~ *are you* turning here?
          1.

Marta: I need to stop at the pharmacy. A lot of cars are waiting *C* at the drive-through. Let's go inside.
          2.

Amy: But usually you're using the drive-through. Why are we go inside now?
          3.   **4.**

Marta: The drive-through is very busy, and I want to talk to a pharmacy clerk.

Amy: That woman's wearing a white coat. Is she a doctor?
          5.

Marta: No. She's a pharmacist. She's busy. She talking to a customer. We have to wait.
          6.

Amy: What are they talking about?
          7.

Marta: That customer's buying aspirin. Maybe he asking about different brands of aspirin.
          8.   **9.**

          Or maybe the pharmacist's giveing the customer advice. Now it's our turn.
          10.

Marta: What are you doing, Amy?
          11.

Amy: I'm hungry. I'm eat my grilled cheese sandwich now.
          12.

PART 3 Write

Look at the picture. Write five or six sentences about what is or isn't happening.

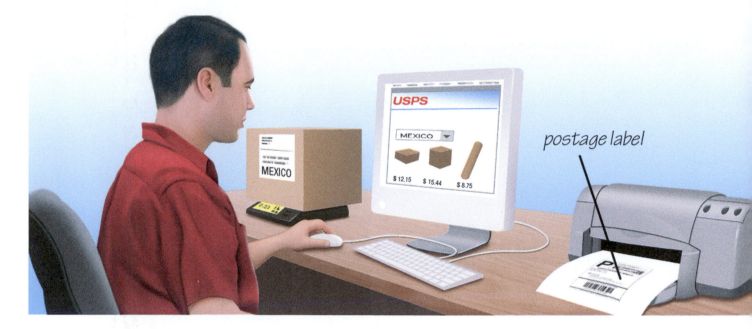

postage label

Simon is working on his computer. He isn't going to the post office today.

PART 4 Learner's Log

1. Write one sentence about each of these topics:
   - U.S. post office services
   - drive-through businesses

2. Write any questions you still have about the post office or drive-through businesses in the United States.

The Future (*Be Going To* Form)
Time Expressions

A bird approaches a yellow crocus, which
signals the change from winter to spring.

CHANGES

To improve is to change; to be perfect
is to change often.

WINSTON CHURCHILL

BEFORE YOU READ

1. What do parents have to buy for a new baby?

2. What changes in family life are necessary for a new baby?

READ

Read the following conversation. Pay special attention to the affirmative and negative statements with *be going to* and time expressions in bold. 🎧 9.1

Shafia and her husband, Ali, **are going to have** a baby in November. Dorota and Halina are visiting Shafia. Ali is at work.

Shafia: Our baby**'s going to arrive in two months**. I'm not ready.

Dorota: Let's see. You**'re going to need** a crib, a high chair, and a car seat.

Halina: You can use my daughter's crib. She's two now, and she has a bed. She also has a new car seat. We**'re not going to need** the crib or the car seat anymore.

Shafia: That's wonderful, Halina. Thank you. I**'m not going to need** the car seat **for a while**. We don't have a car right now.

Dorota: Actually, you need one to take the baby home from the hospital. And you**'re going to need** a stroller to take the baby outside. There's a resale shop in my neighborhood. You can get a high chair and a stroller there. Resale shops are not expensive.

Shafia: What's a resale shop?

Dorota: It's a store with used items. People take their used clothing and furniture there. The shop sells them at a low price. The money often goes to a charity. Resale shops are very popular.

Shafia: That's a great idea. We can go on Thursday.

Dorota: Good idea. But don't buy too many clothes for the baby. People **are going to give** you gifts.

Shafia: You're right. We have a lot of relatives. We**'re not going to buy** too much.

Halina: You**'re going to need** some help **for the first weeks**, too. New babies are a lot of work. And you**'re not going to get** much sleep.

Shafia: I know. My mother**'s going to help**. She**'s going to stay** with us **for the first month**. She's so excited. She**'s going to be** a grandmother for the first time.

> ### DID YOU **KNOW?**
> The average age of first-time mothers in the U.S. is going up. Today it is about 26 years old.

COMPREHENSION Based on the reading, write T for *true* or F for *false*.

1. _____ Shafia and Ali need a car seat.

2. _____ Shafia doesn't need a high chair.

3. _____ Shafia needs to buy a lot of clothes.

WORDS TO KNOW 🎧 9.2

arrive	Ali isn't home now. He's going to **arrive** at 6 p.m.
crib	Babies sleep in **cribs**.
high chair	A baby often sits in a **high chair** to eat.
wonderful	I'm so happy about your new job. That's **wonderful** news.
for a while	She's going to stay here **for a while**. I don't know how long.
stroller	You can take a baby outside in a **stroller**.
resale shop	You can buy used items at a **resale shop**. It is sometimes called a "thrift store."
used	This furniture is not new. It's **used**.
furniture	She needs baby **furniture**: a crib and a high chair.
charity	The resale shop gives money to a **charity**. The **charity** helps sick children.
gift	Relatives and friends are going to buy **gifts** for the baby.
relative	She is my husband's sister. She is a **relative** of our family.
get some sleep	I'm tired. I need to **get some sleep**.
excited	My family is **excited** about the baby. They're very happy.

LISTEN

Listen to the sentences about the conversation. Circle *True* or *False*. 🎧 9.3

1. True   (False)   5. True   False

2. True   False   6. True   False

3. True   False   7. True   False

4. True   False   8. True   False

9.1 The Future—Affirmative Statements

Be Going To Forms

SUBJECT	BE	GOING TO	VERB (BASE FORM)	
I	am		need	some help.
My mother	is		help	me.
We			have	a baby.
You		going to	give	us a crib.
Shafia and Ali	are		buy	a used high chair.
Their relatives			help	them.
There	is		be	a change in Shafia's life.

Pronunciation Note:

In informal speech, we pronounce *going to* as /gənə/. Listen to your teacher pronounce the sentences in the chart above. We do not write *gonna* in formal writing.

EXERCISE 1 Fill in the blanks with the affirmative of the verb given. Use the future with *be going to*. Use contractions when possible.

1. Shafia <u>'s going to get</u> some things for the baby.
    get

2. Halina and Dorota _____ Shafia again on Thursday.
    see

3. Shafia's mother _____ her with the new baby.
    help

4. The new baby _____ soon.
    arrive

5. Shafia's relatives _____ a lot of gifts for the baby.
    bring

6. Halina and Dorota _____ Shafia to the resale shop.
    take

7. Shafia _____ a stroller for the baby.
    need

8. Shafia and Ali _____ parents for the first time.
    be

9. With the help of her friends, Shafia _____ ready for the baby.
    be

10. Shafia's mother _____ her daughter for a month.
    visit

9.2 The Future—Negative Statements

SUBJECT	BE + NOT	GOING TO	VERB (BASE FORM)	
I	am not		need	a new car seat.
Shafia's father	is not		visit	her in January.
We		going to	buy	a lot of things.
You			give	us a stroller.
Shafia's relatives	are not		come	to the resale shop on Thursday.
There			be	many people at the resale shop.

GRAMMAR IN USE

Remember that you can form the negative contraction with *be* two different ways:

*He**'s not** going to visit her.*
*He **isn't** going to visit her.*

EXERCISE 2 Fill in the blanks with the negative form of *be going to*. Use the verbs given. Use contractions when possible.

1. Shafia <u>isn't going to buy</u> a lot of baby clothes.
    buy

2. With a new baby, Shafia and Ali _____ a lot of sleep.
    get

3. Shafia's mother _____ for a year.
    stay

4. Shafia _____ a lot of time for herself.
                        have

5. Dorota, Halina, and Shafia _____ at the resale store today.
                        shop

6. There _____ enough space in Dorota's car for the baby furniture.
              be

7. Relatives _____ Shafia a crib.
            give

8. The resale shop _____ open next Sunday.
            be

9. Dorota and Halina _____ any baby clothes at the resale shop.
            buy

10. Ali _____ Shafia to the resale shop.
        take

9.3 The Future—Use

EXAMPLES	EXPLANATION
Shafia's **going to buy** some things for the baby.	We use *be going to* with future plans.
You're **not going to get** much sleep.	We use *be going to* with predictions for the future.

EXERCISE 3 Fill in the blanks with the affirmative or negative form of *be going to* and the verb given. Use contractions when possible.

Shafia and Ali _____ *are going to be* _____ parents very soon. They're excited, but a little
                  1. be

worried. Things __ *aren't going to be* __ the same. There _____
             2. not/be   **3. be**

many changes. The baby _____ in two months. Then Ali
                      4. arrive

_____ two weeks off from work. He
        5. take

_____ able to take off any more time because he has a new job.
        6. not/be

Shafia's mother _____ for a month to help. She
                  7. come

_____ so Shafia can take care of the baby.
        8. cook and clean

Shafia and Ali _____ a lot of new things before the baby comes.
                9. buy

For example, they need a crib, a high chair, and a stroller. They _____
                                 10. not/have

a lot of money after the baby arrives. Shafia _____ to English classes for
                           11. not/go

a while, but both Shafia and Ali _____ a special class for new parents at the
                         12. take

community center.

9.4 Time Expressions

Time expressions can go at the beginning or at the end of the sentence. Learn the prepositions with each time expression.

EXAMPLES	EXPLANATION
She's going to visit me **in two weeks**. **In January**, he's going to visit me. They're going to visit me **in 2025**.	We use *in* with numbers of days, weeks, months, or years in the future. It means "after." We use *in* with years or names of months.
I'm going to visit you **on January 12**.	We use *on* with dates.
On Thursday, I'm going to go shopping. I'm going to go shopping **this Thursday**.	We use *on* or *this* with names of days. *This* means a future day in a present week.
This week, I'm going to get some new clothes. My parents are going to visit **next week**.	We use *this* with future time in the same week, month, or year. We use *next* with future time in the week after the present week.
Tomorrow I'm going to help you. I'm not going to help you **tonight**.	We use *tomorrow* for the day after today. *Tonight* means "this night."
She's going to live here **for a year**.	We use *for* with a time period.
She's going to stay with us **for a while**.	*For a while* means for an indefinite amount of time.
Ali's going to come home from work **at 6:00 p.m.**	We use *at* for a specific time in the future.
We're going to see our relatives **soon**.	We use *soon* for a near future time that is not specific.

EXERCISE 4 Fill in the blanks with the correct preposition for each time expression. Use *in, on, at,* and *for*.

1. Shafia's going to have her baby _____*in*_____ two months.

2. Shafia's going to visit the resale shop _____ Thursday.

3. Shafia and Ali are going to stay in their apartment _____ a while.

4. Ali's going to be home _____ 6:00 p.m. tonight.

5. Ali's life is going to change a lot _____ November.

6. Shafia's mother is going to stay with her _____ a month.

7. Shafia's mother is going to arrive _____ November 10.

8. Shafia and Ali's child is going to be in school _____ 2025.

ABOUT YOU Make predictions about your future. Think about your life in ten years. Use the verbs given in the affirmative or negative with *be going to*. Add more information where possible.

1. live in an apartment

   <u>In ten years, I'm not going to live in an apartment.</u>

   <u>I'm going to have a house.</u>

2. live in this city

   _____

   _____

3. be a student

   _____

   _____

4. work in an office

   _____

   _____

5. have a big family

   _____

   _____

6. be a U.S. citizen

   _____

   _____

7. forget my language

   _____

   _____

8. return to my country to live

   _____

   _____

9. have a car OR have a different car

   _____

   _____

EXERCISE 5 Look at part of Shafia's calendar. Write about her activities. Make affirmative and/or negative statements with *be going to* and the words given. Add a time expression in the future. Then rewrite the sentence with a different time expression. Use the expressions on page 200.

SEPTEMBER				
MONDAY	**TUESDAY**	**WEDNESDAY**	**THURSDAY**	**FRIDAY**
1 TODAY Errands 10 a.m. to 1 p.m.	2 Exercise class 9 a.m. to 11 a.m.	3	4 Resale shop 1 p.m.	5
8	9 Doctor's appointment 3 p.m.	10	11	12 Visit Ali's parents
15 Errands 10 a.m. to 1 p.m.	16 Exercise class 9 a.m. to 11 a.m.	17	18	19 Dinner with Ali, Halina, and Peter 7 p.m.
22	23 Doctor's appointment 3 p.m.	24	25 Get ready for the trip to New York—Ali	26 Movie at home with Dorota—Ali out of town

1. Ali/be out of town

   Ali's going to be out of town on Friday, September 26.

   He isn't going to be out of town this week.

2. Shafia/take an exercise class

   _____

   _____

3. Dorota/come to Shafia's house

   _____

   _____

4. Shafia/see the doctor

   _____

   _____

5. Ali/get ready for a trip to New York

   _____

   _____

6. Shafia, Halina, and Dorota/go to the resale shop

_____

_____

7. Shafia and Ali/have dinner with Halina and Peter

_____

_____

8. Shafia and Ali/visit Ali's parents

_____

_____

9. Shafia/have free time

_____

_____

10. Shafia/run errands

_____

_____

EXERCISE 6 Complete the conversations. Use the verbs given in the affirmative or negative with *be going to*. Use contractions when possible. Then listen and check your answers. 🎧 9.4

CONVERSATION A: Halina and Shafia are talking about the new baby's room.

Halina: Where's the baby's room?

Shafia: We have an extra room. It's small. But there _'s going to be_ enough
                                                          1. be

space for a crib.

Halina: What's in the room now?

Shafia: There's a desk and a computer. But we _____ them there.
                                                          2. leave

Ali _____ them to the living room next week.
        3. move

His brother _____ him. The desk is very heavy.
                4. help

Halina: What about the color of the walls?

Shafia: We _____ them yellow. But not now.
                5. paint

There _____ enough time.
            6. be

CONVERSATION B: Halina, Dorota, and Shafia are talking about the baby's name.

Halina: Shafia, do you have a name for the baby?

Shafia: No. Ali and I _____ a name right now. After the baby's birth,
　　　　　　　　　　　　　　　7. choose

we _____ some of our relatives for ideas. It's very important to choose
　　　　　　8. ask

the right name.

Dorota: There are long lists of names on the Internet. Just search for *baby names*. You can even find the

meaning of each name.

Shafia: That's interesting. But the baby _____ an American name.
　　　　　　　　　　　　　　　　　　　　9. have

We _____ the baby a name from our country.
　　10. give

Dorota: There are names from other countries online, too. There are thousands

of names for boys and girls.

Dorota means "gift from God."
Halina means "light." *Shafia*
means "mercy."

Shafia: Thanks, Dorota. But we _____ to see the
　　　　　　　　　　　　　　　　　11. wait

baby first.

In the U.S., green and yellow
are considered neutral colors
for a baby's room. Pink is often
used for girls, and blue is used
for boys.

1. Is it hard to move? Why or why not?

2. How do people prepare to move?

READ

Read the following conversation. Pay special attention to the *yes/no* **questions and** *wh-* **questions with** *be going to* **in bold.** 🎧 9.5

Victor and Simon are on the phone. Victor and his family are moving soon.
Simon is giving him some advice.

Victor: We're going to move in two weeks. There's so much to do!

Simon: You're right. **Are you going to hire a mover?**

Victor: No, I'm not. I'm going to rent a truck. The new apartment is in our neighborhood. Lisa and I don't have a lot of things. But we're going to need some help. Are you available on the 27th of this month?

Simon: Sure. I can help you.

Victor: Thanks, Simon. What should I do about our mail?

Simon: You can fill out a change-of-address form at the post office. Or you can fill it out online. It's easy! The post office sends your mail to your new address for one year.

Victor: What else do we need to do?

Simon: **Are you going to get Internet service in your new apartment?**

Victor: Yes, we're definitely going to need Internet service.

Simon: Then you can call and make an appointment. The company can come and set it up. They often have good rates if you get phone, Internet, and TV together. It's called a "package."

Victor: That sounds good. **How long is it going to take for the new service?**

Simon: You can make an appointment for the day after you move in. They can usually set it up within an hour or so.

Victor: Oh, great.

Simon: **When are you going to pack?** Do you need boxes?

Victor: I'm starting to pack now. We have some boxes, but not enough.

Simon: You should go to some stores in your neighborhood. You can ask them for their old boxes.

Victor: That's a good idea. We also have a lot of old things. **What are we going to do with them?** I don't want to move them.

Simon: You can give them to charity. There's a resale shop in this neighborhood.

DID YOU KNOW?

Common reasons for moving are family-related, employment-related, and housing-related.

COMPREHENSION Based on the reading, write T for *true* or F for *false*.

1. _____ Simon is going to help Victor hire a mover.

2. _____ Victor is going to pack on the 27th.

3. _____ Victor wants to give some old things away.

WORDS TO KNOW 🎧 9.6

move	We're going to **move** to a new apartment in two weeks.
mover	We need a **mover** to help us with the furniture.
hire	The school needs a new English teacher. It's going to **hire** a new teacher.
rent	I can **rent** a truck for one day. It's not expensive.
truck	The car isn't big enough. You're going to need a **truck**.
neighborhood	Victor and Lisa are moving close to their old apartment. Their new apartment is in the same **neighborhood**.
address	They live on Madison Street. Their **address** is 1245 Madison Street.
wireless	I have **wireless** Internet service at home. I don't need any cords to get online.
package	I am going to order a **package**. It comes with different services.
pack	I'm going to **pack** my things. I'm going to put them in boxes.

LISTEN

Listen to the sentences about the conversation. Circle *True* or *False*. 🎧 9.7

1. (True)   False   5. True   False

2. True   False   6. True   False

3. True   False   7. True   False

4. True   False   8. True   False

9.5 The Future—*Yes/No* Questions

BE	SUBJECT	GOING TO	VERB (BASE FORM)		SHORT ANSWER
Am	I		**need**	a change-of-address form?	Yes, you are.
Are	you		**get**	Internet service?	Yes, I am.
Is	Victor		**move**	to another city?	No, he isn't.
Are	we	**going to**	**give**	our old items to charity?	Yes, we are.
Are	Victor and Lisa		**hire**	a mover?	No, they aren't.
Are	there		**be**	any problems?	No, there aren't.

Compare the word order in statements and *yes/no* questions:

STATEMENT	YES/NO QUESTION
You are going to move.	**Are you** going to move to a new neighborhood?
I am going to need a truck.	**Am I** going to need boxes?

EXERCISE 7 Write *yes/no* questions about Victor and Simon's conversation on page 205. Use *be going to* and the words given. Give a short answer.

1. Victor's family/move soon

   Is Victor's family going to move soon? Yes, they are.

2. Victor/hire a mover

   _____

3. he/buy some boxes

   _____

4. their new apartment/be in the same neighborhood

   _____

5. he/get Internet service

   _____

6. it/take a long time to get Internet service

   _____

7. the post office/send Victor and Lisa's mail to their new address

   _____

8. Victor/have to pay for boxes

   _____

9. they/move all their things to their new apartment

   _____

10. Simon/help Victor

    _____

EXERCISE 8 Complete the short conversations. Write a *yes/no* question with *be going to*.

1. **A:** We're going to move.

   B: *Are you going to move this week?*
   <small>this week</small>

2. **A:** I'm going to change my address.

   B: _____
   <small>your phone number, too</small>

continued

3. A: He's going to pay for that service.

   B: _____
more than $50

4. A: They're going to move.

   B: _____
to a house

5. A: Simon's going to help.

   B: _____
Marta, too

6. A: They're not going to move all their things.

   B: _____
give some things to charity

7. A: Victor and Lisa are going to rent a new apartment.

   B: _____
in a different city

8. A: Victor's going to get a change-of-address form.

   B: _____
online

9.6 The Future—*Wh*- Questions

QUESTION WORD(S)	BE	SUBJECT	*GOING TO*	VERB (BASE FORM)		ANSWER
Why	**are**	you		**move?**		Because my apartment is too small.
Where	**are**	Victor and Lisa		**live?**		In the same neighborhood.
What	**is**	he		**give**	to charity?	Their old things.
When	**are**	they	going to	**get**	boxes?	Next week.
How many boxes	**are**	they		**need?**		About fifty.
What kind of truck	**is**	he		**rent?**		A big one.
What kinds of supplies	**are**	you		**buy**	at the store?	A pad of paper, pens, and pencils.

Note:

Remember, some question words can contract with *is*.

    Where's *Victor going to live?*   **Why's** *he going to move?*

Compare the word order in statements and *wh*- questions.

STATEMENT	*WH*- QUESTION
You are going to move.	When **are you** going to move?
I am going to need boxes.	How many boxes **am I** going to need?

EXERCISE 9 Write a *wh-* question about each statement. Use *be going to* and the question words given.

1. **A:** Victor's going to get a change-of-address form.

   B: _Where's he going to get it?_____
                                        where

2. **A:** I'm going to rent a truck.

   B: _____
                                        when

3. **A:** Victor's going to go to stores in his neighborhood.

   B: _____
                                        why

4. **A:** There are going to be some problems.

   B: _____
                                     what kind of

5. **A:** I'm going to move this furniture to my new apartment.

   B: _____
                                        how

6. **A:** You're going to need boxes.

   B: _____
                                        how many

7. **A:** The truck is going to cost money.

   B: _____
                                      how much

8. **A:** I'm going to give some items to charity.

   B: _____
                                      which

9. **A:** We're going to get some boxes.

   B: _____
                                      where

10. **A:** We're going to hire some movers.

    B: _____
                                       how many

EXERCISE 10 Complete the conversations. Look at the short answer to each question. Then write a question with the words given. Use the correct question word with *be going to*. Use contractions when possible.

1. **A:** _When's Victor going to move?_
   _{Victor/move}

   B: In about two weeks.

2. **A:** _____
   _{Victor and Lisa/rent}

   B: A truck.

3. **A:** _____
   _{the cost/be for new Internet service}

   B: Less than $100.

4. **A:** _____
   _{they/move}

   B: Because their apartment is too small.

5. **A:** _____
   _{Simon/help Victor}

   B: On the 25th of this month.

6. **A:** _____
   _{Victor/get boxes}

   B: From a store in the neighborhood.

7. **A:** _____
   _{Victor and Lisa/rent}

   B: A large, three-bedroom apartment.

8. **A:** _____
   _{Victor and Lisa/pack}

   B: Fifty boxes.

On average, people in the U.S. move more than 11 times in their life.

9. A: _____
Victor/do with his old items

B: Give them to charity.

10. A: _____
the phone company/change your service

B: On moving day.

11. A: _____
you/have the same phone number

B: Because I'm going to live in the same neighborhood.

12. A: _____
you/give to charity

B: Some old clothes and some furniture.

9.7 The Future—Questions with *How Long*

EXAMPLES	EXPLANATION
A: How long are you going to stay? **B: Until** next week.	We use *how long* to ask about specific amounts of time. We can use *until* in answers to *how long* questions. Use *until* when the action ends at a specific time.
A: How long are they going to wait? **B: For** 15 minutes.	We can use *for* in answers to *how long* questions. Use *for* when the action takes an amount of time.

ABOUT YOU Find a partner. Use the words given to ask questions with *how long* and *be going to*. Your partner will answer with *for* or *until*. Write the questions and answers for practice.

1. you/be in this class

   A: *How long are you going to be in this class?*

   B: *I'm going to be in this class until the end of the semester.*

2. our class/work on this exercise

   A: _____

   B: _____

3. we/use this book

   A: _____

   B: _____

4. you/stay at school today

   A: _____

   B: _____

continued

5. this school/be open today

    A: _____

    B: _____

6. you/be a student

    A: _____

    B: _____

9.8 The Future—Subject Questions

QUESTION WORD(S)	BE	GOING TO	VERB (BASE FORM)		ANSWER
What	is	going to	happen?		I'm going to move.
Who			help	you?	My friends are.
How many friends	are		help	you?	Four.
Which services			come	with the package?	Phone, Internet, and TV.

EXERCISE 11 Write a subject question for each statement. Use *be going to* and the question word(s) given. Use contractions when possible.

1. Somebody's going to visit me.

    _Who's going to visit you?_____
                                                   who

2. Something's going to change.

    _____
                                                  what

3. Many people are going to move this year.

    _____
                                             how many

4. Some services are going to be expensive.

    _____
                                             which

5. Somebody's going to give me some boxes.

    _____
                                             who

6. Something's going to happen on Thursday.

    _____
                                             what

7. A mover's going to help me.

_____
which

8. Some apartments are going to be available.

_____
how many

EXERCISE 12 Victor is calling a truck rental company. He wants to rent a truck for his move. Complete Victor's conversation using *yes/no* questions and *wh-* questions with *be going to*. Use the words given. Then listen and check your answers. 🎧 9.8

Employee: Avery Truck Rental. How can I help you?

Victor: I need to rent a truck. I'm going to move, and I need some information about prices.

Employee: Sure. ___*Are you going to return*___ the truck here or in another city?
1. you/return

Victor: I'm going to return it here.

Employee: OK. _____?
2. what kind of truck/you/need

Victor: Uh ... I don't know.

Employee: Well, _____?
3. how many rooms/you/move

Victor: It's a two-bedroom apartment.

Employee: A 15-foot truck is enough.

Victor: _____?
4. it/have/room for my sofa

Employee: Oh, yes. It's going to be fine. _____?
5. when/you/move

Victor: In two weeks.

Employee: Is that on the weekend or during the week?

Victor: I'm not sure. Why is that important?

Employee: It's $20 a day more on the weekend. And we don't have many trucks available on the weekends.

Victor: _____ any trucks available two weeks from today?
6. there/be

Employee: _____ enough?
7. one day/be

Victor: Yes. I need it for just one day.

Employee: OK. It's going to be $59.99 a day and 99 cents a mile. I need a credit card number to reserve it.

_____?
8. what kind of card/you/use

Victor: I'm not ready to reserve it now. I'm only calling about prices. Thank you.

EXERCISE 13 Complete the conversation between Victor and Simon. Use the phrases from the box. Then listen and check your answers.  9.9

are going to help	I'm going to invite	aren't going to move	we're going to meet
I'm going to get	are you going to pack ✓	are you going to be	

Simon: When _____are you going to pack_____ the rest of your things?
1.

Victor: This week. _____ more boxes today.
2.

Simon: Ed and I can help you move on Saturday, the 27th. We're available all day.

Victor: Thanks, but the people in my new apartment _____ until
3.

Sunday. _____ available on Sunday?
4.

Simon: I think so. How many people _____ you?
5.

Victor: Just two of my friends. _____ at my apartment at 1:00.
6.

Then later, _____ you all for pizza.
7.

Movers load a sofa onto a moving truck.

214   Unit 9

EXERCISE 14 Read the following frequently asked questions, or FAQs, about moving. Complete the FAQs with *yes/no* questions and *wh-* questions with *be going to,* and the verbs given. Use contractions when possible.

MOVING FAQS

1. Q: When is the best time to move?

   A: That depends. May through September _____*are going to be*_____ the busiest months for
   _{**a. be**}

   moving companies. _____ yourself, or are you going to hire a mover?
   _{**b. move**}

   Either way, it _____ easier in the off-season.
   _{**c. be**}

2. Q: How long _____ to get ready?
   _{**a. take**}

   A: For most people, it _____ six to eight weeks to do everything. Start
   _{**b. take**}

   planning early. If you wait, you _____ enough time.
   _{**c. not/have**}

3. Q: How much _____?
   _{**a. cost**}

   A: It _____ more if you hire movers and if you have a lot of stuff.
   _{**b. cost**}

   A moving company _____ someone to your house about four weeks
   _{**c. send**}

   before the move. They _____ at how much stuff you have and give
   _{**d. look**}

   you a price.

4. Q: What should I do before the moving company comes?

   A: Get rid of everything you _____ with you to your new home.
   _{**a. not/take**}

   You _____ it. Give it to a charity or throw it away.
   _{**b. not/want**}

FUN WITH GRAMMAR

Play a chain activity. Student A begins by asking Student B a question about the future, using *be going to*:

   A: What are you going to eat for dinner tonight?

Student B answers the question and then asks Student C a new question using *be going to*. Continue around the circle. Answer the question and then ask a new question. Each correct question and each correct answer is worth 1 point. You get an extra point if you use a time expression.

   A: Rana, what are you going to eat for dinner tonight?

   B: I'm going to eat pasta. Mario, are you going to go to work tomorrow?

   C: No, I'm not. Ana, when are you going to …

SUMMARY OF UNIT 9

The Future—Affirmative and Negative Statements

SUBJECT	BE OR BE + NOT	GOING TO	VERB (BASE FORM)	
I	am / am not		need	some help.
My mother	is / is not		help	me.
We	are / are not		have	a baby.
You	are / are not	going to	give	us a crib.
They	are / are not		buy	a used high chair.
There	is / is not		be	a change.

Time Expressions

She's going to visit me **in two weeks**.	**Tomorrow** I'm going to help you.
I'm going to visit you **on January 12**.	She's going to stay **for a while**.
I'm going to go shopping **this Thursday**.	We're going to see them **soon**.
They're going to visit **next week**.	I'm going to come home at **6 p.m.**

The Future—*Yes/No* Questions

BE	SUBJECT	GOING TO	VERB (BASE FORM)		SHORT ANSWER
Am	I		need	a form?	Yes, you are.
Are	you		get	Internet service?	Yes, I am.
Is	Victor		move	to another city?	No, he isn't.
Are	we	going to	give	things to charity?	Yes, we are.
Are	they		hire	a mover?	No, they aren't.
Are	there		be	any problems?	No, there aren't.

The Future—*Wh-* Questions and Questions with *How Long*

QUESTION WORD(S)	BE	SUBJECT	GOING TO	VERB (BASE FORM)		ANSWER
Why	are	you		move?		Because my apartment is small.
Where	are	they		live?		In this city.
What	is	he		give	to charity?	Their old things.
When	are	they	going to	get	boxes?	Next week.
What kind of truck	is	he		rent?		A big one.
How long	are	you		stay?		Until next week.

The Future—Subject Questions

QUESTION WORD(S)	BE	GOING TO	VERB (BASE FORM)		ANSWER
What	is		happen?		I'm going to move.
Who			help	you?	My friends are.
How many friends		going to	help	you?	Four.
Which services	are		come	with the package?	Phone, Internet, and TV.

REVIEW

Fill in the blanks with *be going to* and the words given. Use contractions when possible.

A: Hi, Pam.

B: Hi, Janet! How are you?

A: I'm good. I have some news. Paul and I _____ .
　　　　　　　　　　　　　　　　　　　　　　1. move

B: Wow! _____ ?
　　　　　2. where/you/move

A: We _____ to Alaska.
　　　　　　3. go

B: Alaska? _____ there? It _____ so cold!
　　　　　　　　4. why/you/go　　　　　　　　　5. be

A: It _____ cold all year. The summer _____ warm . . .
　　　　　　6. not/be　　　　　　　　　　　　　　　　　　　7. get

B: _____ there?
　　　　8. how long/you/stay

A: We _____ there for only a year. I _____ for a company in Fairbanks for a
　　　　　9. live　　　　　　　　　　　　　　　10. work

year. But then we _____ back here.
　　　　　　　　　　11. come

B: _____?
　　　12. when/you/move

A: We _____ next week. We _____ everything. We _____
　　　　　13. pack　　　　　　　　　　　14. not/take　　　　　　　　　　15. give

some things to charity.

B: _____ a truck? Or _____ movers?
　　　16. you/rent　　　　　　　　　17. you/hire

A: Definitely movers! They _____ our stuff in two weeks.
　　　　　　　　　　　　　　　　18. pick up

B: _____ with your cat?
　　　19. what/happen

A: She _____ with us! Paul _____ with the cat, and I _____.
　　　　　20. come　　　　　　　　　　21. drive　　　　　　　　　　22. fly

B: Well, I _____ you. But I'm glad you _____ back next year. Actually,
　　　　　23. miss　　　　　　　　　　　　　　24. come

I have some news, too . . .

A: What? _____, too?
　　　　　25. you/move

B: No. I _____ a baby!
　　　　　26. have

A: Congratulations! That's wonderful! _____ the baby?
　　　　　　　　　　　　　　　　　　　27. when/you/have

B: In August.

A: _____ a boy or a girl?
　　　28. you/have

B: We don't know yet. It _____ a surprise.
　　　　　　　　　　　　　　29. be

A: You _____ very busy! _____ you?
　　　　　30. be　　　　　　　　　　31. who/help

B: My mom _____ us when the baby is born.
　　　　　　　　　32. visit

A: That's great. I'm so happy for you!

B: Thank you!

FROM GRAMMAR TO WRITING

PART 1 Editing Advice

1. Use a form of *be* with *going to*.

    We ^ 're going to shop at a resale shop.

2. Use the correct word order in questions.

    Where ~~they are~~ *are they* going to work?

3. Use the correct preposition with time expressions.

    We are going to move ~~after~~ *in* two weeks.

4. Don't forget *to* after *going*.

    Victor's going ^ *to* rent a truck.

5. Don't forget the *-ing* in *going to*.

    I'm ~~go~~ *going* to move next week.

PART 2 Editing Practice

Some of the shaded words and phrases have mistakes. Find the mistakes and correct them.
If the shaded words are correct, write *C*.

Dorota: We ^ 're going to have a party for Shafia. It's going to be *C* at my house. Can you help me?
   1.   2.

Halina: Sure. What kind of party are you go to have?
                                          3.

Dorota: A baby shower.

Halina: A baby shower? What's that?

Dorota: At a baby shower, people have lunch together. And everyone brings a gift for the baby.

Halina: When it's going to be?
                 4.

Dorota: The party going to be next weekend, on Saturday, the 13th.
               5.   6.

Halina: Who's going be there?
                 7.

Dorota: Shafia's relatives and good friends.

Halina: Are we going to cook?
                 8.

Dorota: We're going to cook some things. But we're go to buy prepared food at the deli.
               9.   10.

            I'm going order a cake, too!
               11.

Halina: What time the party going to start?
                                12.

Dorota: In 2 p.m.
        13.

Halina: But Peter has to work until 4 p.m. on Saturday.
                           14.

Dorota: Don't worry. This shower's for women only.

PART 3 Write

Write a paragraph of six to eight sentences about the picture. Write about what is happening right now and what is going to happen.

Victor is coming out of his apartment building. He is moving today.

PART 4 Learner's Log

1. Write one sentence about each of the topics:
   - preparing for a new baby
   - resale shops
   - preparing to move
   - renting a truck

2. Write any questions you still have about each topic above.

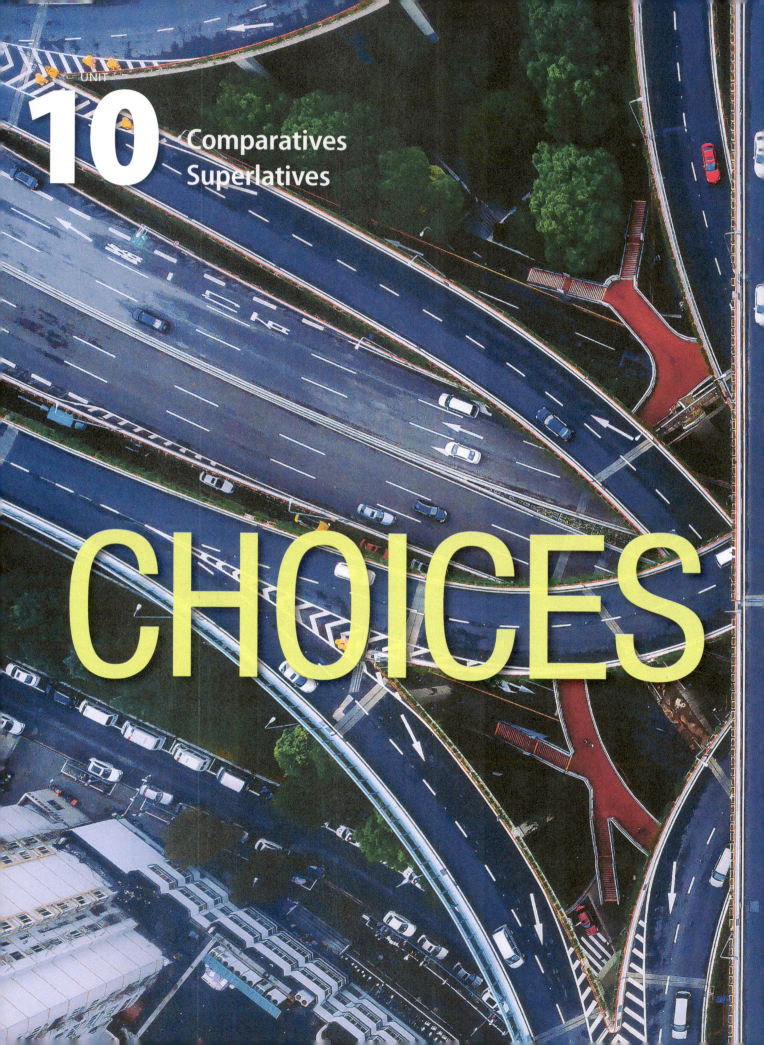

10

Comparatives
Superlatives

CHOICES

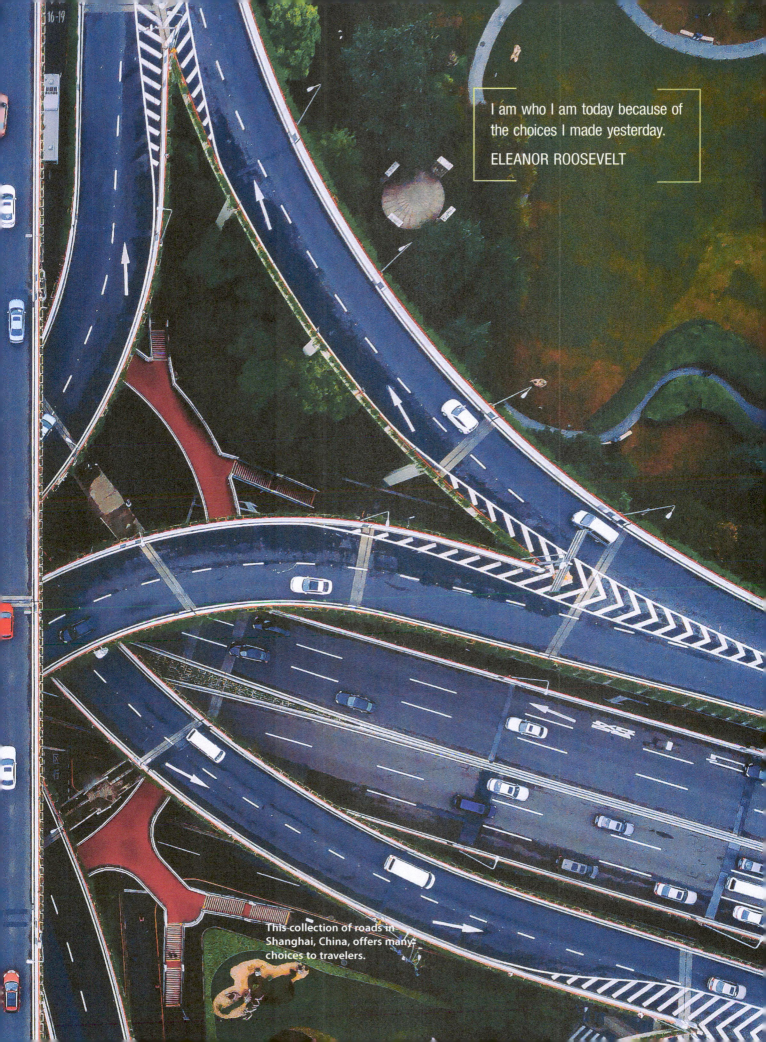

I am who I am today because of the choices I made yesterday.

ELEANOR ROOSEVELT

This collection of roads in Shanghai, China, offers many choices to travelers.

BEFORE YOU READ

1. Where are the state universities in your state?

2. What community colleges do you know about in your area?

READ

Read the following article. Pay special attention to the comparative forms in bold. 🎧 10.1

In the United States, many students choose to go to a community college. Students can get a two-year certificate or degree. Some students start their education at a community college. Then they go to a four-year college or university to get a bachelor's degree.

A four-year university is **more expensive than** a community college. The average tuition at a community college is $3,347 a year. At a four-year state university, it's $9,970 a year.[1] A community college is often **closer** to home **than** a four-year college. Community colleges in big cities often have several campuses.

There are other differences, too. A community college often has **smaller classes than** a university. Some university classes can have **more than** 100 students. Also, students at a community college are usually **older than** students at a four-year college. The average age of students at a community college is 29. At a university, most students are between the ages of 18 and 24.

Community college students are often **busier**, too. Many students have full- or part-time jobs and families. Community colleges are **more convenient than** universities for students with small children. Many community colleges offer childcare. There are more night and weekend classes, too.

Which is **better** for you: a community college or a four-year college?

DID YOU **KNOW?**
There are different levels of college degrees: associate's degree, bachelor's degree, master's degree, and PhD (or doctorate).

COMPREHENSION Based on the reading, write T for *true* or F for *false*.

1. _____ You can go to a university after a community college.

2. _____ Universities have more night classes than community colleges.

3. _____ Many community college students go to work and go to school.

certificate	My cousin has a **certificate** from a community college to work with children.
education	We go to school to get an **education**.
bachelor's degree	My brother has a **degree** from a four-year college. He has a **bachelor's degree**.
average	I'm 23, my brother is 25, and my sister is 27. Our **average** age is 25.
tuition	College is not free. Students have to pay **tuition** to go to college.
campus	My college has several **campuses**. There is a **campus** near my house.
between	The number 20 is **between** 19 and 21.
offer	The college **offers** good services for students. It has childcare and weekend classes.
childcare	People with small children need **childcare** when they work or go to school. It is sometimes called "day care."

LISTEN

Listen to the sentences about the article. Circle *True* or *False*. 📖 10.3

1. (True)   False
2. True   False
3. True   False
4. True   False

5. True   False
6. True   False
7. True   False
8. True   False

10.1 Comparative Forms of Adjectives

Notice how we compare two people or things.

SIMPLE FORM	COMPARATIVE FORM	EXAMPLES	EXPLANATION
old tall cheap	old**er** tall**er** cheap**er**	Community college students are **older than** university students.	After a one-syllable adjective, we add -*er*.
late nice	late**r** nice**r**	English class begins **later than** my computer class.	If the adjective ends in *e*, we add -*r* only.
big hot	big**ger** hot**ter**	Classes at universities are often **bigger than** classes at community colleges.	After a one-syllable adjective with a consonant + vowel + consonant, we double the final consonant before adding -*er*.
busy happy easy	bus**ier** happ**ier** eas**ier**	Community college students are often **busier than** university students.	In a two-syllable adjective that ends in *y*, we change the *y* to an *i* and add -*er*.
simple quiet friendly	simpl**er**, **more** simple quiet**er**, **more** quiet friendl**ier**, **more** friendly	My new neighborhood is **quieter than** my old one. My new neighborhood is **more quiet than** my old one.	Some two-syllable adjectives have two forms.

continued

SIMPLE FORM	COMPARATIVE FORM	EXAMPLES	EXPLANATION
helpful crowded expensive flexible	**more** helpful **more** crowded **more** expensive **more** flexible	University tuition is **more expensive than** community college tuition. Online classes are **more flexible than** regular classes.	With most other two-syllable adjectives and all three-syllable adjectives, we add *more* before the adjective.
good bad	**better** **worse**	The movie *Star Wars* is **better than** *Star Trek*. A bad grade is **worse than** a good grade.	Some comparative forms are irregular. We change the word completely.

Notes:

1. We use *than* to complete the comparison. We omit *than* if we do not mention the second item of comparison.

   *The university is **bigger than** the college, but the college is **more convenient**.*

2. We can put *much* before a comparative form.

   *Those students are **much younger** than we are.*

GRAMMAR IN USE

Using the subject pronoun after *than* is very formal. Most Americans use the object pronoun.

FORMAL: *You are busier than I am.*   INFORMAL: *You are busier than me.*

EXERCISE 1 Write the comparative forms of the adjectives. Use correct spelling with *-er* endings. In some cases, there are two answers.

1. busy _____busier_____

2. excited _____more excited_____

3. friendly _friendlier OR more friendly_

4. convenient _____

5. big _____

6. fine _____

7. lazy _____

8. hard _____

9. funny _____

10. expensive _____

11. large _____

12. interesting _____

13. quiet _____

14. hot _____

15. good _____

16. kind _____

17. mad _____

18. late _____

19. bad _____

20. cheap _____

21. simple _____

22. long _____

23. beautiful _____

24. cold _____

25. small _____

26. angry _____

27. boring _____

28. healthy _____

EXERCISE 2 Compare Wilson Community College and Jackson University, using the information in the chart. Fill in the blanks with the comparative form of one of the adjectives from the box. Add *than* where necessary. The numbers in the chart go with the item numbers in the exercise.

	WILSON COMMUNITY COLLEGE	JACKSON UNIVERSITY
1.	night and weekend classes	no night or weekend classes
2.	tuition: $3,200 per year	tuition: $8,990 per year
3.	average class size = 16 students	average class size = 30 students
4.	80 percent of students have jobs	10 percent of students have jobs
5.	childcare	no childcare
6.	all classes in one building	more than 60 buildings
7.	opened in 1985	opened in 1910
8.	good for me	good for my sister

busy   good   big   flexible ✓   old   small   expensive   convenient

1. Wilson is ____more flexible than____ Jackson for people with day jobs.

2. Jackson is _____ Wilson.

3. Classes at Wilson are _____ classes at Jackson.

4. Most students at Wilson work full-time. Students at Wilson are _____ students at Jackson.

5. Wilson is _____ Jackson for parents with small children.

6. Jackson is _____ Wilson.

7. Jackson is _____ Wilson.

8. Wilson is good for me, but Jackson is _____ for my sister because she's finishing her bachelor's degree.

Childcare is important for some students when choosing between a community college or a university.

EXERCISE 3 Use the comparative form of the adjectives from the boxes to fill in the blanks. Add *than* where necessary. Then listen and check your answers. 🎧 10.4

convenient	close	cheap ✓	old	busy	young

CONVERSATION 1

A: I don't plan to go to Cassidy University. I prefer Central Community College.

B: Why?

A: The tuition's only $2,050 a semester. It's _____*cheaper than*_____ a four-year college.
1.

Also, it's _____ to my home, so I can walk there. And the students are
2.

_____. I'm 32. A lot of the students are in their 30s and 40s.
3.

B: You're right. Most of the students at Cassidy are _____ the students at Central.
4.

They're under 22 years old.

CONVERSATION 2

A: A lot of the community college students have small children. Central has childcare. So it's

_____ for people with small children.
5.

B: You don't have kids.

A: No. But my sister does. We're planning to take classes together. She has a full-time job. Her kids are

young. So she's much _____ I am. The childcare is really great for her.
6.

expensive	bad	hard	convenient	interesting	important	good

CONVERSATION 3

A: I prefer Cassidy University.

B: Why? The tuition is high. Cassidy is _____ Central.
7.

A: I know. But I want to be a nurse, and Cassidy's nursing program is _____
8.

Central's nursing program.

B: Yes, that's true. But Central is also _____ Cassidy. You need to take two buses
9.

to get to Cassidy. It's only one to Central.

A: To me, getting a good education is _____ an extra bus ride.
10.

CONVERSATION 4

A: I'm having a problem with my grades. My classes this semester are _____
11.
my classes last semester. And my grades aren't very good. My grades this semester are

_____ my grades last semester.
12.

B: You should go to your teachers for help.

A: You're right. How are your classes this semester?

B: I love my history class, but my math class is just numbers. It's boring. My history class is

_____ my math class.
13.

ABOUT YOU Compare yourself to another person.

1. tall

   I am taller than my best friend. OR My brother is taller than me.

2. responsible

_____

3. helpful

_____

4. busy

_____

continued

5. funny

_____

6. friendly

_____

7. polite

_____

8. strong

_____

9. quiet

_____

10.2 Comparisons with Nouns and Verbs

EXAMPLES	EXPLANATION
Part-time students need **more time** to finish college **than** full-time students do.	We can use _more_ before nouns to make a comparison statement. Use _than_ before the second item of comparison.
You spend **less money** at a community college than at a university. My math class has **fewer students** than my biology class.	We can use _less_ or _fewer_ with nouns to make a comparison: • Use _less_ with noncount nouns. • Use _fewer_ with count nouns. _Less_ and _fewer_ are the opposites of _more_.
I prefer the city college because it **costs less**. You **pay** much **more** at a university. I **study harder** on the weekends.	We can use a comparative form after verbs.

ABOUT YOU Find a partner. Tell your partner about yourself, using the words given. Then write sentences about you and your partner.

1. have books

   I have more books than Jalilah.

2. work hard

_____

3. take classes

_____

4. walk

_____

5. have time to relax

_____

6. study

_____

7. have brothers and sisters

_____

8. exercise

_____

EXERCISE 4 Compare Central Community College and Cassidy University, using the information in the chart. Add _than_ where necessary. The numbers in the chart go with the item numbers in the exercise.

		CENTRAL COMMUNITY COLLEGE	CASSIDY UNIVERSITY
1.	students	2,000	10,000
2.	tuition	$4,100 per year	$7,650 per year
3.	night classes	150	50
4.	books in library	8,000	50,000
5.	campuses	5	2
6.	average number of students in a class	16	30
7.	students over the age of 40	215	77
8.	married students	800	200

1. Cassidy has _____ _more students than_ _____ Central.

2. Central costs _____ Cassidy.

3. Central has _____ Cassidy.

4. Central has _____ in its library.

5. Central has _____ Cassidy.

6. Central has _____ in a class.

7. Central has _____ over the age of 40.

8. Cassidy has _____ Central.

EXERCISE 5 Read the article. Complete the sentences with *more, less,* or *fewer.*

College is a big change for many students. In high school, there is _____*less*_____ homework,
1.

but students often spend _____ time in class. In college, students are sometimes only in
2.

classes for three hours a day, while high school students are in classes six or seven hours. In college, students

study _____ outside of class. They often spend as much as four hours in the library.
3.

Another difference is the size of the classes. High-school classes often have _____
4.

students, maybe 20–25 in each class. In college, some classes are small, but most classes have

_____ students than classes in high school. Sometimes there are as many as
5.

200 students! College students have _____ freedom, but they also have
6.

_____ work and _____ stress. They are often
7.   8.

_____ worried than high school students and sleep_____ than
9.   10.

high school students do.

The University of Texas at Austin U.S.

BEFORE YOU READ

1. Do you have a car? Is it a new car or a used car? What kind of car is it?

2. What's your favorite car? Why?

READ

Read the following conversation. Pay special attention to the superlative forms in bold. 📺 10.5

Victor: I want to buy a used car. My coworker, Sam, wants to sell me his 2014 car. He wants $6,000. Is that a good price?

Simon: I don't know. **The best way** to get information about used car prices is in the *Kelley Blue Book®*.

Victor: What's that?

Simon: The *Kelley Blue Book®* shows prices and other information about new and used cars. It can help you. We can look at it online. Then you can make a decision.

(after Simon goes online)

Simon: Look. Here's your coworker's car.

Victor: There are three prices for the same car. Why?

Simon: The price depends on several things: condition of the car, mileage, and extras, such as heated seats and a hands-free phone system. Cars in **the best condition** with **the lowest mileage** and **the most extras** are **the most expensive**. Cars with **the highest mileage** and **the most problems** are **the cheapest**.

Victor: Sam says his car is in good condition.

Simon: **The best way** to know for sure is to take it to a mechanic. You need a good car. Repairs are very expensive.

Victor: But it costs money to go to a mechanic.

Simon: It's better to lose $300 than $6,000. But the price of the car is not the only thing to consider. Also look at fuel economy. There's a website that compares fuel economy. Here it is. Look. Your coworker's car gets only 19 miles per gallon[1]. Look at these other two cars. This car gets 30 miles per gallon. This one gets 35 miles per gallon. Your coworker's car is **the cheapest** to buy, but it isn't **the most economical** to use.

Victor: There's a lot to know about buying a used car!

---

1 An abbreviation for *miles per gallon* is *mpg*.

COMPREHENSION Based on the reading, write T for *true* or F for *false*.

1. _____ The *Kelley Blue Book®* shows prices of new cars and used cars.

2. _____ The price of a used car depends only on the mileage of the car.

3. _____ A mechanic can help you decide about a used car.

WORDS TO KNOW 🎧 10.6

coworker	Victor works with Sam. Sam is Victor's **coworker**.
make a decision	There are many choices. Victor has to **make a decision**.
depend on	The price of the car **depends on** miles, condition, etc.
condition	My car is in good **condition**. I have no problems with it.
mileage	How many miles does the car have? What is its **mileage**?
extras	This model has a lot of **extras**. It has heated seats, a remote starter, and a hands-free phone.
mechanic	A **mechanic** fixes cars.
repair	An old car needs a lot of **repairs**.
consider	You have to **consider** a lot of things before you buy a car.
fuel economy	This car doesn't use a lot of gas. This car has good **fuel economy**.
economical	It is very **economical**. It isn't expensive and it's good quality.

LISTEN

Listen to the sentences about the conversation. Circle *True* or *False*. 🎧 10.7

1. True   (False)   5. True   False

2. True   False   6. True   False

3. True   False   7. True   False

4. True   False   8. True   False

10.3 Superlative Forms of Adjectives

We use the superlative form to compare three or more items. We add *the* before the superlative form.

SIMPLE FORM	SUPERLATIVE FORM	EXAMPLES	EXPLANATION
low tall	**the** low**est** **the** tall**est**	Car A has **the lowest** mileage.	After a one-syllable adjective, we add *-est*.
easy happy	**the** eas**iest** **the** happ**iest**	**The easiest** way to compare prices is with the *Kelley Blue Book®*.	In a two-syllable adjective that ends in *y*, we change the *y* to *i* and add *-est*.
simple quiet friendly	**the** simpl**est** **the most** simple **the** quiet**est** **the most** quiet **the** friendl**iest** **the most** friendly	Car A is **the most quiet**. Car A is **the quietest**.	Some two-syllable adjectives have two forms.
helpful expensive	**the most** helpful **the most** expensive	Car A is **the most expensive** car.	With most other two-syllable adjectives and all three-syllable adjectives, we add *the most* before the adjective.
good bad	**the best** **the worst**	Which car is in **the best** condition? Car C is in **the worst** condition.	Some superlative forms are irregular. We change the word completely.

Notes:

1. We often add a prepositional phrase after a superlative phrase.

    Your car is the oldest car **in the parking lot**.

2. You can use *one of the* before a superlative form. The noun after it is plural.

    The blue car **is one of the** *worst <u>cars</u> in the parking lot.*

3. Omit *the* after a possessive form.

    My best *friend has a new car.*   Not: *My the best friend has a new car.*

10.4 Spelling of the *-est* Form

SIMPLE ADJECTIVE	SUPERLATIVE ADJECTIVE	EXPLANATION
old cheap	old**est** cheap**est**	We add *-est* to short adjectives.
big hot	big**gest** hot**test**	If the adjective ends with consonant + vowel + consonant, we double the final consonant before adding *-est*.
nice late	nice**st** late**st**	If the adjective ends in *e*, we add *-st* only.
busy easy	bus**iest** eas**iest**	If a two-syllable adjective ends in *y*, we change the *y* to an *i* and add *-est*.

EXERCISE 6 Write the superlative form of the adjectives. Use correct spelling with -*est* endings. In some cases, there are two answers.

1. interesting ___the most interesting___
2. early ___the earliest___
3. convenient _____
4. big _____
5. fine _____
6. lazy _____
7. funny _____
8. expensive _____
9. friendly _____
10. quiet _____

11. hot _____
12. good _____
13. kind _____
14. mad _____
15. late _____
16. helpful _____
17. busy _____
18. beautiful _____
19. healthy _____
20. small _____

EXERCISE 7 Victor is comparing three cars. Write superlative sentences about these cars, using the information in the chart and the adjectives from the box.

	CAR A	CAR B	CAR C
Cost	$5,000	$12,000	$10,000
Size	big enough for four passengers	big enough for five passengers	big enough for six passengers
Year	2010	2016	2014
Mileage	28 mpg	25 mpg	20 mpg
Condition	needs work	very good condition	average condition

expensive   big   economical   old   good   cheap ✓   bad   new

1. Car A costs $5,000. It's _____the cheapest_____ .

2. Car B costs $12,000. It's _____ .

3. Car C is _____ inside.

4. Car A is from 2010. It's _____ .

5. Car B is from 2016. It's _____ .

6. Car A gets 28 miles per gallon. In terms of gas, it's _____ .

7. Car B is in very good condition. It's _____ .

8. Car A is in very bad condition. It's _____ .

EXERCISE 8 Fill in the blanks with the superlative form of one of the adjectives from the boxes. Then listen and check your answers. 🎧 10.8

big	hard	close	good	smart	convenient

PART A

1. On the phone:

Shafia: I need your help. I want to buy a car. This is one of _____the biggest_____ decisions

   1.

of my life. What's _____ car?

   2.

Dorota: I can't answer that question. It depends on your needs.

2. At home:

Marta: This is your last year of high school. Let's talk about college for you. I prefer Lake College for

you because it's _____ to home. It's _____

   3.   4.

because you can walk there.

Tina: But Lake College isn't very good. I want to go to _____ college here

   5.

in the United States. I want to be a doctor.

Marta: It takes many years to become a doctor. You have to go to medical school and then practice

in a hospital. You are choosing one of _____ professions.

   6.

Tina: I know, but I really want to be a doctor. I'm _____ student in my

   7.

biology class.

hard	slow	early	economical	fast	late	expensive

PART B

3. At the college:

Halina: Which English class should we take?

Shafia: How about this one? It starts at 8:00 a.m. It's _____ class of the day.

   8.

Halina: I don't like morning classes. How about this one?

Shafia: No, no. Not that one! That teacher is _____ at the school. Also, there's

   9.

a 7 p.m. class. It's _____ class of the day.

   10.

4. At the electronics store:

Halina: I need to buy a new computer. My old computer is slow. I want to buy

_____ one. How about this one?

   11.

continued

Peter: Yes, it's fast. But look at the price! It's _____ computer in the store!

12.

5. *At the post office:*

Halina: What's _____ way to send this package? I need to save money.

13.

Clerk: You can send it by third-class mail. But it's _____ way. It can take a

14.

week.

ABOUT YOU Write about people in your family for each of these items. Use superlatives.

1. tall

My brother Tim is the tallest person in our family.

2. helpful

_____

3. beautiful

_____

4. nice

_____

5. interesting

_____

6. serious

_____

7. funny

_____

8. old

_____

9. young

_____

10. good at sports

_____

10.5 Superlatives with Nouns and Verbs

EXAMPLES	EXPLANATION
Which car uses **the most gas**?	We can use *the most* before nouns to make superlative statements.
I want to spend **the least money** possible. This car has **the fewest extras**.	We can use *the least* and *the fewest* before nouns: • Use *the least* with noncount nouns. • Use *the fewest* with count nouns.
Which car **costs the least**? Who **drives the best** in your family?	We can use a superlative form after verbs.

GRAMMAR IN USE

As with the comparative form, do not use *the* if you use a possessive.

*Eva is **her best** friend.*   NOT: *Eva is her the best friend.*

EXERCISE 9 Victor and Simon are looking at car prices online. Fill in the blanks with the superlative forms of the words from the box. You can use some items more than once. Then listen and check your answers. 🎧 10.9

repairs	cheap	good	economical	extras	expensive

Victor: Look at these ten cars. Should I get _____the cheapest_____ car?

1.

Simon: _____ is sometimes _____.

2.   3.

Victor: How is that possible?

Simon: The cheapest car sometimes needs _____. You should also

4.

consider fuel economy. Look at this car here. It gets 35 miles per gallon.

It's _____.

5.

Victor: But I like this one _____.

6.

Simon: That one gets only 22 miles per gallon.

Victor: But it has _____: heated seats, a hands-free phone system,

7.

a sunroof, and more.

Simon: You want my advice, right? This is my _____ advice.

8.

ABOUT YOU Form a group with three or more classmates. Find the answers to these questions. Report your answers to the class. Write the answers for practice.

1. Who speaks the most languages?

   Ivan speaks the most languages. He speaks four languages.

2. Who's the youngest?

   _____

3. Who has the longest last name?

   _____

4. Who's the newest immigrant?

   _____

5. Who has the largest family?

   _____

6. Who lives the closest to the school?

   _____

7. Who's taking the most classes?

   _____

8. Who talks the most in class?

   _____

EXERCISE 10 Circle the correct comparative or the superlative to complete the sentence.

1. Gas in Europe is (*more expensive than*/*the most expensive*) gas in the United States.

2. There are three kinds of gas. Premium gas is (*the most expensive*/*more expensive*).

3. Can you help me buy a used car? You have (*the most information*/*more information than*) I do.

4. I have many choices. I'm thinking of buying (*the most economical*/*the most economical than*) car.

5. Is a Japanese car (*better than*/*the best*) an American car?

6. This car is (*cheapest*/*cheaper than*) that car.

7. I'm looking at four cars. This car is (*nicer*/*the nicest*) one. And it is in (*the best*/*better*) condition.

   It probably needs (*fewer*/*the fewest*) repairs.

8. My new car is (*the most beautiful*/*more beautiful than*) my old car.

9. A bicycle is (*the best/better*) for the environment than a car.

10. It's hard to find parking in a city. A car is (*the least convenient/less convenient than*) a bicycle.

EXERCISE 11 Read the article about hybrid cars. Fill in the blanks with the comparative or superlative form of the adjectives given. Add *than* or *the* where necessary.

Hybrid cars are becoming _____more popular_____. One reason for this is their fuel
1. popular

economy. Hybrid cars use both gas and electricity. They use less gas than regular cars but more gas than

electric cars. Electric cars are _____ in terms of gas usage, but they are
2. economical

_____ for people who drive a lot, because you have to recharge their batteries.
3. convenient

Of the three, electric cars are _____. Gas cars have
4. quiet

_____ engines. Hybrid cars are in the middle—they are
5. noisy

_____ than gas cars and _____ than electric cars.
6. quiet   7. noisy

Electricity is _____ than gas, so gas-powered cars are
8. cheap

_____ to operate than either hybrid or electric cars. However, gas-powered cars
9. expensive

cost less than hybrid and electric cars—they are _____ of the three types.
10. expensive

FUN WITH GRAMMAR

Play Bingo. Your teacher will give you a blank Bingo card. Write the following categories in the squares. Some squares will have the same categories. Put them in any order.

comparative of an adjective	comparison with a noun	comparison with a verb
superlative of an adjective	superlative with a noun	superlative with a verb

Your teacher will call out a category. Find a square with that category and write a sentence that belongs to the category in the square. To win, you need to get sentences in four squares in a row, either horizontally (→), vertically (↓), or diagonally (↗). The first person to get four correctly written sentences in a row says, "Bingo!" and wins the game.

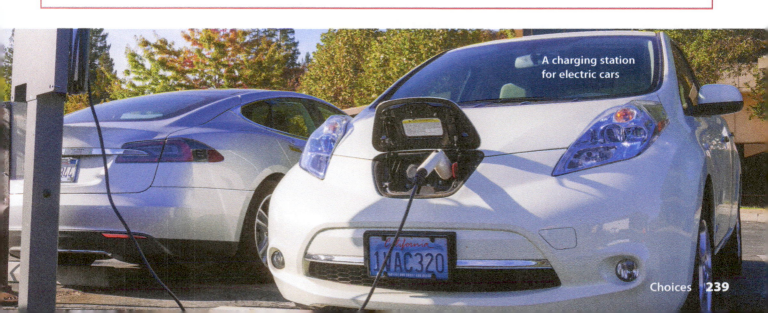

A charging station for electric cars

SUMMARY OF UNIT 10

Comparative Forms of Adjectives

USE	SIMPLE FORM	COMPARATIVE FORM
After a one-syllable adjective, and most other adjectives, we add -er.	old	older
If a one-syllable adjective ends with consonant + vowel + consonant, we double the final consonant before adding -er.	big	bigger
If the adjective ends in e, we add -r only.	nice	nicer
In a two-syllable adjective that ends in y, we change the y to an i and add -er.	busy	busier
Some two-syllable adjectives have two forms.	simple	simpler, more simple
With most other two-syllable adjectives and all three-syllable adjectives, we add more before the adjective.	helpful	more helpful
Some comparative forms are irregular. We change the word completely.	good bad	better worse

Superlative Forms of Adjectives

USE	SIMPLE FORM	SUPERLATIVE FORM
After a one-syllable adjective, and most other adjectives, we add -est.	old	the oldest
If a one-syllable adjective ends with consonant + vowel + consonant, we double the final consonant before adding -est.	big	the biggest
If the adjective ends in e, we add -st only.	nice	the nicest
In a two-syllable adjective that ends in y, we change the y to an i and add -est.	busy	the busiest
Some two-syllable adjectives have two forms.	simple	the simplest the most simple
With most other two-syllable adjectives and all three-syllable adjectives, we add the most before the adjective.	helpful	the most helpful
Some superlative forms are irregular. We change the word completely.	good bad	the best the worst

Comparatives and Superlatives with Nouns and Verbs

USE	COMPARATIVES	SUPERLATIVES
More/The Most	This car uses **more gas than** that car.	Which car uses **the most** gas?
Less/The Least *Fewer/The Fewest*	You spend **less money** at a community college **than** at a university. My math class has **fewer students than** my biology class.	I want to spend **the least money** possible. This car has **the fewest extras**.
After Verbs	I prefer the city college because it **costs less**. You **pay** much **more** at a university. I **study harder** on the weekends.	Which car **costs the least**? Who **drives the best** in your family?

REVIEW

Fill in the blanks with the comparative or superlative form of the words given.

A: I need to buy a car. I'm not sure what to get—a new car or a used car.

B: Well, used cars are _____ than new cars.

1. cheap

A: Yes. But new cars need _____ than used cars. So new cars are

2. repairs

_____ in terms of repairs.

3. expensive

B: Right. And new cars are _____ to maintain than used cars. They also use

4. easy

_____ . Also, they have _____ than used cars.

5. gas　　　　　　　　　　　　　　　　　　　6. extras

A: OK, maybe I'll get a new car. Now, should I get a gas-powered car, a hybrid, or an electric car?

This car, the gas-powered car, is _____ of the three. It's $10,000.

7. beautiful

The hybrid is $12,000. And the electric car is $15,000.

B: So the gas-powered car is _____ to buy. But what about fuel economy?

8. expensive

A: It gets 25 mpg. That's _____ than the hybrid—it gets 45 mpg.

9. bad

But the electric car is _____ of the three—it doesn't use any gas!

10. good

It's _____ in terms of fuel.

11. economical

B: The electric car is also _____ , isn't it?

12. quiet

A: Yes. It makes almost no noise. The gas-powered car is _____ .

13. loud

B: The electric car and the hybrid are also _____ for the environment than

14. good

the gas-powered car.

A: True . . .

B: Which car do you like _____ out of the three?

15. good

A: The electric car. But it's _____ .

16. expensive

B: Let's look online. Maybe there's a _____ used electric car.

17. cheap

A: That's a good idea. Look—here's one. It's only two years old. It's _____ than

18. simple

the new car, but it costs _____ . It's $10,000.

19.

B: I actually think the used car is _____ than the new car!

20. nice

A: Why do you say that?

B: It's a _____ color . . .

21. beautiful

A: Ha ha. OK. I'm going to buy the used car.

FROM GRAMMAR TO WRITING

PART 1 Editing Advice

1. Don't use *-er* and *more* together.

    My new car is ~~more~~ better than my old car.

2. Don't use *-est* and *most* together.

    I want to buy the ~~most~~ cheapest car.

3. Use *than* before the second item of comparison.

    This car is more expensive ^than^ that car.

4. Don't confuse *then* and *than*.

    My English class is easier ~~then~~ than my math class.

5. Use *the* before a superlative form.

    Which is ^the^ best college in this city?

6. Don't use *more* in superlative statements.

    My sister is the ~~more~~ most interesting person in my family.

7. Use correct spelling with comparative and superlative forms.

    My brother is the ~~lazyest~~ laziest student in his class.

    My English class is ~~biger~~ bigger than my art class.

8. Don't use *the* with a possessive form.

    Math is my ~~the~~ worst subject in school.

PART 2 Editing Practice

Some of the shaded words and phrases have mistakes. Find the mistakes and correct them.
If the shaded words are correct, write *C*.

Halina wants to get a new job soon. She needs childcare for Anna during the day.

Halina: I have to find good childcare for Anna. Can you help me find ~~best~~ the best one for my family?
1.

You know more about this than I do.
2.   **3.**

Marta: Let's look for information on the Internet. That's the easyest way to get information.
4.

Here's a list of ten day care centers in the city.

Halina: Play-Time is the more expensive. It's too expensive for me. What about these two,
5.

Kiddy Place and Tiny Tot?

Marta: I think Kiddy Place is more better for you then Tiny Tot. It's very close to your home.
6.   **7.**

So it's more convenient for you. How old is Anna now?
8.

Halina: She's two and a half.

Marta: Kiddy Place only takes children three years old and older . We have to find a place
9.

that takes more younger children.
10.

Halina: What about this one? It's called Baby Bear. It's cheaper Kiddy Place and closer to my
11.   12.

house. So it's more easy to get to.
13.

Marta: That's a good choice. My sister has three boys, and her the youngest son goes to that
14.

childcare. Her son loves it, and she's very happy with it, too.

Halina: You always give me best advice. Thanks for your help.
15.

PART 3 Write

Look at the photos of two English classrooms. Use the photos to compare the classes. Write a paragraph of five or six sentences.

Classroom A is…

PART 4 Learner's Log

1. Write one sentence about each of the topics:
   - community colleges and four-year universities
   - comparing used cars
2. Write any questions you still have about community colleges, four-year universities, and comparing used cars.

CAREERS

Whatever you are, be a good one.
ABRAHAM LINCOLN

A lobsterwoman at work on a lobster boat

1. What jobs can people get in stores?

2. How do people look for jobs?

READ

Read the following conversation. Pay special attention to the past of the verb _be_ in bold. 🎧 11.1

Halina is talking to Dorota on the phone.

Dorota: Hi, Halina. I stopped by your house several hours ago, but you **weren't** home. Only Anna and Peter **were** there.

Halina: I **was** at BigMart today.

Dorota: **Were** there any good sales?

Halina: I **wasn't** there for the sales. I **was** there to apply for a job as a cashier. Positions are available now for the holidays. A lot of people **were** there, but they **weren't** happy. There **was** a long line to apply for jobs.

Dorota: **Were** there interviews today, too?

Halina: No, there **weren't** any interviews. I **was** surprised. The application **was** on a computer at the front of the store. That's where the line **was**.

Dorota: Many companies have job applications online now. I think you can fill out the application at home.

Halina: I know that now.

Dorota: Employers usually look at the applications and then interview people later if the application is a good one. How **were** the questions on the application? **Were** they hard to answer?

Halina: They **weren't** hard at all. They **were** easy. The first questions **were** about my job history and education. There **were** questions about references, too. You **were** one of my references, Dorota. I hope that's okay. They're going to contact you soon.

Dorota: Of course! You can use me as a reference any time. What **were** some other questions?

Halina: There **were** some tricky questions. One **was**: "Your shift starts at 8:00. Where should you be at 8:00? A) in the parking lot, B) in the employees' room, or C) in your department."

Dorota: That is tricky! What **was** your answer?

Halina: It **wasn't** A or B. Time is important here. It **was** C, of course.

DID YOU KNOW?

For jobs at stores and small businesses, there is at least one interview with future employees. For professional jobs, there are often two and sometimes three interviews.

COMPREHENSION Based on the reading, write T for _true_ or F for _false_.

1. _____ A lot of people want a job at BigMart.

2. _____ Halina filled out the application at home.

3. _____ Halina didn't know the answers to some questions.

WORDS TO KNOW 🔊11.2

stop by	I often **stop by** my neighbor's house to visit for a few minutes.
apply for	I want to **apply for** a new job. I have to fill out an application.
position	There are many jobs available right now. What **position** do you want to apply for?
the holidays	Store employers often hire extra cashiers in November and December before **the holidays**.
interview (v.) interview (n.)	People from the store are going to talk to me. They are going to **interview** me. The **interview** is tomorrow.
employer/ employee	My **employer** has a big business. He hires new people each year. These people are his **employees**.
as	They work **as** cashiers. She wants a job **as** a manager.
reference	Dorota is a **reference** for Halina. Employers are going to call her to ask questions about Halina.
contact	The employer is going to **contact** Mr. Suarez. They are going to call him.
tricky	Some of the questions are **tricky**. They're hard to answer.
shift	My work **shift** starts at 8 a.m. and ends at 5 p.m. The evening **shift** is from 5 p.m. to 1 a.m.

LISTEN

Listen to the sentences about the conversation. Circle *True* or *False*. 🔊11.3

1. (True)   False   5. True   False

2. True   False   6. True   False

3. True   False   7. True   False

4. True   False   8. True   False

A cashier helps a customer check out.

11.1 The Past of *Be*—Affirmative Statements

SUBJECT	BE	
I		at the store this morning.
It		crowded.
Dorota		at home.
She	**was**	busy.
Peter		at home.
He		with Anna.
There		a long line at the store.
You		at home.
We		in line.
The questions		easy.
They	**were**	sometimes tricky.
Peter and Anna		in the kitchen.
There		a lot of questions.

EXERCISE 1 Fill in the blanks with *was* or *were*. Use the information from the conversation on page 246.

1. Halina _____ *was* _____ at BigMart today.

2. Peter and Anna _____ home.

3. Halina's job application _____ on a computer.

4. Some of the questions _____ tricky.

5. The application _____ easy to fill out.

6. There _____ questions about Halina's job history

   on the application.

7. People _____ in line for jobs at BigMart today.

8. Dorota _____ at Halina's house today.

9. Positions _____ available today for the holidays.

10. There _____ a question about time.

11.2 The Past of *Be*—Negative Statements

SUBJECT	*BE + NOT*	
I	**was not**	late.
The store	**wasn't**	open until 8:00 a.m.
We	**were not**	happy in line.
The questions	**weren't**	hard.

Notes:

1. We use *not* to form the negative. The contractions are *wasn't* and *weren't*.
2. After *there*, you can use *wasn't/weren't any* or *was/were no*.

　　There **weren't any** interviews today. = There **were no** interviews today.

　　There **wasn't any** time for questions. = There **was no** time for questions.

EXERCISE 2 Fill in the blanks with the affirmative or negative form of *be* in the past. Use the ideas from the conversation on page 246. Use contractions when possible.

1. Halina _____was_____ at the store to apply for a job.

2. She _____wasn't_____ there to shop.

3. The questions on the application _____ hard.

4. The question about time _____ tricky for Halina.

5. Anna _____ with Halina at the store today. Anna _____

   at home with Peter.

6. Some people _____ happy because the lines were long.

7. There _____ questions about references.

8. Peter _____ one of Halina's references. References cannot be people

   in your family.

9. There _____ some positions available for the holidays.

10. There _____ any interviews today.

11. The application _____ a paper application.

12. The questions _____ about Anna.

11.3 Time Expressions in the Past

EXAMPLES	EXPLANATION
I was at BigMart two **days ago**. Halina was there two **hours ago**.	We use *ago* with numbers of minutes, hours, days, weeks, months, or years. It means *before now*.
Dorota wasn't at work **yesterday**.	*Yesterday* is the day before today.
We were at the store **last week**. They weren't with us **last night**.	We use *last* with the words *night*, *week*, *month*, and *year*. It means the night, week, month, or year before the present one.

ABOUT YOU Write statements about yourself. Use the words given. Use the affirmative or negative form of *be* in the past.

1. in a department store two hours ago

   I wasn't in a department store two hours ago.

2. late for work (or class) last week

   _____

3. at a job interview yesterday

   _____

4. an employee at a store last year

   _____

5. an employer in my country

   _____

6. in my country last month

   _____

7. confused at the beginning of this class

   _____

8. with my family last weekend

   _____

9. at a different school a few months ago

   _____

10. in college in my country

    _____

11.4 The Past of *Be*—*Yes/No* Questions

BE	SUBJECT		SHORT ANSWER
Was	I	on time today?	Yes, you were.
Was	Halina	at home this morning?	No, she wasn't.
Were	you	surprised by the questions?	Yes, I was.
Were	Anna and Peter	with you?	No, they weren't.
Was	there	a line at the store?	Yes, there was.
Were	there	any interviews today?	No, there weren't.

Compare statements and *yes/no* questions.

STATEMENT	*YES/NO* QUESTION
You were at BigMart.	**Were you** on time?
There was an application online.	**Was there** a paper application?

EXERCISE 3 Write a *yes/no* question about each statement. Use the words given. Answer with a short answer. Use the ideas from the conversation on page 246.

1. Halina was at BigMart today.

   Was she at a job interview? No, she wasn't.
   at a job interview

2. Many people were at BigMart today.

   _____
   to apply for jobs

3. There were questions on Halina's application.

   _____
   about her family

4. The job application was on a computer.

   _____
   easy to fill out

5. Halina was surprised.

   _____
   by some of the questions

6. Many people were in line.

   _____
   for interviews

7. Halina wasn't home this morning.

   _____
   with Dorota

8. Halina was at BigMart today.

   _____
   for the sales

11.5 The Past of *Be*—*Wh-* Questions

QUESTION WORD(S)	BE	SUBJECT		ANSWER
When		BigMart	open?	Early this morning.
How long	was	Halina	at BigMart?	For about an hour.
Who		your last employer?		Community Bank.
How		your job	at Community Bank?	It was great!
Where	were	the job applications?		Online.
Why		there	a lot of people at BigMart?	Because there were jobs available.

Compare a statement and a *wh-* question.

STATEMENT	WH- QUESTION
The line was long.	How long **was the line**?

EXERCISE 4 Complete the short conversations. Ask a *wh-* question about each statement. The underlined words are the answers.

1. **A:** I wasn't at work today.

   B: _Where were you?_

   A: I was <u>at a job interview</u>.

2. **A:** My employer was surprised.

   B: _____

   A: <u>Because I was an hour late for work</u>.

3. **A:** There were a lot of questions on the application.

   B: _____

   A: <u>They were easy</u>.

4. **A:** They were out of town for the holidays.

   B: _____

   A: <u>In Florida</u>.

5. **A:** I was at BigMart several days ago.

   B: _____

   A: <u>On December 23</u>.

11.6 The Past of *Be*—Subject Questions

QUESTION WORD(S)	BE		ANSWER
What kinds of questions	**were**	on the application?	Questions about education and job history.
How many employees		late today?	Only one.
Which employee	**was**	late?	The new employee.
Who		at BigMart?	Halina was.
What		on the website?	The job application was.

EXERCISE 5 Complete the short conversations with *wh-* questions as subjects. Use *be* in the past.

1. **A:** Some employees were at the office yesterday.

   B: Who _____ *was there* _____?

2. **A:** Many questions were on the application.

   B: What kinds of _____?

3. **A:** Some people were surprised.

   B: Who _____?

4. **A:** Positions were available last month.

   B: How many _____?

5. **A:** Something was wrong with your application.

   B: What _____?

6. **A:** Some of the questions were tricky.

   B: Which _____?

EXERCISE 6 Shafia is interested in Halina's job application. She is asking a lot of questions. Fill in the blanks in their conversation with items from the box. You can use some items more than once. Then listen and check your answers. 🎧 11.4

there were	were	was	what was
were there	weren't	wasn't	were you

Shafia: So, your application for BigMart was on a computer. _____ *Were you* _____ OK with that?
1.

Halina: Sure. I know a lot about computers. The computer was an important part of my job in Poland.

Shafia: _____ your job in Poland?
2.

continued

Halina: I was a department manager in the shoe department of a big store. Part of my job was to write reports and order supplies.

Shafia: _____ a lot of questions about your job history? American employers
                                 3.
are very interested in that.

Halina: Yes, but I have a very short job history. That was my only job for ten years.

Shafia: _____ it difficult to find references? I worry about that. I don't know
                                 4.
many people here.

Halina: You can ask Dorota. She's one of my references. And two references

_____ my college teachers. It _____ difficult to
                    5.   6.
find references. People are happy to be a reference for you.

Shafia: _____ any questions about U.S. work customs? Those are difficult.
                         7.
I don't know much about work customs here.

Halina: _____ some questions. But they _____ difficult
                         8.   9.
to answer. There were three possible answers. It _____ easy to choose
                                                                      10.
the correct answer most of the time.

A playground in the Cherry Creek
Shopping Mall in Denver, Colorado, US

1. Do you want a job in an office? Why or why not?

2. Where do you want to work? Why?

READ

Read the following conversation. Pay special attention to the simple past verbs, affirmative and negative, in bold. 🎧 11.5

Halina: I **had** a job interview today.

Dorota: Great! Was it at BigMart?

Halina: No. I **applied** for a job in an office. I **saw** a job posting online for a sales position a few weeks ago. I **sent** my résumé. And they **called** me yesterday. I **had** the interview this morning.

Dorota: That was fast. How was the interview?

Halina: It **didn't go** well. I **didn't get** there on time. I **didn't find** parking close to the office. I **parked** five blocks away.

Dorota: How late were you?

Halina: Only 15 minutes. I **ran** to the office.

Dorota: That's too late for an interview. Next time, go to the place the day before the interview. You can check travel time and parking then.

Halina: I **didn't like** the interview, Dorota. It **took** an hour. There were two people behind a desk. They **asked** me a lot of questions. And I **felt** nervous.

Dorota: What were some of the questions?

Halina: Well, one question was, "Why do you want this job?" I **told** them the truth. My last job was difficult. I **worked** a lot of hours. I **didn't make** enough money.

Dorota: You shouldn't complain about your past jobs. Instead, say positive things about this new company.

Halina: I **did**. I **told** them some good things. I **said** their company was easy to get to. I **didn't complain** about the parking.

Dorota: But you **didn't say** anything about the company. Find out some information on the company's website. What does the company do? What do you like about it? It's important to know something about the company.

Halina: I **made** a lot of mistakes in this interview. I **said** the wrong things.

Dorota: Don't worry. It was good practice. The next time is going to be easier. You're going to be more prepared.

DID YOU KNOW?
Sometimes companies hire people for 90-day trial periods. If the employee does a good job, he or she can become a regular employee.

COMPREHENSION Based on the reading, write T for *true* or F for *false*.

1. _____ Halina had a good interview.

2. _____ Halina knew a lot about the company.

3. _____ The company is not going to hire Halina.

WORDS TO KNOW 🎧 11.6

job posting	There are some good websites with job **postings**. I'm applying for some I found there.
sales position	Halina wants a **sales position**. She wants to sell things in a store.
résumé	Your **résumé** is very important. It shows your job history and your education history.
go well	Her test **went well**. She got a perfect grade. It **didn't go well** for a few students. They didn't pass.
get (to a place)/there	It's easy to **get to** the office. I can **get there** by bus.
block	Halina parked three **blocks** from the office.
nervous	It's my first time on an airplane. I am **nervous**.
difficult	My last job was **difficult**. It was hard for me.
instead	Don't drive. Take the bus **instead**.
positive	Don't complain. Say something **positive** instead.
make a mistake	One of her answers was wrong. She **made a mistake**.
prepared	It's important to be **prepared** for a job interview. Learn about the company before the interview.

LISTEN

Listen to the sentences about the conversation. Circle *True* or *False*. 🎧 11.7

1. (True)   False   5. True   False

2. True   False   6. True   False

3. True   False   7. True   False

4. True   False   8. True   False

11.7 The Simple Past of Regular Verbs—Affirmative Statements

We add *-ed* to the base form of the verb to form the simple past of regular verbs.

SUBJECT	VERB + -ED	
I	**complained**	about my last job.
Halina	**filled out**	the application.
She	**needed**	a reference.
We	**talked**	about my job history.
You	**wanted**	a better job.
The employers	**asked**	me a lot of questions.

Note:

The simple past of regular verbs is the same for all persons:

*I **worked** hard.*   *She **worked** hard.*   *They **worked** hard.*

Pronunciation Note:

The *-ed* ending has three sounds: /d/, /t/, and /ɪd/. We pronounce the /ɪd/ sound if the verb ends in a
t or *d* sound. The /id/ sound adds an extra syllable to the word. Listen to your teacher pronounce the
following sentences:

/d/	/t/	/ɪd/
Peter **stayed** home.	She **parked** three blocks away.	You **expected** to get the job.
Halina **used** the car.	I **talked** about my last job.	I **decided** to try again.

EXERCISE 7   Fill in the blanks with the simple past of the verb given.

1. Halina _____ parked _____ five blocks from the office building.
   park

2. Halina _____ an application for a sales position.
   fill out

3. The company _____ Halina for an interview.
   call

4. Two people _____ Halina.
   interview

5. The people _____ Halina about her job history.
   ask

6. Halina _____ about her old job.
   complain

7. Dorota and Halina _____ about the interview.
   talk

8. Halina _____ references for this position.
   need

9. She _____ Dorota as a reference.
   use

10. Halina _____ a lot of hours at her old job.
    work

11.8 Spelling of the *-ed* Form

BASE FORM	PAST FORM	EXPLANATION
work	work**ed**	For most verbs, we add *-ed* to the base form.
live	live**d**	If the verb ends in *e*, we add *-d* only.
study	stud**ied**	If the verb ends in consonant + *y*, we change the *y* to *i* and add *-ed*.
stay	stay**ed**	If the verb ends in a vowel + *y*, we do not change the *y* to *i*.
shop	shop**ped**	If a one-syllable word is a consonant + vowel + consonant, we double the final consonant before adding *-ed*.

EXERCISE 8 Fill in the blanks with the simple past of the verb given. Use the spelling rules from Chart 11.8.

1. I _____ liked _____ my job in that company.
   like

2. Halina _____ for the sales position.
   apply

3. Employees at that company _____ business in college.
   study

4. You _____ the car in front of the office building.
   stop

5. Several employees _____ to work on Saturday.
   plan

6. We _____ at the interview for half an hour.
   stay

7. BigMart _____ extra workers for the holidays.
   hire

8. I _____ the application online.
   complete

11.9 The Simple Past of Irregular Verbs—Affirmative Statements

Some verbs do not use -ed to form the past. Here are some common irregular verbs.

BASE FORM	PAST FORM	BASE FORM	PAST FORM
do	**did**	make	**made**
feel	**felt**	run	**ran**
get	**got**	say	**said**
give	**gave**	see	**saw**
go	**went**	send	**sent**
have	**had**	take	**took**
know	**knew**	tell	**told**

*For a list of irregular past forms, see Appendix C.

EXERCISE 9 Fill in the blanks with the simple past of a verb from the box. Use Chart 11.9 to check for irregular forms of the simple past.

have	go	feel	see ✓	get	send	run	tell	give	take

1. Halina _____ saw _____ two people at her interview.

2. Halina _____ a job interview last week.

3. She _____ her résumé to a company.

4. She _____ to the office for an interview.

5. The interview _____ an hour.

6. Halina _____ information about the job online.

7. Halina _____ Dorota about her interview.

8. Dorota _____ Halina some good advice.

9. Halina _____ to the interview.

10. Halina _____ nervous before the interview.

11.10 The Simple Past—Negative Statements

We use *didn't* + the base form for the negative of both regular and irregular verbs in the past.
Didn't is the contraction for *did not*.

SUBJECT	DID + NOT	VERB (BASE FORM)	
I		work	at BigMart last year.
Halina		arrive	on time.
My employer	**did not**	hire	any new employees.
You	**didn't**	apply	for the job.
We		know	all the answers.
They		give	the right answer.

Compare affirmative and negative statements.

AFFIRMATIVE	NEGATIVE
She **worked** on Saturday.	She **didn't work** on Sunday.
They **went** by car.	They **didn't go** by bus.

GRAMMAR IN USE

Make sure to use the base form in negative statements with *didn't*. Don't use *didn't* + past form.

*They **didn't give** the right answer.*

NOT: *They didn't gave the right answer.*

EXERCISE 10 Use the words given to make a negative statement about the sentence.

1. Halina said many things.

   But _she didn't say positive things about the company._
   <u>positive things about the company</u>

2. Halina parked her car.

   But _____
   <u>close to the office</u>

3. Halina had an interview for an office job.

   But _____
   <u>at BigMart</u>

continued

4. Dorota went with Halina to the supermarket.

But _____
to her job interview

5. The new employees worked during the week.

But _____
on the weekend

6. Halina used Dorota as a reference on her application.

But _____
Simon

EXERCISE 11 Complete the short conversations with the affirmative or negative of the verb given. Use the simple past.

1. A: I used you and Dorota as references on a job application.

B: Yes, I know. The company _____ *called* _____ Dorota yesterday. But they
call

_____ *didn't contact* _____ me.
contact

2. A: Halina applied for a job at BigMart last month.

B: Yes, but she _____ the job. She's still looking for a job.
get

3. A: You look nervous. What's wrong?

B: I _____ a big mistake at work yesterday. I'm going to talk
make

to my boss about it today.

4. A: You didn't apply for the sales position. Why?

B: I _____ time. I'm going to apply next week.
have

5. A: I was surprised by the news.

B: We were all surprised. We _____ to hear this news.
expect

6. A: Why did you leave your last job?

B: The company _____ me out of town on business too often.
send

I _____ my family enough.
see

7. A: We are going to hire a new office manager.

B: I know. Mr. Parker _____ me.
tell

8. A: How was your interview?

B: It was good. I _____ the job!
get

ABOUT YOU Use the words given to talk about what you did in the past. Make an affirmative or negative past sentence.

1. work on weekends in my country

   I worked on weekends in my country. OR I didn't work on weekends.

2. apply to come to this school

   _____

3. apply online

   _____

4. go to high school in my country

   _____

5. take a test to enter this class

   _____

6. study English in my country

   _____

7. get a job in my first month in the United States

   _____

8. take classes at a different school last year

   _____

9. see my friends last night

   _____

10. need to buy a book for this class

    _____

11. go to the library last week

    _____

12. go to interesting places last year

    _____

EXERCISE 12 Complete the conversation between Dorota and Halina about another job interview three weeks later. Use the affirmative or negative of the verb given. Use the simple past. Then listen and check your answers. 🎧 11.8

Halina: Thanks for your advice about interviews, Dorota. Unfortunately, I _____*didn't get*_____
                                                                                          1. get

the sales position. But I _____ another interview this morning.
                                  2. have

Dorota: That's great!

Halina: Yes! It was for a position at another company. I _____ any mistakes this time.
                                                                       3. make

Dorota: Good for you. I _____ you would be better prepared this time.
                                  4. know

Halina: Yes, I was. I _____ to the building the day before the interview.
                                5. drive

I _____ a parking lot nearby. I was on time because
       6. find

I _____ where to park.
       7. know

Dorota: I'm sure you _____ more relaxed because you were on time.
                              8. feel

Halina: Yes, and because I _____ prepared. I _____
                                      9. be   **10. learn**

about the company online first. I _____ the interviewers positive things
                                          11. tell

about their company. I _____ about my old job.
                              12. complain

Dorota: Were their questions tricky?

Halina: They _____ about my work experience.
                      13. ask

They _____ about children.
          14. ask

Dorota: Don't worry, Halina. They can't ask any personal questions in a job interview.

Halina: Really? Why not?

Dorota: It's against the law.

Halina: I _____ that. I'm glad, because personal questions can be tricky.
                  15. know

Dorota: I'm glad you _____ such a good interview.
                              16. have

Halina: Me, too. I _____ them an email to thank them as soon as
                          17. send

I _____ home. I _____ them I really
       18. get   **19. tell**

want the job.

Dorota: I hope you get it!

BEFORE YOU READ

1. Do you know some people with interesting jobs? What kinds of jobs do they have?

2. In your opinion, what jobs are going to be important in the future?

READ

Read the following conversation. Pay special attention to the *yes/no* **and** *wh-* **questions in the simple past in bold.** 🎧 11.9

Matt helped Marta's father in the hospital. Simon and Marta became friends with Matt. Now Matt is visiting, and they are talking about Matt's job.

Simon: So, Matt, you have an interesting career. You are a physical therapist, right?

Matt: Well, not exactly. I'm a physical therapist assistant, or PTA. I help the physical therapists, or PTs, at the hospital.

Marta: **Why did you choose** this career, Matt?

Matt: Well, I like physical activity. I like to help people. And **did you know** that a job in health services is a good job for the future?

Simon: Yes. I read something about it last week. It's because the U.S. population is getting older.

Matt: That's right. And older people need more health care.

Marta: **What did you do** to prepare for this job?

Matt: First, I took classes at a community college. I was in a special program for physical therapist assistants.

Simon: **How long did it take**?

Matt: Two years. I got a certificate from the college.

Marta: **Did you have** on-the-job training also?

Matt: Yes. We had training at the hospital for 16 weeks. I worked with several physical therapists and their patients. I was so busy those days. I had another job, too.

Marta: **What did you do**?

Matt: I was a part-time fitness instructor at an athletic club. I thought about a career in fitness.

Simon: **How long did you stay** there?

Matt: Only a year. It was a temporary position.

DID YOU KNOW?
Jobs in service industries like health care and hospitality are increasing, while jobs in farming and the postal service are decreasing.

COMPREHENSION Based on the reading, write T for *true* or F for *false*.

1. _____ Matt is a physical therapist assistant.

2. _____ Matt went to college for two years.

3. _____ Matt wants to be a fitness instructor.

WORDS TO KNOW 🎧 11.10

career	Matt studied for his **career**. He likes his job in health services.
physical therapist (PT)	A **physical therapist** helps patients move and exercise after an accident or injury.
assistant	An **assistant** helps another person with his/her job.
on-the-job training	Companies often give new employees **on-the-job training**. The employees work and learn about the job at the same time.
patient	Marta's father was in the hospital. He was a **patient**.
injure (v.) injury (n.)	She fell and broke her leg. She **injured** her arm, too. The **injuries** are serious.
fitness instructor	A **fitness instructor** works at a health club. He or she helps people with exercise and exercise machines.
athletic club	People go to an **athletic club** to exercise. Other names for an **athletic club** are health club or gym.
temporary	Matt's job was **temporary**. He stayed for only one year.

LISTEN

Listen to the sentences about the conversation. Circle *True* or *False*. 🎧 11.11

1. True (False)   5. True   False

2. True   False   6. True   False

3. True   False   7. True   False

4. True   False   8. True   False

11.11 The Simple Past—*Yes/No* Questions

The question pattern for regular and irregular verbs is the same. We use *did* + the base form.

DID	SUBJECT	VERB (BASE FORM)		SHORT ANSWER
	I	**choose**	a good career?	Yes, you did.
	Matt	**visit**	Simon and Marta?	Yes, he did.
Did	they	**invite**	Matt to their home?	Yes, they did.
	you	**work**	last Saturday?	No, I didn't.
	we	**know**	about your last job?	No, you didn't.

Pronunciation Note:

In fast, informal speech, we sometimes pronounce *did you* as /dɪdʒə/, and *did he* as /dɪdi/.

Listen to your teacher pronounce the following sentences:

Did you choose a career?   *Did he get the job?*

Did you make a good choice?   *Did he have any training?*

Compare the affirmative statements and questions.

STATEMENT	QUESTION
He **worked** on Saturday.	**Did** he **work** on Sunday?
She **got** the job.	**Did** she **get** a good salary?

EXERCISE 13 Write *yes/no* questions with the words given. Answer them with a short answer. Use the ideas in the conversation on page 263.

1. Matt/need/an education for his job

   Did Matt need an education for his job? Yes, he did.

2. Matt/get/a bachelor's degree

   _____

3. Matt's employer/offer/on-the-job training

   _____

4. Simon and Marta/ask/about Matt's family

   _____

5. Simon/hear/about health careers on TV

   _____

6. Matt/help/Simon's father in the hospital

   _____

7. Simon and Marta/ask/Matt a lot of questions

   _____

8. Matt/work/at the athletic club for many years

   _____

11.12 Other Irregular Verbs in the Simple Past

BASE FORM	PAST FORM	BASE FORM	PAST FORM	BASE FORM	PAST FORM
become	**became**	hear	**heard**	read	**read**
choose	**chose**	keep	**kept**	spend	**spent**
come	**came**	leave	**left**	think	**thought**
eat	**ate**	meet	**met**	write	**wrote**

Pronunciation Note:

The past of *read* sounds like the color *red*.

EXERCISE 14 Fill in the blanks about the conversation on page 263 with the affirmative of a simple past verb. Choose verbs from Chart 11.12 and from Chart 11.9 on page 258. Answers may vary.

1. Matt _____ *spent* _____ two years at a community college.

2. Marta and Simon _____ Matt in the hospital.

3. They all _____ friends.

4. Matt _____ to Simon and Marta's house.

5. Matt _____ a career in health services.

6. Matt _____ about a career as a fitness instructor.

7. Simon _____ about careers in health services last week.

8. It _____ Matt two years to get a certificate from college.

9. Then Matt _____ a full-time job at a hospital.

10. The hospital _____ him on-the-job training.

11. During his training, Matt _____ a temporary job at an athletic club.

12. He _____ his job at the athletic club for only a year. Then he _____ it.

13. Matt _____ Simon and Marta all about his training.

14. At the hospital, Matt _____ many people with injuries.

15. After his training, Matt _____ how to help people with injuries.

16. Marta's father _____ better after Matt helped him.

11.13 The Simple Past—*Wh-* Questions

QUESTION WORD(S)	DID	SUBJECT	VERB (BASE FORM)		ANSWER
Why		I	**make**	mistakes?	Because you weren't prepared.
What kind of job		Matt	**find?**		A job as a PTA.
Where	**did**	you	**hear**	about the job?	From a friend.
How		you	**prepare**	for the job?	I took courses at a community college.
How many people		they	**interview**	today?	Five.
How long		they	**work**	at the hospital?	For five years.

Compare affirmative statements and *wh-* questions.

AFFIRMATIVE STATEMENT	WH- QUESTION
Matt **got** his job last year.	How **did** he **get** his job?
Matt **went** to Simon and Marta's house.	Why **did** he **go** to their house?
He **worked** at an athletic club.	When **did** he **work** at an athletic club?

EXERCISE 15 Write a *wh-* question for each answer in the short conversations. The underlined words are the answers. Answers may vary.

1. **A:** _How many jobs did he apply for?_____

   B: He applied for <u>three</u> jobs.

2. **A:** _____

   B: I took classes <u>at Central Community College</u>.

3. **A:** _____

   B: Simon read about <u>careers in health services</u>.

4. **A:** _____

   B: Matt met <u>four</u> physical therapy assistants in that hospital.

5. **A:** _____

   B: They helped <u>people with injuries</u>.

6. **A:** _____

   B: Marta's father stayed in the hospital <u>for three weeks</u>.

7. **A:** _____

   B: Matt got a part-time job <u>as a fitness instructor</u>.

continued

8. A: _____

   B: He kept that job <u>for a year</u>.

9. A: _____

   B: <u>Because it was a temporary position</u>.

10. A: _____

   B: Simon and Marta met Matt <u>at the hospital</u>.

11.14 The Simple Past—Subject Questions

In a subject question, we use the past form of the verb.

QUESTION WORD(S)	VERB+ -ED OR IRREGULAR FORM		ANSWER
What	**happened**	to the patient?	She went home.
Who	**helped**	the new patient?	Matt did.
How many students	**got**	a certificate in PT?	Thirty students did.
Which newspaper	**had**	information about health careers?	Last week's newspaper did.

EXERCISE 16 Write questions with the words given. Use the question word as the subject.

1. Who/take/those people to the hospital

   Who took those people to the hospital?

2. What/happen/at work yesterday

   _____

3. Who/tell/you about that job

   _____

4. How many people/apply/for the job as a fitness instructor

   _____

5. Which patient/spend/two weeks at the hospital

   _____

6. Which student/choose/a job in health services

   _____

7. Who/write/about jobs of the future

_____

8. What kinds of patients/need/help with their injuries

_____

9. How many physical therapists/go/to community colleges

_____

10. What/came/in the mail yesterday

_____

11.15 More Irregular Verbs in the Simple Past

BASE FORM	PAST FORM	BASE FORM	PAST FORM
break	**broke**	hurt	**hurt**
buy	**bought**	lose	**lost**
cost	**cost**	pay	**paid**
drive	**drove**	put	**put**
fall	**fell**	sell	**sold**
find	**found**	understand	**understood**

Note:
For some verbs, the base form and the past form are the same. For example, *hurt* and *cost*.

EXERCISE 17 Write a question and an answer for each short conversation with the words given.

1. **A:** _Where did the patient hurt her arm?_
   Where/the patient/hurt her arm

   B: _She hurt it at the gym._
   at the gym

2. **A:** _____
   How/she/hurt her arm

   B: _____
   fall and break

3. **A:** _____
   Which arm/she/break

   B: _____
   her right arm

4. **A:** _____
   Who/drive/her to the hospital

   B: _____
   her husband

continued

5. A: _____
How long/the woman/stay at the hospital

B: _____
only a few hours

6. A: _____
What kind of help/she/get later

B: _____
physical therapy

7. A: _____
Who/help/her in her house

B: _____
a home health care assistant

8. A: _____
How much/this service/cost

B: _____
$20 an hour

9. A: _____
Where/she/find this service

B: _____
online

10. A: _____
How much time/she/miss at work

B: _____
a week

ABOUT YOU Use the words given to write questions . Think about your answers. Then ask and answer the questions with your partner.

1. _____?
what/you/study/last year

2. _____?
where/you/live/three years ago

3. _____?
who/help you/learn English

4. _____?
you/work/yesterday

5. _____?
how many/classes/you/take/last semester

6. _____?
how/you/get to school/today

EXERCISE 18 Halina wrote an email to Lisa about her different interviews. Complete the email using the words given. Use contractions when possible.

Hi Lisa,

I just _____ *got* _____ your message. I'm so sorry that I _____
　　　　　　　1. get　　　　　　　　　　　　　　　　　　　　　　　　**2.** not/call

you back. I am so busy! You _____ about my job search.
　　　　　　　　　　　　　　　　3. ask

I _____ you the details. I _____ an interview three
　　4. want/tell　　　　　　　　　　**5.** have

weeks ago for an office job. This morning, I _____ an interview at another
　　　　　　　　　　　　　　　　　　　　　　　　6. have

company. The first interview _____ well. The second interview
　　　　　　　　　　　　　　7. not/go

_____ much better. I _____ confident, and I
　　8. be　　　　　　　　　　**9.** feel

_____ nervous.
　　10. not/be

When _____ your job search? _____ your résumé
　　　11. you/start　　　　　　　　　　　**12.** you/send

anywhere yet? Where _____ ? What about references?
　　　　　　　　　　　13. you/apply

_____ for references? How many references _____ ?
　14. the company/ask　　　　　　　　　　　　　　　　**15.** you/need/give

_____ you for an interview yet? Which employers _____
　16. the employer/call　　　　　　　　　　　　　　　　　**17.** contact

you? Dorota _____ me some great advice: Don't wait to send in your application.
　　　　　　18. give

Halina

FUN WITH GRAMMAR

Play a chain activity. Write the irregular verbs from charts 11.9, 11.12, and 11.15 on slips of paper. (You do not have to write all the verbs.) Also write *be* on a slip of paper. Put all the slips in a bag. Student A begins by drawing a slip of paper. Ask any classmate (Student B) a question about the past, using the past form of the verb on the paper:

　A: *Nina, where did you go last year?*

Student B answers the question and then draws a new slip of paper and asks another student (Student C) a question. Continue around the circle. Answer the question and then ask a new question. Each correct question and each correct answer is worth 1 point. You get an extra point if you use a time expression.

　A: *Nina, where did you go last year?*

　B: *I went to Florida. Tim, did you make dinner last night?*

　C: *No. My sister made dinner. Martin, . . .*

SUMMARY OF UNIT 11

The Past of *Be*

	EXAMPLES	ANSWER
Affirmative Statement	I **was** at the store this morning. It **was** crowded. She **was** busy. We **were** at home. There **was** a long line. There **were** a lot of questions.	
Negative Statement	She **was not** late. They **were not** happy. She **wasn't** late. They **weren't** happy.	
Yes/No **Question**	**Was** she at home? **Were** they surprised? **Was** there a line at the store? **Were** there any interviews today?	Yes, she was. No, they weren't. Yes, there was. No, there weren't.
Wh- **Question**	When **was** BigMart open? How **was** your job? Where **were** the applications?	This morning. It was great! Online.
Subject Question	How many employees **were** late? Who **was** at BigMart?	Only one. Halina was.

The Simple Past

	EXAMPLES	ANSWER
Affirmative Statement	I **filled out** the application. She **had** a good job. We **talked** about my job. They **gave** me good advice.	
Negative Statement	Halina **didn't arrive** on time. You **didn't apply** for the job.	
Yes/No **Question**	**Did** I **choose** a good career? **Did** they **visit** Matt?	Yes, you did. No, they didn't.
Wh- **Question**	Why **did** I **make** mistakes? How long **did** they **work** there? How **did** you **prepare** for the job?	Because you weren't prepared. For five years. I studied at a community college.
Subject Question	What **happened** to the patient? Which newspaper **had** the information?	She went home. Last week's newspaper did.

Time Expressions in the Past

I was at BigMart two **days ago**.

Dorota wasn't at work **yesterday**.

We were at the store **last week**.

REVIEW

Fill in the blanks with the past of *be* or the simple past of the verbs given.

A: Hi, Jake. How _____ your job interview?
                                          1. be

B: Well, I _____ two interviews last week. The first interview
              2. have

_____ very well.
  3. not/go

A: Oh really? _____ ?
            4. what/happen

B: First, I _____ late.
          5. arrive

A: _____ late?
     6. why/you/be

B: I _____ stuck in traffic. And then I _____ really far away.
    7. get   8. park

A: _____ so far away?
    9. why/you/park

B: Because I _____ parking near the office. They
          10. not/find

_____ a parking lot nearby, but I _____ it.
  11. have   12. not/see

A: That's too bad. It's not good to be late for an interview.

B: I know. It _____ me nervous.
          13. make

A: _____ you?
  14. how many people/interview

B: There _____ three people. They _____
        15. be   16. ask

a lot of questions. They _____ down all my answers.
              17. write

But I _____ it wasn't a very good interview.
    18. know

A: Well, it _____ good practice. What about the second interview?
      19. be

_____ on time?
  20. you/be

B: Yes, I _____ . That _____ much better.
      21. be   22. go

I _____ stuck in traffic. And I _____ parking close.
   23. not/get   24. find

A: Good. What kinds of questions _____ ?
         25. the interviewers/ask

B: They _____ about my job history. They also _____
    26. ask   27. tell

me a little bit more about the job. I _____ even more interested in the job.
        28. become

A: Great! I hope you get the job. _____ them a thank-you email?
        29. you/send

B: Yes, I _____ . And guess what? They _____ me
    30. do   31. call

this morning. I _____ the job!
    32. get

A: Congratulations!

FROM GRAMMAR TO WRITING

PART 1 Editing Advice

1. Don't use the simple past after *to* (the infinitive).

   He wanted to ~~spent~~ *spend* some time at the athletic club.

2. Use the base form after *did* and *didn't*.

   Where did she ~~went~~ *go* after work?

   They didn't ~~found~~ *find* good jobs.

3. Use the correct verb form and word order in questions.

   Where ~~your brother went~~ *did your brother go* to college?

4. Don't use *did* in subject questions about the past. Use the past form.

   What ~~did happen~~ *happened* at your interview today?

5. Use the correct spelling of the *-ed* forms.

   She ~~applyed~~ *applied* for a job as a fitness instructor.

6. Use the correct verb form. Remember, some verbs are irregular.

   I ~~hurted~~ *hurt* my leg. He ~~breaked~~ *broke* his arm.

PART 2 Editing Practice

Some of the shaded words and phrases have mistakes. Find the mistakes and correct them.
If the shaded words are correct, write C.

Matt is talking to a new patient, Teresa, about her injury.

Matt: Teresa, did your doctor ~~gave~~ *give* you a note for me?
1.

Teresa: Yes. He gave me this note. *C*
2.

Matt: Thanks. What happen? How you hurt your shoulder?
3.   4.

Teresa: I falled during my walk. I broke my shoulder. There was something on the sidewalk,
5.   6.

and I didn't saw it.
7.

Matt: That's terrible! Did you called 911?
8.

Teresa: I wanted to called 911, but I didn't have my cell phone. But someone help me.
9.   10.   11.

Matt: Who did help you?
12.

Teresa: A nice woman stoped her car to help me.
13.

Matt: What the woman did? Did she took you to the hospital?
14.   15.

Teresa: No. She call 911 and waited with me. Then the ambulance come and taked me to the
16.   17.   18.   19.

hospital. I feeled very nervous. The woman told me not to worry.
20.   21.

Matt: Did the woman goed with you?
22.

Teresa: No, she didn't. I wanted to thanked her later, but she didn't tell me her name.
23.   24.

PART 3 Write

Rewrite the following conversation between Matt and Teresa. Change *now* to *last year*. Make the necessary changes to the verbs.

Matt: Do you have a job now, Teresa?

Teresa: Yes, I do. I work in the employment services department at Adams Trucking Company.

Matt: What do you do there?

Teresa: I keep information about employees. I help employees with their problems. And I write

reports. I use the computer a lot.

Matt: How do you get a job like that?

Teresa: Well, it isn't difficult. It takes only two years to get a certificate in human resources.

Matt: Do you like your job?

Teresa: No, I don't. I don't want to work for a company anymore.

Matt: Did you have a job last year, Teresa?

PART 4 Learner's Log

1. Write one sentence about each topic:
   - ways to apply for a job
   - job interviews
   - training and education for physical therapist assistants

2. Write any questions you still have about the topics above.

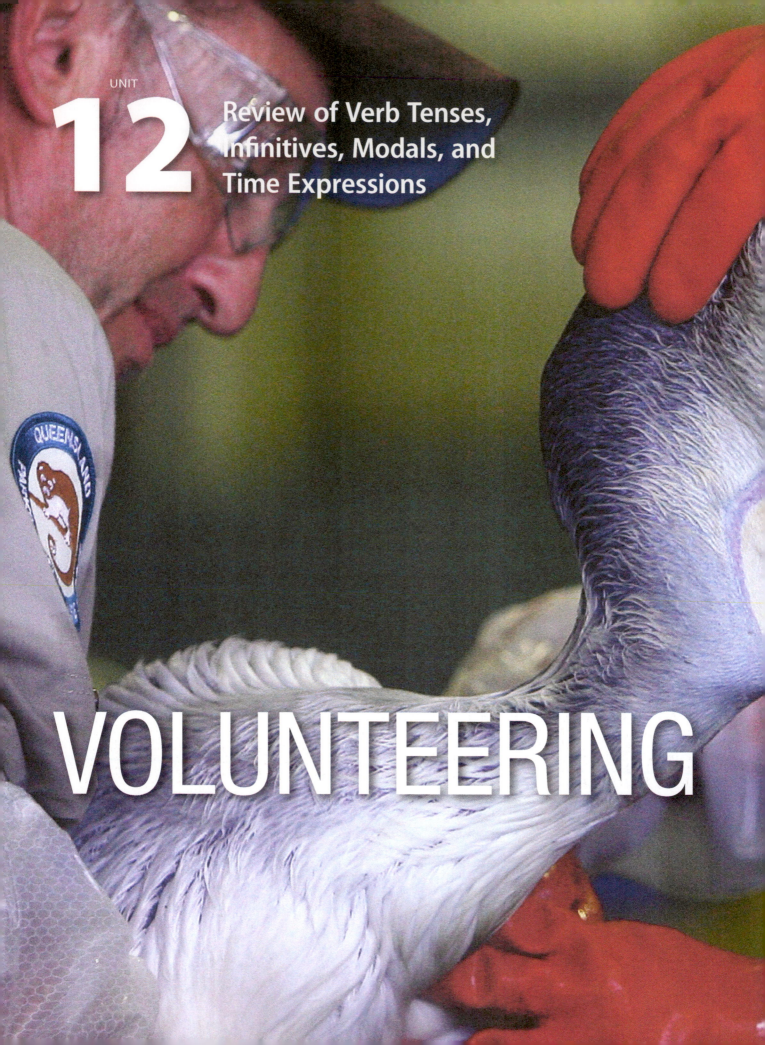

VOLUNTEERING

Our prime purpose in this life is to help others. And if you can't help them, at least don't hurt them.

THE DALAI LAMA

Volunteers clean a pelican after an oil spill, Brisbane, Australia.

BEFORE YOU READ

1. What help did you need as a newcomer? Who helped you? How?

2. What do you do to help other newcomers?

READ

Read the following conversation. Pay special attention to the verb tenses and modals, affirmative and negative, in bold. 🎧 12.1

Simon, Dorota, Victor, Lisa, and Halina **are** in a coffee shop.

Victor: Simon, thanks for your help on moving day. With your help, it **didn't take** us a long time. You **gave** me some good advice about used cars, too. I **don't have** a car yet. I'm still **looking**, but I **hope to buy** one soon.

Simon: You're welcome. How's your new apartment? **Are** you adjusted yet?

Lisa: We're very comfortable there. It's big and sunny. Maya **likes** the location because she **didn't have to change** schools. She **doesn't have to walk** far to school. We're all **enjoying** life in the United States now. We **don't feel** like newcomers anymore. Thanks for all your help. We're **not going to forget** it.

Simon: No problem. Any time.

Halina: And Dorota, I **want to thank** you. With your help, I **learned** about many important places in this city. Also, you **helped** me with my Social Security card. And your advice about job interviews **was** very helpful. I really **like** my new job. I'm **going to stay** with this company for a while.

Dorota: I **was** happy to help, Halina.

Halina: My life **is** easier now. I **don't feel** confused. I **feel** comfortable now. Maybe I **can help** you in your work with newcomers. I **can be** a volunteer. I'm **going to have** some free time on weekends from now on.

Victor: You **can count on** my help, too. I **want to volunteer**. Both you and Dorota **were** so helpful when we **arrived**.

Simon: That's good. Marta and I **are going to have** a meeting for volunteers next week. We **have to meet** in the evening. Many people **work** during the day. You **should come**. You **can learn** about other volunteer opportunities, too. There **are** many ways to help others.

> **DID YOU KNOW?**
> In 2017, 77.3 million Americans volunteered a total of nearly 7 billion hours.

COMPREHENSION Based on the reading, write T for *true* or F for *false*.

1. _____ Simon helped Victor and Lisa move.

2. _____ Dorota helped Halina move.

3. _____ Victor and Lisa aren't going to volunteer.

yet	Victor has a driver's license, but he doesn't have a car **yet**. He's going to buy a car soon.
comfortable	Halina feels **comfortable** here now. Her life here is easier for her.
newcomer	My friend just arrived in the United States. He is a **newcomer**.
no problem	**No problem** is another way of saying *you're welcome*.
really	Halina **really** likes her new job. She likes it very much.
volunteer (n.) volunteer (v.)	Simon and Dorota are **volunteers**. They do not get paid for their work. They **volunteer** with newcomers.
from now on	Halina has an easier life now. **From now on**, she is going to have more free time.
count on	You always help us. We can always **count on** you.
opportunity	There are many volunteer **opportunities**. You have a choice of many things.

LISTEN

Listen to the sentences about the conversation. Circle *True* or *False*. 🎧 12.3

1. True   (False)   5. True   False

2. True   False   6. True   False

3. True   False   7. True   False

4. True   False   8. True   False

12.1 Review of Verb Tenses—Affirmative and Negative

The Simple Present

	EXAMPLES	EXPLANATION
Be	a. Dorota **is** forty years old. b. Halina **isn't** a manager now. c. Dorota **is** from Poland. d. The five friends **are** in a coffee shop. e. It **isn't** cold today. f. It **is** 3:00 p.m. g. Halina and Victor **are** happy. Their lives **aren't** difficult now. h. It **is** hard to start life in a new country.	a. Age b. Occupation/work c. Place of origin d. Location e. Weather f. Time g. Description h. After *it* in impersonal expressions
There + Be	a. There **is** a need for volunteers. b. There **aren't** many people in the coffee shop.	a. Use *there is* to introduce a singular subject. b. Use *there are* to introduce a plural subject.
Other Verbs	a. Halina **works** in an office. b. Dorota **doesn't work** every day.	a. Facts b. Habits, customs, regular activity

continued

The Present Continuous

EXAMPLES	EXPLANATION
Halina **is thanking** Dorota. They **are meeting** in a coffee shop.	Actions at the present moment
Halina **isn't looking** for a job at this time. She **is thinking** about volunteer activities.	Actions at a present time period

The Future

	EXAMPLES	EXPLANATION
Be	They **are going to be** volunteers.	Future plans and predictions
There + Be	There **isn't going to be** a volunteer meeting tomorrow.	
Other Verbs	Halina **is going to help** newcomers. Halina **is going to have** more free time soon.	

The Simple Past

	EXAMPLES	EXPLANATION
Be	Halina **was** a department manager in Poland.	Actions completed in the past
There + Be	There **weren't** many people in the coffee shop yesterday.	
Regular Verbs	Victor and Lisa **moved** to a new apartment two weeks ago. They **didn't move** far away.	
Irregular Verbs	Halina **got** a job in an office. She **didn't get** a job in a store.	

EXERCISE 1 Complete each sentence about the conversation on page 278 with the correct form of the verb given. Use affirmative verbs.

1. Halina _____'s talking_____ to Dorota now.

talk

2. Simon, Dorota, Halina, Lisa, and Victor _____ together in a coffee shop.

sit

3. Victor's family _____ a bigger apartment.

find

4. Lisa _____ the new apartment.

like

5. Victor and Halina _____ life in America now.

enjoy

6. Simon _____ Victor good advice about used cars.

give

7. Victor _____ a used car soon.

buy

8. Halina and Victor _____ newcomers several months ago.

be

9. Halina _____ a Social Security card.

have

10. Dorota _____ Halina with her Social Security card.

help

11. Halina _____ Dorota with other newcomers from now on.

help

12. There _____ a volunteer meeting at Marta and Simon's house soon.

be

EXERCISE 2 Read each sentence. Write sentences, using the negative form of the verb and the words given. Use contractions when possible.

1. The five friends are having coffee now.

They aren't having lunch.

lunch

2. Victor and Halina are talking about their lives now.

_____

their problems

3. Victor wanted to move.

_____

stay in his old apartment

4. His old apartment was too small.

_____

big enough for his family

5. Lisa feels comfortable in the United States now.

_____

strange anymore

6. Simon gave Victor advice about cars.

_____

about jobs

7. Halina and Victor had a lot to do at first.

_____

much free time then

8. Victor and Lisa need a used car.

_____

a new car

9. Halina's going to work in the same company for a while.

_____

look for another job soon

10. Victor and Lisa are going to attend a meeting next week.

_____

move into a new apartment

12.2 Review of Infinitives

EXAMPLES	EXPLANATION
Halina started **to work** for a new company. She expects **to stay** there for a while. I'm happy **to help** you. It's fun **to be** a volunteer. It takes time **to learn** about a new country. Halina wants **to help** other people. Victor is trying **to buy** a used car.	The infinitive is *to* + the base form of the verb. The tense is always in the verb before the infinitive. Infinitives can go after: • verbs • adjectives • impersonal expressions with *it*

EXERCISE 3 Complete each sentence with an infinitive phrase. Use the ideas from the conversation on page 278 and your own ideas. Answers will vary.

1. It's good *to help other people.*

2. Victor wants _____

3. Halina needed _____

4. Halina is planning _____

5. It's not easy _____

6. Simon and Marta like _____

7. Simon and Marta are planning _____

8. Dorota was happy _____

9. I want _____

10. Most immigrants expect _____

11. Students often try _____

12. It's fun _____

Company employees give back to the community on Employee Volunteer Day, Bronx, New York U.S.

12.3 Review of Modal Verbs—Affirmative and Negative

	EXAMPLES	EXPLANATION
Can	a. Victor **can speak** Spanish. Dorota **can't speak** Spanish. b. Simon has a license. He **can drive**. Ed **can't drive**. c. Victor and Halina **can volunteer** now. Peter is too busy. He **can't volunteer** now.	a. Ability/No ability b. Permission/No permission c. Possibility/Impossibility
Should	a. We **should be** on time. b. You **shouldn't arrive** late to an interview.	a. Advice or suggestion to do something b. Advice not to do something
Must	a. Workers **must have** a Social Security card. b. You **must not drive** without a driver's license.	a. Strong obligation because of a rule or law b. Strong obligation not to do something because of a rule or law
Have To	a. Victor's daughter **has to go** to school. b. She **doesn't have to buy** her lunch at school. She can bring a lunch from home.	a. Necessity (by law, custom, rule, or personal obligation) b. Not necessary

ABOUT YOU Fill in the blanks. Write sentences that are true about you. Use the affirmative or negative of the modals given. Use contractions when possible.

1. I _____ *have to* _____ work tonight.

             have to

2. I _____ *can't* _____ read the newspaper without a dictionary.

             can

3. I _____ speak English every day.

             should

4. I _____ go to a meeting today.

             have to

5. I _____ speak English like an American.

             can

6. I _____ listen to English-language radio to improve my listening skills.

             should

7. I _____ drive.

             can

8. I _____ work.

             have to

EXERCISE 4 Simon, Dorota, Victor, Lisa, and Halina continue their conversation. Fill in the blanks with the correct form of the verbs given. Use the different tenses from Charts 12.1-12.3, infinitives, and modals. Use contractions when possible. Then listen and check your answers. 🎧 12.4

PART 1

Dorota: We _____ *need* _____ more volunteers this year. There's a lot to do. Sometimes

             1. need

   we _____ enough volunteers to help all the newcomers.

             2. not/get

Victor: What else do volunteers do?

continued

Simon: Well, many newcomers _____ how to drive in the United States.
3. not/know

They _____ sure about the rules on American roads.
4. not/be

Volunteers _____ people with their driving practice. Tomorrow,
5. can/help

Dorota and I _____ with a group of newcomers. One young
6. meet

man _____ to work every day. I _____
7. have to/drive   8. practice

with him yesterday. But I _____ busy next week.
9. be

Lisa: I _____ him. But I _____ a car yet.
10. want/help   11. not/have

Simon: That's OK. This newcomer _____ a good used car last month.
12. buy

He _____ someone else's car.
13. not/need/use

PART 2

Dorota: Next Thanksgiving, we _____ a holiday dinner for newcomers.
14. prepare

We _____ volunteers now. It's difficult _____
15. look for   16. find

people right before a holiday. Everyone is so busy then.

Halina: Peter and I _____ you. I _____ .
17. want/help   18. can/cook

Dorota: Thanks, Halina. I _____ my friend Sue about you. Sue and her
19. tell

husband, Rick, _____ holiday meals every year in a school in
20. prepare

her neighborhood. Their holiday dinners are very popular with newcomers. Last year,

fifty newcomers _____ . There _____
21. come   22. not/be

enough volunteers. They _____ enough food. So I
23. not/have

_____ them. I _____ the extra food from
24. volunteer/help   25. get

the deli. Everyone _____ a wonderful time.
26. have

12.4 Review of Time Expressions

FREQUENCY		PRESENT	PAST	FUTURE
always	hardly ever	today	yesterday	tomorrow
usually	rarely	at the moment	two weeks ago	soon
often	never	right now	last week	in two weeks
sometimes	every week	this week		

EXERCISE 5 Circle the time expressions in the following sentences. Then fill in the blanks with an affirmative verb from the box. Use the correct tense. Use contractions when possible. You can use some items more than once. Answers may vary.

help	move	tell	try to get	give	have
be	enjoy	teach	come	find	invite

1. At the coffee shop (yesterday,) Dorota _____*told*_____ Halina more about her friend Sue.

2. Sue often _____ newcomers.

3. These newcomers hardly ever _____ all the items necessary for their new life in the United States.

4. Sue usually _____ them clothes and things for their house.

5. And she always _____ them about American life.

6. Last year, five new families from Africa _____ into Sue's neighborhood.

7. In just a month, Sue _____ them enough items for a comfortable home.

8. She _____ jobs for them later, too.

9. These families _____ their new life in the United States now.

10. Sue _____ all the newcomers to her family's famous holiday dinner later this year.

11. Last year, a city news reporter _____ to Sue's dinner.

12. His report _____ on TV a week later.

13. A lot of people _____ her now.

14. Sue _____ them to work with newcomers now.

A Syrian community volunteer shows a newly arrived family how to adjust the heat in their apartment in Bloomfield Hills, Michigan, U.S.

EXERCISE 6 Look at the photo. Write a paragraph about the photo. Use all the tenses you learned in this book: simple present, present continuous, future (*be going to*), simple past, and modal verbs. Use affirmative and negative sentences.

Newcomers are going to have an American Thanksgiving dinner. Volunteers cooked a Thanksgiving meal.

Volunteers serve Thanksgiving dinner.

BEFORE YOU READ

1. What volunteer opportunities do you know about?

2. Why do people volunteer?

READ

Read the following conversation. Pay special attention to the question forms in bold. 🎧 12.5

There's a volunteer meeting at Marta and Simon's house.

Marta: Good evening, everyone. These are my friends Rhonda, Amir, Elsa, and Haru. They're volunteers. They're going to tell you about volunteer work. Rhonda, **are you** ready? **What's your volunteer group doing** this month?

Rhonda: I work for an airline, and I'm a member of a volunteer organization. We have a program to help poor children in other countries. This month, we're planning a trip to South America. We're going to bring wheelchairs, eyeglasses, and medical supplies to people in small villages. We're going to fly there with the supplies.

Marta: **Who gives** you these supplies?

Rhonda: Doctors and hospitals donate medical supplies. Volunteers save their old eyeglasses for us. Charities help us, too. And airlines pay for the flights.

Marta: **Do you bring** anything else to these people?

Rhonda: Yes. We bring clothing for children and adults, too. And we also have special projects each year.

Marta: **What did your group do** last year, Rhonda? **Was it** another project in South America?

Rhonda: Yes, it was. We brought a sick little boy from Colombia here to the United States. He needed an operation. They didn't have medical care in his village. Two months later, I brought a healthy boy back to his parents. They were so happy. And I was, too.

Marta: **Do volunteers have to work** full time?

Rhonda: No. They give as many hours as they can.

Marta: **How can we help**?

Rhonda: You can collect supplies for us.

Marta: **What are you going to do** next?

Rhonda: Right now, we're collecting clothing and toys for a holiday party for Colombian children.

Marta: Rhonda can answer your questions now. **Does anyone have** a question for Rhonda?

> **DID YOU KNOW?**
> Most volunteers in the United States are between the ages of 35 and 44. But volunteers over age 65 give the most hours of their time.

COMPREHENSION Based on the reading, write T for *true* or F for *false*.

1. _____ The airline donates medical supplies.

2. _____ The volunteer organization helps children and adults.

3. _____ The organization is collecting clothing right now.

airline	What **airline** flies to Colombia?
bring	What did you **bring** to the volunteer meeting?
wheelchair	Some people can't walk. They need a **wheelchair**.
village	Only 500 people live in his **village**.
fly	Rhonda is going to **fly** from New York to Colombia next week.
donate	The wealthy woman is generous. She **donates** a lot of money to charities.
flight	Her **flight** leaves at 5 p.m.
project	Rhonda's **project** is to collect clothing for poor people.
operation	A little boy was very sick. He needed an **operation** at a hospital.
collect	Rhonda **collects** donations to give to poor people.
toy	Children like to play with **toys** such as dolls, cars, and board games.

LISTEN

Listen to the sentences about the conversation. Circle *True* or *False*. 12.7

1. True	(False)		**4.** True	False		**7.** True	False
2. True	False		**5.** True	False		**8.** True	False
3. True	False		**6.** True	False		**9.** True	False

12.5 Review of *Yes/No* Questions

The Simple Present

	YES/NO QUESTIONS	SHORT ANSWERS
Be	**Is** Rhonda a volunteer? **Are** the volunteers from South America?	Yes, she is. No, they aren't.
Be + There	**Is** there a meeting at Marta and Simon's house? **Are** there any Colombians at the meeting?	Yes, there is. No, there aren't.
Other Verbs	**Does** Dorota **work** for an airline? **Do** charities **help** with supplies?	No, she doesn't. Yes, they do.

The Present Continuous

YES/NO QUESTIONS	SHORT ANSWERS
Is Rhonda **talking** about her career?	No, she isn't.
Are you **listening** to Rhonda?	Yes, I am.
Are the volunteers **asking** for money?	No, they aren't.
Are we **learning** about volunteer activities?	Yes, we are.

The Future

YES/NO QUESTIONS	SHORT ANSWERS
Is Rhonda **going to need** help?	Yes, she is.
Is there **going to be** a party for the volunteers?	No, there isn't.
Are new volunteers **going to help**?	Yes, they are.

The Simple Past

	YES/NO QUESTIONS	SHORT ANSWERS
Be	**Were** you a volunteer last year? **Was** Rhonda in South America last week? **Were** the volunteers helpful last year?	No, I wasn't. No, she wasn't. Yes, they were.
Be + There	**Was** there a problem with the volunteers? **Were** there enough volunteers to help?	No, there wasn't. Yes, there were.
Regular and Irregular Verbs	**Did** Rhonda **help** a sick boy? **Did** volunteers **go** to Mexico?	Yes, she did. No, they didn't.

Modal Verbs and *Have To*

	YES/NO QUESTIONS	SHORT ANSWERS
Should	**Should** we **volunteer** for that project?	Yes, we should.
Can	**Can** I **volunteer**?	Yes, you can.
Have To	**Did** Rhonda **have to volunteer** for this project? **Do** volunteers **have to come** to the meeting?	No, she didn't. Yes, they do.

GRAMMAR IN USE

Questions with *must* are not common and sound very formal. We use *have to* for questions.

> *Do I have to go to school today?*
>
> NOT: *Must I go to school today?*

EXERCISE 7 Write a *yes/no* question about the conversation on page 287. Use the words given. Use the same tense as in the statement. Answer your question with a short answer.

1. Rhonda has a job.

   Does she have a job with an airline? Yes, she does.
   with an airline

2. Rhonda is talking.

   _____
   about her job with the airline

3. Rhonda brings medical supplies to poor children.

   _____
   wheelchairs

continued

4. A little boy needed medical care last year.

_____

an operation

5. The sick boy was from a village.

_____

from the United States

6. Rhonda brought the boy to the United States.

_____

back to his parents

7. The volunteers are going to have a party.

_____

in the United States

8. There are many people at Marta and Simon's house today.

_____

any volunteers

9. People should save their medical supplies for Rhonda's projects.

_____

toys, too

10. People can ask Rhonda questions.

_____

about other projects

12.6 Review of *Wh-* Questions

The Simple Present

	WH- QUESTIONS	ANSWERS
Be	Who **is** Rhonda? Where **are** the volunteers?	Marta's friend. At Marta and Simon's house.
Be + There	Why **is** there a meeting today? How many people **are** there at the meeting?	To give information about volunteer work. About twenty.
Subject Questions	Who **collects** eyeglasses? Which airline **helps** people?	Many people do. Rhonda's airline does.
Other Questions	Where **does** Rhonda **work**? How **do** doctors **help**?	At an airline. They give medical supplies.

The Present Continuous

	WH- QUESTIONS	ANSWERS
Subject Questions	How many volunteers **are speaking** at the meeting?	Three.
Other Questions	What kind of trip **is** Rhonda **planning**? What **are** volunteers **collecting** now?	A trip to bring supplies to South America. Children's clothing and toys.

The Future with *Be Going To*

	WH- QUESTIONS	ANSWERS
Be	What **is** the new project **going to be**? When **are** you **going to be** a volunteer?	A holiday party for kids. Next month.
Be + There	When **is** there **going to be** another meeting? How many meetings **are** there **going to be**?	Next week. Only two more.
Subject Questions	Which children **are going to get** the gifts? Who **is going to be** at the next meeting?	The children in one small village. Many new volunteers.
Other Questions	What **is** Rhonda **going to do** with the toys? When **are** the volunteers **going to give** the toys to the children?	She's going to give them to kids. In December.

The Simple Past

	WH- QUESTIONS	ANSWERS
Be	Where **was** the last meeting? Why **were** the sick boy's parents worried?	We don't know. Because there was no medical care in their village.
Be + There	Why **were** there people at their house? What kind of help **was** there for the boy?	Because there was a meeting about volunteer work. Medical help.
Subject Questions	Which volunteers **brought** the boy to the United States? Who **came** to the meeting?	Rhonda and her friends did. Victor and Lisa did.
Other Questions	What **did** the boy **need**? When **did** the boy **have** his operation?	He needed an operation. He had it last year.

Modal Verbs and *Have To*

	WH- QUESTIONS	ANSWERS
Subject Questions	Who **can help** Rhonda? How many children **had to get** an operation last year?	All of us can. One did.
Other Questions	When **can** we **help** Rhonda? What **should** we **bring** to Rhonda? When **does** Rhonda **have to get** the toys?	Right now. Clothing and toys. Before her next trip.

EXERCISE 8 Write a *wh-* question about each sentence. Use the question word(s) given. Then write the answer. Use the ideas in the conversation on page 287.

1. Rhonda has a job.

   <u>What kind of job does she have? She works for an airline.</u>
   what kind

2. Rhonda does volunteer work.

   _____
   what kind

3. Her organization helps people.

   _____
   who

4. Rhonda went to South America last year.

   _____
   why

5. Someone pays for the flights to South America.

   _____
   who

6. The volunteers are going to have a party for children.

   _____
   when

7. A sick boy had to come to the United States.

   _____
   why

8. People can help with the holiday project.

   _____
   how

9. We should collect things for Rhonda.

   _____
   what

10. Rhonda is explaining something to the new volunteers.

    _____
    what

ABOUT YOU Choose a partner. Write *yes/no* questions and *wh-* questions for your partner. Use a different tense in each question: simple present, present continuous, future, and past. You can use modal verbs, too. Exchange books with your partner and write your answers.

1. <u>How many people are there in your family? There are five people in my family.</u>

2. _____

3. _____

4. _____

5. _____

EXERCISE 9 Amir, another volunteer, is talking now. People are asking him questions. Complete each question with the words given. Use the answer to help you choose the tense.

Victor: Where _____*do you volunteer*_____ ?
　　　　　　　　　　　　　　1. you/volunteer

Amir: I volunteer in my neighborhood. I work at a childcare center once a week for low-income families.

There are other volunteers, too. We help with the children. We also plan projects for them.

Halina: How many _____ at the center?
　　　　　　　　　　　　2. children/there

Amir: Every day is different. There are usually about fifteen or twenty kids.

Simon: How many hours _____ ?
　　　　　　　　　　　　　3. each volunteer/have to/work

Amir: Usually four to six hours. But sometimes we work more. Last week was one of those weeks.

Victor: What _____ last week?
　　　　　　　　　　4. happen

Amir: We had ten new kids, so I worked an extra day to help.

Halina: What _____ ?
　　　　　　　　　　5. you/do

Amir: I helped with the art activities, I served the meals, and I played with the children a lot.

Simon: How _____ about this day care center?
　　　　　　　　　　6. you/learn

Amir: It was on our city's website. That's a good place to look for volunteer opportunities.

Marta: What project _____ now?
　　　　　　　　　　　7. the volunteers/plan

Amir: We're planning a talent show and sale of the children's art. We're going to charge admission.

Victor: What _____ for the show?
　　　　　　　　　　8. children/learn/do

Amir: They're learning to sing several songs, and they also dance.

Simon: When _____ ?
　　　　　　　　　　9. the show/be

Amir: In three months. I can tell you the date later.

Halina: What _____ with the money?
　　　　　　　　　　10. center/do

Amir: We're going to buy books for the children's library. We're also going to buy new art supplies.

EXERCISE 10 Elsa, another volunteer, is talking now. People are asking Elsa questions. Complete each question with the words given. Use the answers to help you choose the tense. Then listen and check your answers. 🎧 12.8

Marta: This is Elsa. She volunteers to help older people. She works with a neighborhood group.

She works one week each month.

Woman: _____*Are you going to work*_____ this week, Elsa?
  1. you/work

Elsa: Yes, I am. I'm going to help an older woman in my neighborhood. She can't see very well,

and she lives alone.

Man: How _____ her?
  2. you/help

Elsa: I'm going to take her to a doctor's appointment tomorrow, and I'm going to take her to the

supermarket on the weekend.

Woman: What _____ all day?
  3. this woman/do

Elsa: She goes to the gym two days a week. She exercises in a swimming pool.

Woman: _____ the bus to the gym?
  4. she/have to/take

Elsa: No, she doesn't. Another volunteer takes her.

Woman: _____ ?
  5. she/can/swim

Elsa: She doesn't exactly swim. She takes an exercise class for seniors. It's exercise in the water.

Woman: When _____ these classes?
  6. she/start

Elsa: She started the classes twenty years ago. She says, "This class is responsible for my long life."

She's ninety years old!

Man: How _____ this job, Elsa?
  7. find

Elsa: I heard about it from a friend in the neighborhood. We're always looking for more volunteers.

Who _____ us?
    8. want/help

Woman: I do! When _____ ?
    9. I/can/start

Elsa: You can start tomorrow.

Woman: Great. Where _____ to sign up?
    10. I/should/go

EXERCISE 11 Read the FAQs (Frequently Asked Questions) from a volunteer organization's website. Complete the sentences with the correct form of the words given.

1. **Q:** What _____*does our organization do*_____ ?
    a. our organization/do

   A: We are an umbrella organization, which means we _____ with a lot
    b. work

   of smaller groups. We _____ volunteers with opportunities.
    c. help/match

2. **Q:** How _____ ?
    a. volunteers/help

   A: Our volunteers _____ all kinds of things: build houses, translate at
    b. do

   hospitals, clean up parks, and serve food at the homeless shelter. If someone

   _____ something special, we _____
    c. can/do   **d.** try/find

   a place for him or her.

3. **Q:** When _____ ?
    a. you/need/volunteers

   A: Our community _____ volunteers all the time. Last year, more than
    b. need

   8,000 volunteers _____ about 40,000 hours to different projects.
    c. give

   We think we _____ even more volunteers in the next twelve months.
    d. have

   Many people _____ around the holidays, but we actually
    e. want/volunteer

   _____ volunteers year-round.
    f. use

FUN WITH GRAMMAR

Play in groups of 3–5 students. Write the following categories on slips of paper:

the simple present	the present continuous	the future
the simple past	infinitives	modal verbs and *have to*
time expressions		

Put all the slips in a bag. Take turns. Take a slip of paper out of the bag. Make a statement or question, using the form that matches the category you chose. Each correctly worded sentence is worth 1 point. Whoever ends up with the most points wins.

SUMMARY OF UNIT 12

Review of Verb Tenses—Statements and Questions

		STATEMENT	YES/NO QUESTION	WH- QUESTION
THE SIMPLE PRESENT		She **is** from Poland. They **aren't** from Mexico.	**Are** they from Poland?	Where **are** they from? Who **is** from Poland?
		There**'s** a meeting today.	**Is** there a meeting today?	Why **is** there a meeting today?
		Halina **works** every day. Paul **doesn't work** on Saturdays.	**Does** Halina **work** every day?	How often **does** Tom **work**?
THE PRESENT CONTINUOUS		They **are looking** for jobs. He **isn't looking** for an apartment.	**Is** she **looking** for a job?	Where **are** you **volunteering**?
THE FUTURE		They **are going to be** volunteers.	**Is** she **going to be** a volunteer?	When **are** you **going to be** a volunteer?
		There **isn't going to be** a meeting tomorrow.	**Is** there **going to be** a party?	When **is** there **going to be** another meeting?
		She**'s going to help** newcomers.	**Are** they **going to help** children?	What **are** you **going to do** with the donations?
THE SIMPLE PAST		I **wasn't** at home yesterday.	**Were** you in South America last year?	Why **were** they worried?
		They **moved** last week.	**Did** they **move** last week?	Where **did** they **move**?
MODAL VERBS AND *HAVE TO*		We **should volunteer**. They **don't have to volunteer**.	**Can** I **volunteer**? Do we **have to volunteer**?	Who **can volunteer**? What **should** we **bring**?

Review of Infinitives

After Verbs	Halina started **to work** for a new company.
After Adjectives	I'm happy **to help** you.
Impersonal Expressions with *It*	It's fun **to be** a volunteer.

Review of Time Expressions

FREQUENCY		PRESENT	PAST	FUTURE
always	hardly ever	today	yesterday	tomorrow
usually	rarely	at the moment	two weeks ago	soon
often	never	right now	last week	in two weeks
sometimes	every week	this week		

REVIEW

Fill in the blanks with the correct form of the words given. In questions, use the answers to help you choose the tense. Use contractions when possible.

A: Hi, Sara. Where _____?
  1. you/go

B: Oh, hi, Julie. I'm going to the community center.

A: I _____ where the community center is.
  2. not/know

B: It _____ on Market Street. _____ where that is?
  3. be   **4.** you/know

A: Oh, yes. It's near the school. Why _____ to the community center?
  5. you/go

B: I _____ there once a month.
  6. volunteer

A: That's great. What _____?
  7. you/do

B: I do a lot of things. My husband does, too. Sometimes we _____ donations.
  8. collect

My husband _____ people how to drive.
  9. teach

A: Where _____?
  10. you/volunteer

B: We volunteer in this city and other places. Last year, _____ a tornado in
  11. there/be

Oklahoma. People _____ a lot of things. We _____
  12. need   **13.** go

there, and we _____ food and clothing.
  14. take

A: Tell me more about the organization. _____ only adults?
  15. you/help

B: No. We help children, too.

A: _____? I like _____ with children.
  16. I/can/volunteer   **17.** work

B: Yes, you can! We _____ for new volunteers right now.
  18. look

A: Great.

B: _____ a meeting tomorrow. You _____
  19. there/be   **20.** should/come

A: OK. How many people _____ at the meeting?
  21. there/be

B: There are going to be about twenty people. Don't worry, they're all nice.

You _____ them.
  22. like

A: What _____ at the meeting?
  23. we/do

B: We're going to talk about our next volunteer project.

A: What _____?
  24. I/should/bring

B: You _____ anything.
  25. not/have to/bring

FROM GRAMMAR TO WRITING

PART 1 Editing Advice

1. Use the base form after *doesn't, don't, didn't, have to,* and modals.

   Peter didn't ~~went~~ go to the meeting last Saturday.

   He had to ~~worked~~ work last Saturday.

   Volunteers should ~~to go~~ go to the meetings.

2. Don't forget to use the base form in an infinitive.

   They wanted to ~~helped~~ help us with the project.

3. Don't use a form of *be* with the simple present or simple past.

   Elsa's neighbor ~~is go~~ goes to the store every week.

   She ~~was walk~~ walked to the store yesterday.

4. Don't use statement word order in a question.

   Where ~~he worked~~ did he work last year?

   When ~~Elsa is going to drive~~ is Elsa going to drive her neighbor to the supermarket?

5. Don't use *do, does,* or *did* in a subject question.

   Who ~~does work~~ works as a volunteer?

6. Be sure each verb is in the correct tense and form for the context.

   Everyone ~~leaves~~ left the meeting at 10 o'clock last night.

   The older woman ~~is going~~ goes to the gym two days a week.

7. Use the correct form in a short answer.

   Are you a volunteer? No, ~~I don't~~ I'm not.

PART 2 Editing Practice

Some of the shaded words and phrases have mistakes. Find the mistakes and correct them.
If the shaded words are correct, write C.

Marta is interviewing another volunteer, Haru, at the meeting.

Marta: What kind of volunteer job do you have?
                                      1.

Haru: I work at a nature museum. I teach children's groups about animals, birds, and plants. Last
              C
              2.

              month, some students come to do a school project. I was helped them. They had to wrote a
                                    3.   4.   5.

              report about the birds in our museum. They didn't knew about these birds before.
                                                           6.

Marta: That's interesting. Where did you heard about this job?
                                        7.

Haru: I finded it through *United We Serve.* It's a way for us to volunteer in our own communities.
8.

There's a great website for volunteers. Go to www.serve.gov.
9.

Marta: How this site works?
10.

Haru: You fill in your interests and your location: your zip code, or city and state. Then the website

list many opportunities. It's easy use. You doesn't have to look at many different sites.
11.   12.   13.

Marta: It's just for young people?
14.

Haru: No, it doesn't. There are opportunities for everyone! Older people can click on the link for
15.

Senior Corps for information.

Marta: I'm have an idea for a volunteer project. What should I do?
16.   17.

Haru: The website has *toolkits.* A toolkit is a list of steps to follow. Before you start, you should to put
18.

your idea on the site and ask for volunteers. Many people are volunteering these days. And
19.

more people going to volunteer in the future. In October 2009, the government pass a law called
20.   21.

the Serve America Act. Now student volunteers can get money for their education. And the

number of older people is going up. That means we going to have more older volunteers, too.
22.   23.

Marta: Thank you for your time, Haru. You're going to stay for coffee with us?
24.

Haru: Yes, I do. Thank you. But I have to leave by 8:30.
25.   26.

PART 3 Write

Answer one of the following questions. Write a paragraph and use affirmative and negative statements in
the correct tense.

- Do you know a volunteer in the United States? What does this volunteer do?
- Do you want to be a volunteer? What are you going to do? Why?
- Were you (or was someone you know) a volunteer in your country? Write about the volunteer activity.
- Did a volunteer help you? How?

My neighbor Javier is a volunteer. He collects donations for the local food bank...

PART 4 Learner's Log

1. Write one sentence about each of the volunteers from this unit. Use a different tense in each sentence.
2. Write any questions you still have about volunteer work.

APPENDIX A

SPELLING RULES FOR VERBS AND NOUNS

Spelling of the *-s* Form of Verbs and Nouns

VERBS	NOUNS	RULE
visit—visit**s** need—need**s** like—like**s** spend—spend**s** see—see**s**	chair—chair**s** bed—bed**s** truck—truck**s** gift—gift**s** bee—bee**s**	Add *-s* to most words to make the *-s* form.
mi**ss**—miss**es** wa**sh**—wash**es** cat**ch**—catch**es** fi**x**—fix**es**	dre**ss**—dress**es** di**sh**—dish**es** mat**ch**—match**es** bo**x**—box**es**	Add *-es* to base forms and words with *ss*, *sh*, *ch*, and *x* at the end.
wor**ry**—worr**ies** **try**—tr**ies** stu**dy**—stud**ies**	par**ty**—part**ies** ci**ty**—cit**ies** ber**ry**—berr**ies**	If the word ends in a consonant + *y*, change *y* to *i* and add *-es*.
p**ay**—pay**s** pl**ay**—play**s** enj**oy**—enjoy**s**	b**oy**—boy**s** d**ay**—day**s** k**ey**—key**s**	If the word ends in a vowel + *y*, do not change the *y*. Just add *-s*.
	lea**f**—lea**ves** kni**fe**—kni**ves**	If the noun ends in *f* or *fe*, change *f* or *fe* to *ves*.

IRREGULAR *-S* FORMS OF VERBS

have—ha**s**
go—go**es**
do—do**es**

IRREGULAR PLURAL FORMS OF NOUNS

man—men woman—women child—children mouse—mice	foot—feet tooth—teeth person—people (or persons) fish—fish

Spelling of the *-ing* Form of Verbs

VERBS	RULE
go—go**ing** eat—eat**ing** spend—spend**ing**	Add *-ing* to most verbs to make the *-ing* form.
tak<u>e</u>—tak**ing** writ<u>e</u>—writ**ing** mak<u>e</u>—mak**ing**	If a verb ends in silent *e*, drop the *e* and add *-ing*. Do NOT double the final consonant. Wrong: writting
pa<u>y</u>—pay**ing** bu<u>y</u>—buy**ing** worr<u>y</u>—worry**ing** stud<u>y</u>—study**ing**	If a verb ends in a *y*, just add *-ing*. Wrong: studing
s<u>top</u>—sto**pping** <u>run</u>—ru**nning** sp<u>lit</u>—spli**tting**	If a one-syllable verb ends in consonant + vowel + consonant, double the final consonant and add *-ing*.
be<u>gín</u>—begi**nning** per<u>mít</u>—permi**tting** oc<u>cúr</u>—occu**rring**	If a two–syllable word ends in consonant + vowel + consonant, double the final consonant and add *-ing* only if the last syllable is stressed.
ó<u>pen</u>—open**ing** háp<u>pen</u>—happen**ing** devé<u>lop</u>—develop**ing**	If a multi-syllable word ends in consonant + vowel + consonant and the final syllable is not stressed, do NOT double the final consonant. Just add *-ing*.

Spelling of the *-ed* Forms of Regular Simple Past Verbs

VERBS	RULE
listen—listen**ed** look—look**ed**	Add *-ed* to most regular verbs to form the simple past.
bak<u>e</u>—bake**d** smil<u>e</u>—smile**d** sav<u>e</u>—save**d**	If a verb ends in silent *e*, just add *-d*.
worr<u>y</u>—worr**ied** stud<u>y</u>—stud**ied**	If a verb ends in a consonant + *y*, change the *y* to *i* and add *-ed*.
enjo<u>y</u>—enjoy**ed** dela<u>y</u>—delay**ed**	If a verb ends in a vowel + *y*, just add *-ed*.
s<u>top</u>—sto**pped** dr<u>ag</u>—dra**gged** sl<u>am</u>—sla**mmed**	If a one-syllable verb ends in consonant + vowel + consonant, double the final consonant and add *-ed*.
per<u>mít</u>—permi**tted** oc<u>cúr</u>—occu**rred**	If a two–syllable verb ends in consonant + vowel + consonant, double the final consonant and add *-ed* only if the last syllable is stressed.
ó<u>pen</u>—open**ed** háp<u>pen</u>—happen**ed** devé<u>lop</u>—develop**ed**	If a multi-syllable verb ends in consonant + vowel + consonant and the final syllable is not stressed, do NOT double the final consonant. Just add *-ed*.

APPENDIX B

SUMMARY OF VERB TENSES

VERB TENSE	FORM	MEANING AND USE
SIMPLE PRESENT	I **have** class Mondays. He **doesn't have** class today. **Do** you **have** class today? **What do** you **do** every day?	• facts, general truths, habits, and customs • used with frequency adverbs, e.g., *always, usually, sometimes, never* • regular activities and repeated actions
PRESENT CONTINUOUS	I **am studying** biology this semester. He **isn't studying** now. **Are** you **studying** this weekend? **What is** she **studying** at college?	• actions that are currently in progress • future actions if a future time expression is used or understood
FUTURE WITH *WILL*	I **will go** to the store. He **won't go** to the store. **Will** you **go** to the store? **When will** you **go** to the store?	• future plans/decisions made in the moment • strong predictions • promises and offers to help
FUTURE WITH *BE GOING TO*	He**'s going to study** all weekend. He **isn't going to study** Saturday. **Are** you **going to study** Saturday? **What are** you **going to study** Saturday?	• future plans that are already made • predictions
SIMPLE PAST	They **liked** the story. I **didn't like** the story. **Did** you **like** the story? **What did** you **like** about the story?	• a single, short, past action • a longer past action • a repeated past action
PAST CONTINUOUS	She **was watching** TV when I called. I **wasn't watching** TV when you called. **Were** you **watching** TV around 10? **What were** you **watching?**	• an action in progress at a specific past time • often with the simple past in another clause to show the relationship of a longer past action to a shorter past action
PRESENT PERFECT	I **have seen** the movie *Black Panther*. He **has seen** *Black Panther* five times. **Have** you **seen** *Black Panther*? **Why have** you never **seen** *Black Panther*?	• action that started in the past and continues to the present • action that repeats during a period of time from the past to the present • action that occurred at an indefinite time in the past
PRESENT PERFECT CONTINUOUS	She **has been working** there for years. I **haven't been working** regularly in a while. **Have** you **been working** here long? **Where have** you **been working** lately?	• an action that started in the past and continues to the present

APPENDIX C

IRREGULAR VERB FORMS

BASE FORM	PAST FORM	PAST PARTICIPLE	BASE FORM	PAST FORM	PAST PARTICIPLE
be	was/were	been	fight	fought	fought
bear	bore	born/borne	find	found	found
beat	beat	beaten	fit	fit	fit
become	became	become	flee	fled	fled
begin	began	begun	fly	flew	flown
bend	bent	bent	forbid	forbade	forbidden
bet	bet	bet	forget	forgot	forgotten
bid	bid	bid	forgive	forgave	forgiven
bind	bound	bound	freeze	froze	frozen
bite	bit	bitten	get	got	gotten
bleed	bled	bled	give	gave	given
blow	blew	blown	go	went	gone
break	broke	broken	grind	ground	ground
breed	bred	bred	grow	grew	grown
bring	brought	brought	hang	hung	hung
broadcast	broadcast	broadcast	have	had	had
build	built	built	hear	heard	heard
burst	burst	burst	hide	hid	hidden
buy	bought	bought	hit	hit	hit
cast	cast	cast	hold	held	held
catch	caught	caught	hurt	hurt	hurt
choose	chose	chosen	keep	kept	kept
cling	clung	clung	know	knew	known
come	came	come	lay	laid	laid
cost	cost	cost	lead	led	led
creep	crept	crept	leave	left	left
cut	cut	cut	lend	lent	lent
deal	dealt	dealt	let	let	let
dig	dug	dug	lie	lay	lain
dive	dove/dived	dove/dived	light	lit/lighted	lit/lighted
do	did	done	lose	lost	lost
draw	drew	drawn	make	made	made
drink	drank	drunk	mean	meant	meant
drive	drove	driven	meet	met	met
eat	ate	eaten	mistake	mistook	mistaken
fall	fell	fallen	overcome	overcame	overcome
feed	fed	fed	overdo	overdid	overdone
feel	felt	felt	overtake	overtook	overtaken

BASE FORM	PAST FORM	PAST PARTICIPLE	BASE FORM	PAST FORM	PAST PARTICIPLE
overthrow	overthrew	overthrown	stick	stuck	stuck
pay	paid	paid	sting	stung	stung
plead	pled/pleaded	pled/pleaded	stink	stank	stunk
prove	proved	proven/proved	strike	struck	struck/stricken
put	put	put	strive	strove	striven
quit	quit	quit	swear	swore	sworn
read	read	read	sweep	swept	swept
ride	rode	ridden	swell	swelled	swelled/swollen
ring	rang	rung	swim	swam	swum
rise	rose	risen	swing	swung	swung
run	ran	run	take	took	taken
say	said	said	teach	taught	taught
see	saw	seen	tear	tore	torn
seek	sought	sought	tell	told	told
sell	sold	sold	think	thought	thought
send	sent	sent	throw	threw	thrown
set	set	set	understand	understood	understood
sew	sewed	sewn/sewed	uphold	upheld	upheld
shake	shook	shaken	upset	upset	upset
shed	shed	shed	wake	woke	woken
shine	shone/shined	shone/shined	wear	wore	worn
shoot	shot	shot	weave	wove	woven
show	showed	shown/showed	wed	wedded/wed	wedded/wed
shrink	shrank/shrunk	shrunk/shrunken	weep	wept	wept
shut	shut	shut	win	won	won
sing	sang	sung	wind	wound	wound
sink	sank	sunk	withdraw	withdrew	withdrawn
sit	sat	sat	withhold	withheld	withheld
sleep	slept	slept	withstand	withstood	withstood
slide	slid	slid	wring	wrung	wrung
slit	slit	slit	write	wrote	written
speak	spoke	spoken			
speed	sped	sped			
spend	spent	spent			
spin	spun	spun			
spit	spit/spat	spit/spat			
split	split	split			
spread	spread	spread			
spring	sprang	sprung			
stand	stood	stood			
steal	stole	stolen			

Note:
The past and past participle of some verbs can end in
-ed or *-t*.

burn	burned or burnt
dream	dreamed or dreamt
kneel	kneeled or knelt
learn	learned or learnt
leap	leaped or leapt
spill	spilled or spilt
spoil	spoiled or spoilt

APPENDIX D

PREPOSITIONS OF TIME

	TIME EXPRESSION	EXAMPLES
in	in the morning in the afternoon in the evening	He eats breakfast **in** the morning. He eats lunch **in** the afternoon. He eats dinner **in** the evening.
	in the [season]	We have vacation **in** the summer. There are many flowers **in** the spring.
	in [month]	Her birthday is **in** March.
	in the _____ century	People didn't use cars **in** the 19th century.
	in [number] minutes, hours, days, weeks, months, years	We'll leave on vacation **in** three days. I will graduate **in** two weeks.
	in the past in the future	**In** the past, people didn't use computers. **In** the future, we will need more health care workers.
	in the beginning	**In** the beginning, I didn't understand the teacher at all.
at	at night	He likes to watch TV **at** night.
	at [time]	My class begins **at** 12:30.
	at present	**At** present, I'm learning French.
	at the beginning of [something] at the end of [something]	The semester starts **at** the beginning of September. The semester ends **at** the end of May.
on	on [date]	His birthday is **on** March 5.
	on [day]	I have to work **on** Saturday.
	on the weekend	I'm going to a party **on** the weekend.
from	from [time] to [time]	My class is **from** 12:30 **to** 3:30.
	from [time] until/till [time]	My class is **from** 12:30 **until** (or **till**) 3:30.
for	for [number] minutes, hours, days, weeks, months, years	She was in Mexico **for** three weeks. We lived in Paris **for** two years.
by	by [time]	Please finish your test **by** six o'clock.
until/till	until/till [time]	I slept **until** (or **till**) 9 a.m. this morning.
	until /till [event]	I lived with my parents **until** (**till**) I got married.
during	during [event]	He fell asleep **during** the meeting.
about	about [time]	The plane will arrive **about** 6 p.m.
around	around [time]	The plane will arrive **around** 6 p.m.
before	before [time, day, date]	You should finish the test **before** 9:30. You should finish the job **before** Friday.
	before [event]	Turn off the lights **before** you leave.
after	after [time, day, date]	Please don't call me **after** 10 p.m. I'll have more free time **after** next Monday.
	after [event]	Wash the dishes **after** you finish dinner.

APPENDIX E

CAPITALIZATION AND PUNCTUATION

Capitalization Rules

RULE	EXAMPLES
The first word in a sentence	**M**y friends are helpful.
The word *I*	My sister and **I** took a trip together.
Names of people	**A**braham **L**incoln; **G**eorge **W**ashington
Titles preceding names of people	**D**octor (**D**r.) **S**mith; **P**resident **L**incoln; **Q**ueen **E**lizabeth; **M**r. **R**ogers; **M**rs. **C**arter
Geographic names	the **U**nited **S**tates; **L**ake **S**uperior; **C**alifornia; the **R**ocky **M**ountains; the **M**ississippi **R**iver **Note:** The word *the* in a geographic name is not capitalized.
Street names	**P**ennsylvania **A**venue (**A**ve.); **W**all **S**treet (**S**t.); **A**bbey **R**oad (**R**d.)
Names of organizations, companies, colleges, buildings, stores, hotels	the **R**epublican **P**arty; **C**engage **L**earning; **D**artmouth **C**ollege; the **U**niversity of **W**isconsin; the **W**hite **H**ouse; **B**loomingdale's; the **H**ilton **H**otel
Nationalities and ethnic groups	**M**exicans; **C**anadians; **S**paniards; **A**mericans; **J**ews; **K**urds; **I**nuit
Languages	**E**nglish; **S**panish; **P**olish; **V**ietnamese; **R**ussian
Months	**J**anuary; **F**ebruary
Days	**S**unday; **M**onday
Holidays	**I**ndependence **D**ay; **T**hanksgiving
Important words in a title	*Grammar in Context; The Old Man and the Sea; Romeo and Juliet; The Sound of Music* **Note:** Capitalize *the* as the first word of a title.

Punctuation Rules

PUNCTUATION	EXAMPLES
A period (.) is used at the end of a declarative sentence.	This is a complete sentence**.**
A question mark (?) is used at the end of a question.	When does the movie start**?**
An exclamation mark (!) is used at the end of an exclamation. It expresses a strong emotion.	This book is so interesting**!**
A comma (,) is used: • before the connectors *and, but, so,* and *or* in a compound sentence. • between three or more items in a list. • after a dependent clause at the beginning of a complex sentence. Dependent clauses include time clauses, *if* clauses, and reason clauses. • between the day and the date and between the date and the year. • between and after (if in the middle of a sentence) city, state, and country names that appear together. • after time words and phrases, prepositional phrases of time, and sequence words (except *then*) at the start of a sentence.	 • She gave Tomas a pen**, but** he wanted a pencil. • He needs **a notebook, a pen, and a calculator**. • **If it's cold outside,** you should wear a coat. • The test will be on **Friday, May 20**. The school opened on **September 3, 2010**. • She lived and taught in **Shanghai, China** for five years. • **Finally,** the test was over and the student could leave. **After the movie,** they decided to go out for coffee.
An apostrophe (') is used to indicate either a contraction or a possession: • Use an apostrophe in a contraction in place of the letter or letters that have been deleted. • Add an apostrophe and the letter *-s* after a word to show possession. If a plural word already ends in *-s*, just add an apostrophe.	 • **I'm** happy to see you. **You've** read a lot of books this year. • That is **Yusef's** book. The **teachers'** books include the answers.
Quotation marks (") are used to indicate: • the exact words that were spoken by someone. Notice that the punctuation at the end of a quote is inside the quotation marks. • language that a writer has borrowed from another source. • when a word or phrase is being used in a special way.	 • Albert Einstein said, **"I have no special talent. I am only passionately curious."** • The dictionary defines punctuation as **"the use of specific marks to make ideas within writing clear."** • The paper was written by a **"professional"** writer.

APPENDIX F

VOWEL AND CONSONANT SOUNDS

Vowels

SYMBOL	EXAMPLES
ʌ	love, cup
a	father, box
æ	class, black
ə	alone, atom
ɛ	ever, well
i	eat, feet
ɪ	miss, bit
ɔ	talk, corn
ʊ	would, book
oʊ	cone, boat
u	tooth, school
eɪ	able, day
aɪ	mine, try
aʊ	about, cow
ɔɪ	join, boy

Consonants

SYMBOL	EXAMPLES
b	bread, cab
d	door, dude
f	form, if
g	go, flag
h	hello, behind
j	use, yellow
k	cook, hike
l	leg, meal
m	month, sum
n	never, win
ŋ	singer, walking
p	put, map
r	river, try
s	saw, parks
ʃ	show, action
ɾ	atom, lady
t	take, tent
tʃ	check, church
θ	thing, both
ð	the, either
v	voice, of
w	would, reward
z	zoo, mazes
ʒ	usual, vision
dʒ	just, edge

APPENDIX G

THE CALENDAR AND NUMBERS

Calendar

MONTHS	DAYS	SEASONS
January (Jan.)	Sunday (Sun.)	Winter
February (Feb.)	Monday (Mon.)	Spring
March (Mar.)	Tuesday (Tues.)	Summer
April (Apr.)	Wednesday (Wed.)	Fall or autumn
May	Thursday (Thurs.)	
June (Jun.)	Friday (Fri.)	
July (Jul.)	Saturday (Sat.)	
August (Aug.)		
September (Sept.)		
October (Oct.)		
November (Nov.)		
December (Dec.)		

Dates

January 6, 1999
Jan. 6, 1999
1/6/1999
1/6/99
1-6-99

March 27, 2017
Mar. 27, 2017
3/27/2017
3/27/17
3-27-17

Numbers

CARDINAL NUMBERS	ORDINAL NUMBERS
1 = one	first
2 = two	second
3 = three	third
4 = four	fourth
5 = five	fifth
6 = six	sixth
7 = seven	seventh
8 = eight	eighth
9 = nine	ninth
10 = ten	tenth
11 = eleven	eleventh
12 = twelve	twelfth
13 = thirteen	thirteenth
14 = fourteen	fourteenth
15 = fifteen	fifteenth
16 = sixteen	sixteenth
17 = seventeen	seventeenth
18 = eighteen	eighteenth
19 = nineteen	nineteenth
20 = twenty	twentieth
21 = twenty-one	twenty-first
30 = thirty	thirtieth
40 = forty	fortieth
50 = fifty	fiftieth
60 = sixty	sixtieth
70 = seventy	seventieth
80 = eighty	eightieth
90 = ninety	ninetieth
100 = one hundred	hundredth
1,000 = one thousand	thousandth
1,000,000 = one million	millionth

Peter Thomas
17 Cherry Tree Lane
New York, NY 10001

6-38/542   7024

DATE _September 6, 2010_

PAY TO THE
ORDER OF _Teresa Jones_ $ _950 00/100_

Nine Hundred Fifty and 00/100 ———— DOLLARS

Summerville Bank

FOR _rent_   _Peter Thomas_

⑆0123456789⑆ 0123456789101⑈   7024

GLOSSARY

- **Adjective** An adjective gives a description of a noun.

   It's a *tall* tree.   He's an *old* man.   My sisters are *nice*.

- **Adverb** An adverb describes the action of a sentence or an adjective or another adverb.

   She speaks English *fluently*.   I drive *carefully*.

   She speaks English *extremely well*.   She is *very* intelligent.

- **Affirmative** means "yes."

- **Apostrophe** ' We use the apostrophe for possession and contractions.

   My *sister's* friend is beautiful. (possession)   Today *isn't* Sunday. (contraction)

- **Article** An article comes before a noun. It tells if the noun is definite or indefinite. The definite article is *the*. The indefinite articles are *a* and *an*.

   I have *a* cat.   I ate *an* apple.   *The* teacher is helpful.

- **Base Form** The base form, sometimes called the "simple" form, of the verb has no tense. It has no ending (*-s* or *-ed*): *be, go, eat, take, write*.

   I didn't *go* out.   He doesn't *know* the answer.

   You shouldn't *talk* in the library.

- **Capital Letter** A B C D E F G . . .

- **Comma** ,

- **Comparative Form** A comparative form of an adjective or adverb is used to compare two things.

   My house is *bigger* than your house.

   Her husband drives *faster* than she does.

- **Complement** The complement of the sentence is the information after the verb if it is not an object. It completes the verb phrase.

   He works *hard*.   I slept *for five hours*.   They are *late*.

- **Consonant** The following letters are consonants: *b, c, d, f, g, h, j, k, l, m, n, p, q, r, s, t, v, w, x, y, z*.

   Note: *y* is sometimes considered a vowel, as in the word *syllable*.

- **Contraction** A contraction is two words joined with an apostrophe.

   He's my brother.   *You're* late.   *What's* your name?

   (*He's* = He is)   (*You're* = You are)   (*What's* = What is)

- **Count Noun** Count nouns are nouns that we can count. They have a singular and a plural form.

   1 pen — 3 pens   1 table — 4 tables

- **Frequency Words** Frequency words (e.g., *always, usually, often, sometimes, rarely, seldom, hardly ever*, and *never*) tell how often an action happens.

   I *never* drink coffee.   We *always* do our homework.

- **Imperative** An imperative sentence gives a command or instructions. An imperative sentence omits the subject pronoun *you*.

    Come here.   *Don't be* late.   Please *sit* down.

- **Infinitive** An infinitive is *to* + the base form.

    I want *to leave*.   You need *to be* here on time.

- **Modal** The modal verbs are *can, could, shall, should, will, would, may, might,* and *must*.

    They *should* leave.   I *must* go.

- **Negative** means "no."

- **Nonaction Verb** A nonaction verb has no action. We do not use a continuous tense (*be* + verb *–ing*) with a nonaction verb. Nonaction verbs include: *believe, cost, care, have, hear, know, like, love, matter, mean, need, own, prefer, remember, see, seem, think, understand, want,* and sense-perception verbs.

    She *has* a computer.   We *love* our mother.   You *look* tired.

- **Noncount Noun** A noncount noun is a noun that we don't count. It has no plural form.

    She drank some *water*.   He ate some *rice*.

    I need *money*.   We had a lot of *homework*.

- **Noun** A noun is a person (*brother*), a place (*kitchen*), or a thing (*table*). Nouns can be either count (*1 table, 2 tables*) or noncount (*money, water*).

    My *brother* lives in California.   My *sisters* live in New York.

    I get *money* from my parents.   I drink *coffee* every day.

- **Object** The object of the sentence follows the verb. It receives the action of the verb.

    He bought *a car*.   I saw *a movie*.   I met *your brother*.

- **Object Pronoun** Use object pronouns (*me, you, him, her, it, us,* and *them*) after a verb or preposition.

    He likes *her*.   I saw the movie. Let's talk about *it*.

- **Parentheses** ( )

- **Period** .

- **Phrase** A group of words that go together.

    Last month my sister came to visit.   There is a red car *in front of my house*.

- **Plural** means "more than one." A plural noun usually ends with *-s* or *-es*.

    She has beautiful *eyes*.   Please wash the *dishes*.

- **Possessive Form** Possessive forms show ownership or relationship.

    Mary's coat is in the closet.   *My* brother lives in Miami.

- **Preposition** A preposition is a connecting word. Some common prepositions are: *about, above, across, after, around, as, at, away, before, behind, below, by, down, for, from, in, into, like, of, off, on, out, over, to, under, up,* and *with*.

    The book is *on* the table.   I live *with* my parents.

- **Present Participle** The present participle of a verb is the base form + *–ing*.

    She is *sleeping*.   They are *laughing*.

- **Pronoun** A pronoun takes the place of a noun.

    Dorota bought a new car. *She* bought *it* last week.

    John likes Mary, but *she* doesn't like *him*.

- **Punctuation** The use of specific marks, such as commas and periods, to make ideas within writing clear.

- **Question Mark** ?

- **Regular Verb** A regular verb forms the simple past with *-ed*.

    He *worked* yesterday.   We *listened* to the radio.

- **-s Form** A simple present verb that ends in *-s* or *-es*.

    He *lives* in New York.   She *watches* TV a lot.

- **Sentence** A sentence is a group of words that contains a subject[1] and a verb and gives a complete thought.

    SENTENCE: She came home.

    NOT A SENTENCE: When she came home

- **Simple Form of Verb** The simple form of the verb, also called the "base" form, has no tense; it never has an *-s*, *-ed*, or *-ing* ending.

    Did you *see* the movie?   I can't *find* his phone number.

- **Singular** means "one."

    She ate a *sandwich*.   I have one *television*.

- **Subject** The subject of the sentence tells who or what the sentence is about.

    My sister bought a new car.   *The car* is beautiful.

- **Subject Pronoun** We use a subject pronoun (*I, you, he, she, it, we, you, they*) before a verb.

    They speak Japanese.   *We* speak Spanish.

- **Superlative** The superlative form of an adjective or adverb shows the number one item in a group of three or more.

    January is the *coldest* month of the year.

    You have the *best* seat in the room.

---

[1] In an imperative sentence, the subject *you* is omitted: *Sit down. Come here.*

- **Syllable** A syllable is a part of a word that has only one vowel sound. (Some words have only one syllable.)

    change (one syllable)   after (af•ter = two syllables)

    look (one syllable)   responsible (re•spon•si•ble = four syllables)

- **Tense** Tense shows when the action of the sentence happened. Verbs have different tenses.

    SIMPLE PRESENT: She usually *drives* to work.

    FUTURE: She *is going to drive* tomorrow.

    PRESENT CONTINUOUS: She *is driving* now.

    SIMPLE PAST: She *drove* yesterday.

- **Verb** A verb is the action of the sentence. The verb *be* connects.

    He *runs* fast.   I *speak* English.   You *are* late.

- **Vowel** The following letters are vowels: *a, e, i, o, u. Y* is sometimes considered a vowel (for example, in the word *mystery*).

INDEX

CREDITS

ILLUSTRATIONS
© Cengage Learning

PHOTOS
2-3 (t) © Carolyn Van Houten/The Washington Post/Getty Images; **5** (b) © Mint Images/Mint Images RF/Getty Images; **8** (bl) © RosaIreneBetancourt 14/Alamy Stock Photo; **11** (b) © All rights reserved-Copyright/Moment/Getty Images; **12** (bl) © Spiroview Inc/Shutterstock.com; **12** (bl) © Spiroview Inc/Shutterstock.com; **12** (bl) © jeffcampbelldigital/ Shutterstock.com; **12** (bl) © Westend61/Getty Images; **14** (b) © Hero Images/Getty Images; **15** (bl) © iStock.com/ Jan_Neville; **15** (br) © David McNew/Getty Images News/Getty Images; **16** (br) © Katrina Wittkamp/The Image Bank/ Getty Images; **19** (b) © Alexander Spatari/Moment/Getty Images; **26-27** (t) © Richard Davis Photography; **28** (b) © Merkuri2/iStock Editorial/Getty Images; **32** (tr) © Andrew Harrer/Bloomberg/Getty Images; **36** (b) © Tomsmith585/ iStock Unreleased/Getty Images; **38** (cr) © Randy Duchaine/Alamy Stock Photo; **43** (b) © Jack Hollingsworth/Stockbyte/ Getty Images; **48–49** (t) © Frazer/Shutterstock.com; **50** (cr) © KRT/Newscom; **54** (cr) © iStock.com/sshepard; **54** (br) © BDoss928/Shutterstock.com; **62–63** (t) © Julia Cumes/Solent News/Shutterstock.com; **64** (cr) © Klaus Vedfelt/ DigitalVision/Getty Images; **70** (b) © H. Mark Weidman Photography/Alamy Stock Photo; **71** (cr) © Dean Drobot/ Shutterstock.com; **78** (b) © Juanmonino/iStock/Getty Images; **83** (tr) © sirtravelalot/Shutterstock.com; **84** (b) © GibsonPictures/E+/Getty Images; **94–95** (t) © REUTERS/Steve Marcus; **96** (tr) © Ryan McVay/PhotoDisc/ gettyimages/Houghton Mifflin Harcourt; **97** (b) © Arnold Media/DigitalVision/Getty Images; **101** (cr) © Micah Bowerbank/ Dreamstime.com; **101** (cr) © iStock.com/Wulfespirit; **101** (br) © iStock.com/Bbostjan; **101** (br) © Mark Aplet/Shutterstock. com; **102** (tr) © iStock.com/Lcoccia; **102** (tr) © iStock.com/Filo; **102** (tr) © iStock.com/Jswinborne; **102** (cr) © iStock.com/ Ra-photos; **102** (cr) © iStock.com/Summersetretrievers; **105** (tr) © MCCAIG/E+/Getty Images; **106** (cr) © Patti McConville/ Alamy Stock Photo; **108** (b) © Brooke Fasani/Stone/Getty Images; **111** (t) © goodluz/Shutterstock.com; **113** (b) © imageBROKER/Alamy Stock Photo; **118–119** (t) © ARNOLD, COREY/National Geographic Image Collection; **120** (c) © DebbiSmirnoff/E+/Getty Images; **123** (b) © Monkey Business Images/Shutterstock.com; **125** (b) © Hero Images Inc./Alamy Stock Photo; **126** (cr) © Peter Cade/Iconica/Getty Images; **129** (tl) © B-D-S Piotr Marcinski/Shutterstock. com; **129** (tc) © Vladir09/Shutterstock.com; **129** (tc) © Anatoly Tiplyashin/Shutterstock.com; **129** (tr) © Allocricetulus/ Shutterstock.com; **129** (tr) © amenic181/Shutterstock.com; **129** (cl) © Maryna Iaroshenko/Alamy Stock Photo; **129** (c) © iStock.com/Sumnersgraphicsinc; **129** (c) © iStock.com/DNY59; **129** (cr) © James Baigrie/Photodisc/Getty Images; **130** (tr) © Daniel Loiselle/iStock/Getty Images; **139** (br) © Hill Street Studios/Blend Images/Getty Images; **144–145** (t) © Corey Arnold/National Geographic Image Collection; **151** (b) © New York City/Alamy Stock Photo; **152** (t) © PeopleImages/E+/Getty Images; **154** (b) © Zuma Press, Inc./Alamy Stock Photo; **159** (b) © Mark Summerfield/ Alamy Stock Photo; **160** (b) © Ingus Kruklitis/Shutterstock.com; **161** (tr) © Patti McConville/Alamy Stock Photo; **165** (cl) © Quang Ho/Shutterstock.com; **165** (c) © Netalieh/iStock/Getty Images; **165** (cr) © ktphotog/iStock/Getty Images; **165** (cr) © iStock.com/DNY59; **167** (b) © Enes Evren/E+/Getty Images; **171** (br) © Maskot/Getty Images; **171** (br) © veryan dale/Alamy Stock Photo; **172–173** (t) © JIJI PRESS/AFP/Getty Images; **174** (tr) © David R. Frazier Photolibrary, Inc./Alamy Stock Photo; **175** (b) © AztecBlue/Alamy Stock Photo; **181** (tr) © Xinhua/Alamy Stock Photo; **183** (tr) © Ryan McVay/ Photodisc/Getty Images; **186** (b) © Mikael Karlsson/Alamy Stock Photo; **188** (br) © Photodisc/Getty Images; **194–195** (t) © Nataba/iStock/Getty Images; **204** (b) © travismanley/iStock/Getty Images; **210** (b) © Klaus Tiedge/Blend Images/Getty Images; **214** (b) © Caia Images/Caia Images/Superstock; **220–221** (t) © Matt Shiffler; **222** (cr) © Helioscribe/ Shutterstock.com; **225** (b) © David Grossman/Alamy Stock Photo; **227** (b) © MoMo Productions/DigitalVision/Getty Images; **230** (b) © dszc/E+/Getty Images; **231** (br) © Ingram Publishing/Getty Images; **232** (b) © Gary Fabiano/Sipa Press/0904221958/Newscom; **239** (b) © Ellen Isaacs/Alamy Stock Photo; **243** (cl) © Patrick Seeger/picture alliance/Getty Images; **243** (cr) © Christian Science Monitor/Getty Images; **244–245** (t) © Cris Crisman; **247** (b) © Peggy Peattie/ZUMA Press/San Diego/CA/USA; **254** (b) © Wiskerke/Alamy Stock Photo; **255** (tr) © Image Source/Getty Images; **263** (tr) © David Grossman/Alamy Stock Photo; **276–277** (t) © Bradley Kanaris/Getty Images News/Getty Images; **282** (b) © Mike Stobe/Getty Images Sport/Getty Images; **285** (b) © Andrew Renneisen/Getty Images News/Getty Images; **286** (b) © Steve Jennings/Getty Images Entertainment/Getty Images; **293** (b) © Hill Street Studios/Eric Raptosh/ AGE Fotostock; **294** (b) © Ariel Skelley/DigitalVision/Getty Images